Using the ISO 56002 Innovation Management System

The Management Handbooks for Results Series

The Organizational Alignment Handbook
A Catalyst for Performance Acceleration
H. James Harrington & Frank Voehl (2011)

The Organizational Master Plan Handbook
A Catalyst for Performance Planning and Results
H. James Harrington & Frank Voehl (2012)

The Lean Six Sigma Black Belt Handbook
Tools and Methods for Process Acceleration
H. James Harrington, Frank Voehl, Chuck Mignosa & Rich Charron (2013)

The Lean Management Systems Handbook
H. James Harrington, Frank Voehl, Hal Wiggin & Rich Charron (2014)

Change Management
Manage the Change or It Will Manage You
H. James Harrington & Frank Voehl (2016)

Lean Triz
How to Dramatically Reduce Product-Development Costs with This Innovative
Problem-Solving Tool
H. James Harrington (2017)

Innovative Change Management (ICM)
Preparing Your Organization for the New Innovative Culture
H. James Harrington (2018)

The Framework for Innovation
A Guide to the Body of Innovation Knowledge
H. James Harrington, Frank Voehl, Rick Fernandez & Brett Trusko (2018)

Total Innovative Management Excellence (TIME)
The Future of Innovation
H. James Harrington & Frank Voehl (2020)

Using the ISO 56002 Innovation Management System
A Practical Guide for Implementation and Building a Culture of Innovation
H. James Harrington & Sid Benraouane (2021)

Using the ISO 56002 Innovation Management System

A Practical Guide for Implementation and Building a Culture of Innovation

Dr. Sid Ahmed Benraouane

Dr. H. James Harrington

Routledge
Taylor & Francis Group

A PRODUCTIVITY PRESS BOOK

First published 2021
by Routledge
600 Broken Sound Parkway #300, Boca Raton FL, 33487

and by Routledge
2 Park Square, Milton Park, Abingdon, Oxon, OX14 4RN

Routledge is an imprint of the Taylor & Francis Group, an informa business

© 2021 Dr. Sid. Ahmed Benraouane & Dr. H James Harrington

The right of Dr. Sid. Ahmed Benraouane & Dr. H James Harrington to be identified as author of this work has been asserted by them in accordance with sections 77 and 78 of the Copyright, Designs and Patents Act 1988.

Trademark notice: Product or corporate names may be trademarks or registered trademarks, and are used only for identification and explanation without intent to infringe.

Library of Congress Cataloging-in-Publication Data
A catalog record for this title has been requested

ISBN: 978-0-367-70140-6 (hbk)
ISBN: 978-0-367-70143-7 (pbk)
ISBN: 978-0-367-70142-0 (ebk)

Typeset in Minion
by MPS Limited, Dehradun

To my father and my mother who don't speak English.

To my son Rayan, my daughter Mona, and my wife Leila who have been my greatest source of inspiration.

Sid Ahmed Benraouane

I'm dedicating this book to Chuck Mignosa – no one could have a better friend.

H. James Harrington

Contents

About the Authors

H. James Harrington, Chief Executive Officer
Harrington Management Systems

In the book, *Tech Trending*, Dr. Harrington was referred to as "the quintessential tech trender." The *New York Times* referred to him as having a "… knack for synthesis and an open mind about packaging his knowledge and experience in new ways -characteristics that may matter more as prerequisites for new-economy success than technical wizardry …"

It has been said about him, "Harrington writes the books that other consultants use."

The leading Japanese author on quality, Professor Yoshio Kondo, stated: "Business Process Improvement (methodology) investigated and established by Dr. H. James Harrington and his group is some of the new strategies which brings revolutionary improvement not only in quality of products and services, but also the business processes which yield the excellent quality of the output."

The father of "Total Quality Control," Dr. Armand V. Feigenbaum stated: "Harrington is one of those very rare business leaders who combines outstanding inherent ability, effective management skills, broad technology background and great effectiveness in producing results. His record of accomplishment is a very long, broad and deep one that is highly and favorably recognized."

William Clinton, past President of the United States, appointed Dr. Harrington to serve as an Ambassador of Goodwill.

In 2010, Newt Gingrich, Former Speaker of the House and General Chairman of American Solutions, had appointed Dr. H. James Harrington to the Advisory Board of his Jobs and Prosperity Task Force.

Harrington Management Systems (formerly Harrington Institute, Inc.) was featured on a half-hour TV program, "Heartbeat of America," which focuses on outstanding small businesses that make America strong. The host, William Shatner, stated: "You (Dr. Harrington) manage an entrepreneurial company that moves America forward. You are obviously successful."

KEY RESPONSIBILITIES

H. James Harrington now serves as the Chief Executive Officer for the Harrington Management Systems. He is also on the Board of Directors for a number of small- to medium-sized companies helping them develop their business strategies. He also serves as:

- President of the Walter L. Hurd Foundation
- Honorary Advisor for Quality for China
- Chairman of the Centre for Organizational Excellence Research (COER)

PREVIOUS EXPERIENCE

Harrington spent 40 years with IBM mostly in management positions. When he retired from IBM, he formed a consulting firm called Harrington, Hurd, & Rieker. He was CEO of the consulting firm until it was purchased by Ernst & Young.

Harrington served as a principal of Ernst & Young with the title of international quality advisor. He retired from Ernst & Young to take over as the CEO of SystemCorp, a small software development company in Montréal with approximately 150 programmers. He managed it until it was sold to IBM.

His next assignment was for the World Bank where he was assigned to restructure their operations in "African Capacity Building Foundation" located in Zimbabwe, Africa.

In 2000, he formed a consulting firm, Harrington Institute, and served as its CEO until 2014 when it was purchased by a software company in Orlando, Florida. Harrington Institute, Inc. established branches in Canada, China, United Arab Emirates (Harrington Middle East) and the United States.

In 2008, Harrington accepted a position as Chief Operating Officer of Define Properties in Dubai UAE, which is a construction, property management, and designer of major water structures from facilities in Dubai. He serves as the chief operating officer until they were purchased by another construction firm in the UAE.

AWARDS AND RECOGNITION

Harrington received many awards and recognition trophies throughout his 60 years activity in promoting quality and high performance throughout the world. He has had many performance improvement awards named after him from countries around the world. Some of them are:

The Harrington/Ishikawa Medal, presented yearly by the Asian Pacific Quality Organization, was named after H. James Harrington to recognize his many contributions to the region.

The Harrington/Neron Medal was named after H. James Harrington in 1997 for his many contributions to the quality movement in Canada.

Harrington Best TQM Thesis Award was established in 2004 and named after H. James Harrington by the European Universities Network and e-TQM College.

Harrington Chair in Performance Excellence was established in 2005 at the Sudan University.

Harrington Excellence Medal was established in 2007 to recognize an individual who uses the quality tools in a superior manner.

H. James Harrington Scholarship was established in 2011 by the ASQ Inspection Division.

PUBLICATIONS AND LECTURES

Harrington is the author of over 55 books and hundreds of papers on performance improvement of which over 150 have been published in major magazines.

Dr. Harrington can be contacted at the following:

Email - hjh@svinet.com
Mailing Address - 15559 Union Ave. # 187 Los Gatos California, 95032
Phone: (408) 358-2476 or (408) 356-7518

Sid Ahmed Benraouane, Ph.D.

I like to think of Innovation Management System as the framework that helps managers discipline serendipity while creating optimum conditions

AREAS OF EXPERTISE

A Leader with 20+ years of experience in multiple sectors, regions, and industries. Dr. Benraouane is a faculty at Carlson School of Management, University of Minnesota. He advises organization on innovation, digital transformation, and AI ecosystems. He is the Lead of the US ISO Working Group 1 on Innovation Management Standard ISO 56002:2019, and a member of the US ISO/SC 42 Working Group 3 Artificial Intelligence – Trustworthiness. With a deep understanding of the economics of digital transformation in the USA and the Middle East and North Africa region, Dr. Benraouane helps decision-makers build decision-making frameworks that enhance innovative thinking and engage the workforce.

Dr. Benraouane advises Dubai Government and is in charge of innovation and foresight. He was a speaker at the World Government Summit on AI and Ethics (UAE 2019) and a frequent keynote speaker at regional events such as Big Data Show (UAE), Cloud and Big Data Show (KSA), Energy Digitization Summit (UAE), Artificial Intelligence Summit (UAE), World Mobility Show and Autonomous Driving (UAE), the Middle East Military Technology Conference and the

Bahrain International Defense Exhibition & Conference (Bahrain). He is a member of the Advisory Board of the Abu Dhabi Digital Authority's Digital Next Conference. Dr. Benraouane holds a Ph.D. from the University of Minnesota, USA, and he is a graduate of l'Ecole Nationale d'Administration, Algiers.

Acknowledgments

We would like to first acknowledge all of the individuals who participated in ISO Technical Committee 279 for their willingness to share their knowledge, ideas, and thoughts with the rest of the team to create an international agreement related to innovation concepts. Without that free exchange of knowledge, the innovation ISO standards would not have been able to be created.

Secondly, we would like to acknowledge the hard work and dedication of Candy Rogers and Michael Sinocchi who have made it possible for translating a rough draft manuscript into a finished book that we both are proud of. Last, but not least, we would like to acknowledge and give deserving special recognition to the International Standards Association and ANSI for their contributions in organizing and contributing to the management of Technical Committee 279.

Authors' Notes

When my co-author Dr. Benraouane approached me in Tokyo about writing a book on innovation management, during the second last meeting of TC 279, the technical committee that generated the standard, I was apprehensive. We had been involved with the writing of the standard 56002:2019 for Innovation Management System and we understood the many thought-provoking and innovative ideas it contained. Although the ISO technical committee was very careful to classify the Standard as a guide, not as a requirement document, this doesn't mean that you cannot use the document to evaluate your innovative processes and upgrade them closer to world standards. The content in the Standard can be used in any combination, in any sequence. More importantly, some of the clauses should be ignored based upon the product and processes that are involved. Innovation can be as simple as reorganizing your work-station to improve your efficiency or as complex as setting up a network of homes on Mars. ISO Standards 56000:2020 defined innovation as "a new or changed entity, realizing or redistributing value."* Based upon this definition, almost every person in the world should be considered an innovator.

There is a basic cycle that all innovation activities should include, independent of the size of the company or the objective of the individual innovation. These are:

1. Identify an opportunity
2. Create a way to take advantage of the opportunity
3. Initiate action to take advantage of the opportunity
4. Change the value of something related to the opportunity (modify or redistribute the value)

God's unique gift to mankind is our desire to improve our surroundings. For example, I'm 92 years old and I woke up this morning wanting to do something that would change the monotony of my daily life. So we made

---

corn soup for lunch. I had never had corn soup before and it was delicious. This met all four criteria for being innovative from identifying the opportunity to the transformation of value.

The manuscript for this book was finished and I decided after lunch to write these paragraphs emphasizing that innovation was not restricted to large organizations, but that it can be applied to everyone's way of life. You can be innovative in the way you tie your fishing husk to your fish line, just as we were creative in figuring out how to land a man on the moon and return him safely to earth. I feel sorry for anyone who is not innovative and creative; they are missing one of the major joys in life. The joy of creating something really interesting and personally satisfying lasts long after the joys and highs from a sexual experience.

Innovation is a state of mind rather than an activity. Now I'll admit that some of the suggested activities in ISO's 56002:2019 do not need to be included in every innovative process. Probably far less than 20% of the actions are needed. For example, you don't need to have a written innovative policy nor do you need to measure the current status. However, you need know what your customer is expecting and requiring from the process. Tesla electric power automobiles leader Elon Musk is known for producing high quality, cutting-edge vehicles with high-end creative features. He was able to accomplish it without the aid of 56002:2019, but he did use many of the suggestions that are included in the standard. An organization, where innovation is deeply rooted as a formal system, has usually made creativity an active part of the organization's culture. This you will often see in companies like Google and Apple. However, a painter of landscapes and music composer will find only a small percentage of the suggestions in 56002:2019 as being essential in their job. Because of the wide range of values that come out of an innovative process, the decision was made to prepare the standard for a complex innovative process that is designing, manufacturing, selling, and maintaining an output. This way, a great deal more potential activities can be presented allowing the user to select the appropriate ones for his needs.

There is no sound reason why everyone in an organization shouldn't be creating ideas that add value to the organization. It is our hope that this book will help make this happen at your organization and in the home lives of your team. To get started, begin by making a list of the three innovative things you've done for your organization in the last five working days. If you're having trouble doing it, be sure to read on. Your goal should be two per day minimum.

Foreword

The *56002:2019 International Standard – Innovation Management System – Guidance* is a guidance document, consisting of an introduction and ten (10) clauses.

Well-organized operational Innovation Management Systems (IMS) will drive sustained growth, economic viability, increase employee morale, maintain a better return on investment, reduce turnover rates and grow the organization's share of the market. Innovative organizations have the ability to understand the market better in order to accurately project future trends. Although this sounds too good to be true, it is true. The innovative organization's focus on quality of design results in minimizing the number of problems that are encountered during the production phase, allowing the organization to focus less on problems and more on improvement opportunities. An innovative organization relies heavily on the creative ability within all employees to make prudent risk decisions.

- Definition of innovation: In the latest version of ISO Standards 56000:2020 innovation is defined as: Innovation is defined as a "new or changed entity, realizing or redistributing value."*
  - Note 1 to entry: Novelty and value are related to, and determined by the perception of, the organization and interested parties
  - Note 2 to entry: An innovation can be a product, service, process, model, method, etc.
  - Note 3 to entry: Innovation is an outcome. The word "innovation" sometimes refers to activities or processes resulting in, or aiming for, innovation. When innovation is used in this sense it should always be used with some form of qualifier, for example "innovation activities."*

- Definition of creativity: Creativity is using the ability to make or think of new things involving the process by which new ideas, stories, products, etc., are created.

  Note: You can have creativity which is not innovative, but you cannot have innovative activities that are not creative.

Management in an organization builds an environment for work innovation, which flourishes as they develop the standards and system to either start the individual's creativity or fertilize it to the point that it blooms on every branch/individual within the organization. To excel at leadership today, you don't have to be the most technically competent, but you do have to be among the very best creative individuals and have the understanding you need to recognize other individuals. Yes, you have to do all the regular tasks like set objectives and goals, prepare mission statements, develop visions, appraise performance, and keep records. You may have to do all these tasks, but you don't have to do them in the same old boring way. Management needs to be more creative than anyone else. Management needs to put a little creativity in what they do daily so that they set the example for their employees to do the same. Every manager should have a goal of making creative/innovative changes in the way they operate every day.

An IMS guides the organization to determine its innovation vision, strategy, policy, and objectives, and to establish the support and processes needed to achieve the intended outcomes. ISO 56002:2019 provides guidance on why it is beneficial to implement an innovation assessment, what you can expect from a good one, how to carry it out, and act upon its results.

THE POTENTIAL BENEFITS FROM UPDATING YOUR IMS

There are many benefits from updating your IMS which include:

- Becoming a leader in your product lines
- Improve stock value
- Improve value-added per employee
- Improve return on assets

- Minimize uncertainties
- Increase employee morale
- Increase market share
- Improve customer satisfaction
- Ability to anticipate customer needs
- Minimize workload fluctuations
- Increase the dividends paid to your investors
- Increase efficiency, effectiveness, and adaptability
- Be more able to manage change with less resistance and build a resilient organization
- Develop a more satisfying reward and recognition system
- Increase bonuses to key personnel
- Improve sustainability and resilience
- Increase satisfaction of the stakeholders
- Engage and empower people in the organization
- Increase ability to attract partners, collaborators, and funding
- Attract challenging and resourceful people to join the organization
- Enhance reputation and valuation of the organization
- Reduce legal expenses
- Develop higher caliber leaders
- Develop a more desirable and challenging culture
- Improve process and system efficiency and effectiveness

IMS PRINCIPLES

- Definition of a management principle: A management principle is a comprehensive and fundamental rule. A management principal is a statement that every manager is committed to govern their interaction and behaviors. Principles are the conditions that the organization promises the stakeholders that these are the laws that the organization will live up to. Many organizations feel that principles are too strict with requirements and instead have a set of beliefs or values.

- Definition of beliefs: Beliefs is an acceptance of something to be true. They, in fact, may or may not be true.
- Definition of values: Values are things that an organization believes are sacred – things that should never be sacrificed.

Do not use the term "principles" unless you and the rest of the management team agree that they are statements that they will never compromise. In fact, it is not unusual for individuals including managers to be fired because they do not live up to one or more of the organization's principles.

Innovation management or governance can be thought of as a system of mechanisms to align goals, allocate resources, and assign decision-making authority for innovation, across the company, and with external parties. In this book we will dive a bit deeper into this topic. What is innovation management governance? What different models are there, and which ones seem to be the most effective? A related topic is: How can companies effectively steer and manage a complex, cross-functional and multidisciplinary activity like innovation?

Most organizations are organized to manage business units, regional operations, and functions. Many have gone further by allocating specific responsibilities and setting up dedicated mechanisms to manage cross-functional processes, for example, new product development. But how can they stimulate, steer, and sustain innovation, an ongoing transformational endeavor that is increasingly becoming a corporate imperative? IBM was able to do it in the 1980s through a program called "Process Compatibility." It required that locations around the world had compatible technical processes and outputs. This eliminated the possibility of customers wanting a product manufactured in a specific country in preference to products manufactured in a different country. At that time, IBM's objective was to provide products and services produced in the region that they were used in. I doubt if there are a handful of medium to large size organizations in the world that could say the same today.

Certainly, innovation consists of several cross-functional processes from generating ideas to taking technologies to market, but there is more to it. It deals with "hard" business issues like growth strategy, technological investments, project portfolios and the creation of new businesses. But it also relates to "softer" challenges, like promoting creativity and discipline, stimulating entrepreneurship, accepting risk, encouraging teamwork, fostering learning and change, and facilitating networking and communications; in short, it requires a special type of organizational culture. Like marketing, innovation is a mindset that should pervade the whole organization.

As often emphasized, we need principles to help us determine the right things to do and understand "why we do what we do." The more specificity we have, the more we get immersed in the detail and lose sight of our objectives – our purpose – our reason for doing what we do. Once we have lost sight of our purpose, our actions and decisions follow the mood of the moment. They are swayed by the political climate or fear of reprisals. We can so easily forget our purpose when in heated discussions, when it's not who you are but what you say and to whom you say it that is deemed to be most important.

Those people who live by a set of principles often find themselves cast out of the inner-circle for saying what they believe. However, with a presence of mind and a recollection of the reasons why the principles are important for survival, they could just redeem themselves and be regarded as an important contributor.

There are eight IMS principles defined by ISO 56002:2019:

1. realization of added -value
2. future-focused leaders
3. strategic direction
4. culture
5. exploiting insights
6. managing uncertainty
7. adaptability
8. system's approach.[*]

The authors suggest there are four additional principles that are worthwhile considering. They are:

1. knowledge-based systems

---

[*]©ISO. This material is excerpted from ISO 56002:2019, with permission of the American National Standards Institute (ANSI) on behalf of the International Organization for Standardization. All rights reserved.

2. opportunity identification
3. integrity
4. there is a better way

The innovation series 56000:2020 of ISO standards for innovation is made up of a number of documents. At the present time, there are eight documents in the mill at various levels of completion (see Table F.1). The quantity of documents, the names of the documents, and the document number as best practices provide more and more insight into the IMS.

- Definition of governance: Governance determines who has power, who makes decisions, how other players make their voice heard and who is accountable. The corporate governance framework consists of (1) explicit and implicit contracts between the company and the stakeholders for distribution of responsibilities, rights, and rewards, (2) procedures for reconciling the sometimes conflicting interests of stakeholders in accordance with their duties, privileges, and roles, and (3) procedures for proper supervision, control, and information flows to serve as a system of checks-and-balances (Wilfong and Ito, 2020).

In a recent management development seminar that we conducted with the International Association of Innovation Professionals (IAOIP) and the US Technical Advisory Group (TAG) for Innovation Management on the theme of innovation governance, the participants (all senior

TABLE F.1

ISO 56000:2020 Standards

ISO 56000:2020	Fundamentals and Vocabulary
ISO 56002:2019	Innovation Management System
ISO 56003:2019	Tools and Methods on Innovation Partnerships
ISO 56004:2019	Innovation Management Assessment
ISO FDIS 56005	Tools and Methods on Intellectual Property Management
ISO DIS 56006	Tools and Methods on Strategic Intelligence Management
ISO AWI 5007	Tools and Methods on Idea Management
ISO AWI 5008	Tools and Methods for Innovation Operation Measurements Guidance

innovation experts vastly experienced in the field of innovation) proposed an excellent list of innovation governance responsibilities:

- Defining the various roles and the many ways of working through the innovation management process;
- Defining decision power, based upon lines of communication and commitments on innovation;
- Defining key responsibilities of the key innovation parties and players;
- Establishing the set of values underpinning all of the company's innovation efforts;
- Making decisions that define expectations, both internal and external parties involved;
- Defining how, when, and why to measure innovation;
- Making strategic and operational decisions on innovation budgets;
- Orchestrating, balancing and prioritizing innovation activities across divisions and working groups; and
- Establishing management routines regarding these decisions.

This list provides a good first description of the scope of innovation governance. But in order to clearly see how it applies in your company, it is worth going a bit further and asking: What questions does innovation governance address? In fact, the most powerful weapon in business today is the alliance between the mathematical smarts of machines and the imaginative human intellect of great leaders. Together they make the mathematical corporation the business model of the future.[1]

We are at a once-in-a-decade breaking point, similar to the quality revolution of the 1980s and the dawn of the internet age in the 1990s, where leaders must transform how they run their organizations, or competitors will bring them crashing to earth, and, in many cases, almost overnight. Mathematical corporations – the organizations that will master the future – will outcompete high-flying rivals by merging the best of human ingenuity with machine intelligence. While smart machines are weapon number one for organizations, leaders are still the drivers of breakthroughs. Only they can ask crucial questions to capitalize on business opportunities newly discovered in oceans of data.

This dynamic combination will make possible the fulfillment of missions that once seemed out of reach, even impossible to attain. According to Jean-Philippe Deschamps, a professor emeritus of technology and innovation

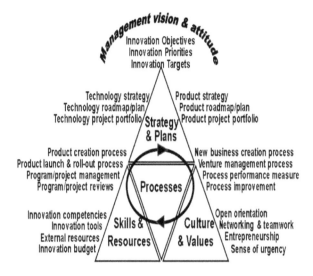

FIGURE F.1
Multiple Dimensions of the Scope of an Innovation Management System.

management at IMD in Lausanne (Switzerland), these issues also deal with both the content and process sides of all innovation activities taking place in a company, as shown in Figure F.1.

An effective IMS should be geared to handle the multiple aspects of the company's innovation masterplan. For most enterprises, it begins or starts with a CEO/Senior Management vision and attitude regarding innovation – reflecting the commitment and engagement mentioned earlier – and the setting of broad innovation objectives and priorities.[2] Additionally, it should also cover:

1. The company's strategies and plans regarding new products and technologies;
2. Its processes, for both the creation and the launch of new products and services, as well as for venturing into new businesses;
3. Its culture and values; and
4. Its resources in terms of people, skills, and budgets.

These innovation dimensions must be mutually compatible and reinforcing. The list of these innovation dimensions, which is summarized in Figure F.1 can be used by management for a quick check, i.e., which of

WHAT MODELS HAVE BEEN ADOPTED? WHO IS REALLY IN CHARGE?

Who is in charge? / At what level?	A SINGLE INDIVIDUAL	A PAIR OR DUO	A SMALL GROUP	A LARGE GROUP
TOP MGMT LEVEL	CEO / CTO/CRO*	CTO/CRO + BU Mger	Subset of top mgmt team	
SENIOR MGMT LEVEL	CxO;CIO** / Innovation Manager	CxO + BU Mger	X-funct'l steering group or "board"	
MIDDLE MGMT LEVEL				Group of champions
		No one specifically!		

* Chief Technology Officer / Chief Research Officer
** Chief Innovation Officer

FIGURE F.2
What Models Have Been Adopted?

these innovation dimensions do we cover in our innovation governance system, and which ones have we somehow left aside? Also, who is in charge of innovation, and what models have been adopted? (See Figure F.2.)

According to Jean-Philippe Deschamps and other experts, a select number of companies, notably in the US, reported that they rely on a group of champions to promote and steer innovation.[3] But one company that stands out for having forcefully empowered a group of champions is PepsiCo, particularly under the leadership of its former CEO, Roger A. Enrico, who was recognized as a charismatic business builder and marketing wizard. Enrico prided himself on not doing things by the book, and he strongly believed that employees are seldom given a chance to fully contribute and show what they can do. So he selected a group of promising young executives to deploy as business development and innovation champions.

CAPACITY OF THE INNOVATION MANAGEMENT MODEL TO EVOLVE

Many companies around the world will either grow and evolve over time, or they will go out of business. Some do it rapidly, reaching many billions of dollars in sales in 20 years or less, while others change more slowly. Some of them expand in terms of product range, and others diversify by entering completely new fields and creating new industries. Furthermore, others maintain the same product range but expand their geographical market coverage, while some others may change their structure over time as they create new business units and/or globalize their operations. Most organizations have to adapt to the radical changes introduced through various forms of technology, or perhaps the internet and the emergence of many of the social networks.

All these changes naturally affect the way innovation needs to be carried out, and therefore is governed. This means that an innovation management model that is well suited to a particular company's current condition may not be adapted to the next stage in its development. This explains, at least in some manner (because changes in management also play a role), why many companies change their innovation management governance models over time. There are many different ways to adapt innovation governance to changes in the company's condition and environment. Some companies may change models altogether, for example, passing from a centralized model to a distributed one, or from relatively loose to much more structured governance.

Other companies keep the same basic governance model, but they try to make it evolve in order to more successfully address their current challenges. It is therefore extremely important for management to regularly review its governance model in order to assess whether the model it has chosen is expandable in terms of scope, product, or geographical coverage, and to better prepare for its evolution.

Whichever innovation management model you choose, it will only be effective to the precise degree that the people responsible for implementing the change obtain the cooperation and support of the remainder of the organization for their innovation initiatives. As a way of distinguishing between the scope of the different types of innovation and innovative activities, we can speak in terms of the degree of "newness" of the product. Several of the following types of innovation management activities can be scoped and classified in this manner:

1. *Focus is on developing entirely new products:* This is often referred to as "new-to-world products," as such innovations perform an entirely new function and/or sometimes even create new markets. Some examples include the famous microwave oven, the cell telephone, and performance enhancing drugs such as Viagra.

While these types of innovations are comparatively rare and pose the highest risks, the downside is that they often incur the highest cost ratio to develop.

2. *Another scope of innovations is on improved performance products:* The scope of these innovations is that of improving the performance of an existing function. This type of innovation is more common than the "new-to-the-world" type and is sometimes the key objective of R&D research activity. An example is the development of digital photography or the "sure-shot" camera. The scope of improved performance encompasses a wide range of various types of innovation. On one hand, the scope may involve the development and use of a brand new technology like digital watches. On the other, it may lead to an extension or improvement of the technology currently used by improved design or better materials. A particular noteworthy example of the scope in this category is the development of the Dyson vacuum cleaner.

3. *Scope of new application products:* A considerable amount of innovative activity involves developing new applications for existing products. The amount of development activity required can vary enormously. In some cases, the high-tech product can be applied in a new context with little or no further development, as was the case of the Hovercraft, whereas for other products or technologies, widening the scope of application requires substantial research and development work.

4. *Additional functions products:* This type of innovation may be used to improve performance or extend functions of existing products. Typical was the addition of internet capabilities on mobile phones and the ability to access Facebook from one's own mobile phone.

5. *Restyled products:* Often, "new products" are no more than an update or change in styling to old ones. This type of innovative activity is prevalent in the car and clothing markets. It is a progressive innovation that generally involves lower costs and risks than "new-to-the-world" types of innovation. However, such low cost, low risk modifications sometimes turn into major investments carrying high risk which may not have been the original intention.

6. *Repackaged or renamed products:* At the opposite extreme to the entirely new product is the "new" product that might simply be a

result of repackaging, renaming, or re-branding. Although requiring careful planning and management, this type of innovation involves fewer management issues than those raised by the development of products which are entirely new. One could argue that such products are not new at all, and should not be treated as innovations. Examples in recent years include the re-branding of Mars candy called the Snickers-Snack product.

We have seen that "innovation" encompasses a broad spectrum of different types of activity, with a focus ranging from development of entirely new products and technologies to repackaging existing ones. It is entirely new products that pose the greatest problems in terms of effective management and attendant risk.

Managing Innovations: Critical Launch Factors

Innovation is crucial to long-term success in an organization, yet the risks are high with significant rates of new product failure. The managerial issues and problems to which this dilemma gives rise are considerable. A combination of the recognized importance of innovation and the high risk of failure has meant that his area of company activity has attracted substantial attention and research in recent years. Much of this has focused on attempts to look for empirical evidence that can establish the key ingredients in the successful management of innovation. There are no "recipes" for certain success, but research has been instrumental in establishing some of the critical factors in the process. By way of example, we have outlined a selection of research programs in this area, together with a brief summary of their findings.

Successful Product launches

Morley's study of over 2,000 new product launches was very comprehensive.[4] It found that only one in seven of the new product launches researched could be considered successful when considering sales and market share. Those that were successful exhibited the following characteristics compared to their less successful counterparts:

✓ sustained heavy promotion during the first three months of launch;
✓ more extensive and rigorous market research;

✓ less reliance on exaggerated claims for the new product to consumers;

✓ more awareness and receptiveness to distributors' needs and wants; and

✓ use of a well-known company and/or brand name.

Conclusions drawn about successful new products were very much along the lines of what one would expect. For example, it is understandable that new products with a well-known company or brand names that are heavily promoted stand more chance of success than their lesser-known weakly promoted counterparts. However, a finding from his study regarding successful new products is perhaps more surprising; namely, that prices for successful new products tended to be above average for the sector (see Figure F.3).

Among the most difficult markets in which to succeed with new products is the grocery, particularly the luxury foods, market. Despite this, Ben & Jerry's brand of ice creams, which is not the cheapest of product ranges in this category on the market, continue to be extremely successful. The

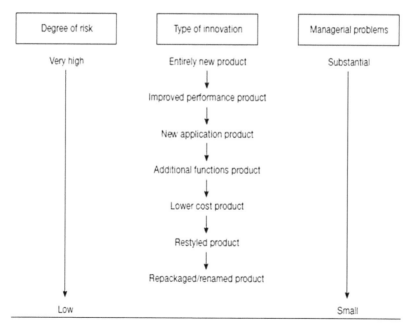

FIGURE F.3
The Continuum of Product Innovation.

brand's marketers have refused to be drawn into a price war against competitors and continue to support the brand's positioning at the top end of the marketplace to good effect.[5]

A FOCUS ON SOME CRITICAL FACTORS IN SUCCESSFUL INNOVATION

These studies are a sample of empirical research done in this area. What emerges from these and other studies is that there are a set of critical factors in successful innovation (Improvement–Novelty–Innovation–Invention) that point the way to key areas for managing and governing this activity as shown in Figure F.4.

A summary of these factors is offered by some experts in terms of the following seven critical factors:

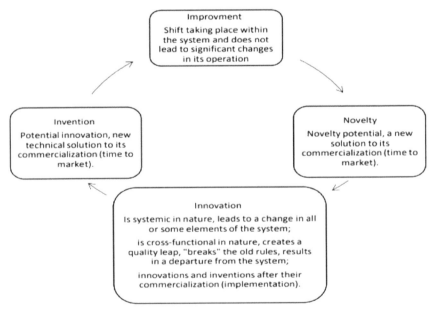

FIGURE F.4
Set of Critical Factors in Successful Innovation.

1. Scope of market orientation
2. Scope of relevance to the organization's corporate objectives
3. Source of creative ideas
4. Effective project selection and evaluation systems
5. Effective project management and control
6. Scope of the organization's reception to innovation
7. Focus of commitment by one individual or a few individuals

Experts often point out that there will be cases where innovations succeed in spite of poor management, but the shortage or absence of one or more of these factors is much more likely to lead to innovation failures and shortcomings. However, some evidence suggests that companies seem to be learning to better manage the process of new product development, especially the idea generation and screening stages, more effectively than in the past, while seeking a better balance between breakthrough and control, as shown in Figure F.5.

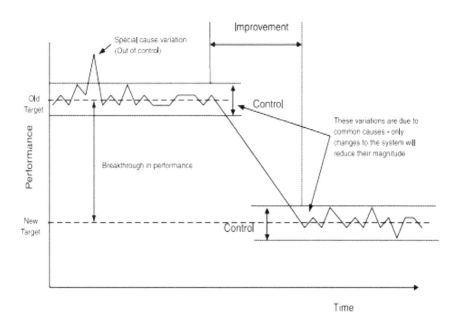

FIGURE F.5
The Balance between Breakthrough and Control.

STRATEGIES FOR ESTABLISHING AN IMS

The first prerequisite for developing and launching new products is to determine the overall scope of the strategic approach to innovation management and its use within corporate strategy. Over the past 20 years or so, many experts have distinguished the following possible strategies for innovation:

1. Offensive strategy
2. Defensive strategy
3. Licensing strategy
4. Market creation strategy
5. Maverick strategy
6. Acquisition of companies
7. Acquisition of personnel

We now examine these more closely to see what the seven innovation strategies consist of:

1. Offensive strategy: This strategy can be high risk, but with high potential pay-off. It requires an effective research and development department, also a positive marketing element that recognizes new market opportunities that can rapidly change new product ideas into commercial products. This type of strategy is usually undertaken by larger players and often occurs in an industry dominated by a small number of major companies. An example of an organization which practices this approach to innovation is Apple which is often at the forefront of new technologies.

2. Defensive strategy: This is the opposite of an offensive strategy. It is a low risk, low pay-off strategy. The company offering it needs an established market share, and has to be able to maintain profit levels through low manufacturing costs even when price competition is intense. At the same time, the company must possess appropriate technological ability to react swiftly to technological advances by competitors. This approach is best suited to companies whose strengths are in marketing rather than

research and development. An example is IBM, which uses its well-established corporate credentials and service and quality levels rather than competing at the edge of technological development.

3. Licensing strategy: A licensing strategy is also known as "absorbtive strategy." This allows the company to make profits by buying technological innovations of another company, so reducing the need for an effective in-house research and development department. There is little to gain from discovering what can be obtained from another source more cheaply. Licensing out your own technology to competing companies also has its advantages. It may reduce the company's market share in the long run, but licensing fees can be obtained from the sale of an innovation, which competition would eventually develop and match itself. Pilkington's have used licensing strategies very effectively and profitably with their "float glass" production technology.[6]

4. Market creation strategy: The organization may be in the position to create a completely new market because of technological advances facilitating the development of entirely new products. This strategy has the advantage of there being little initial competition and it can be very profitable. Sony established a whole new market when they developed their then revolutionary "Walkman" product.

5. Maverick strategy: This strategy is one that is applied to a product, which owing to technological advances, reduces the total market size for the old product. It allows a company to apply new technology to someone else's market, so benefiting their own company, but harming others in the market with a subsequent reduction in total market size. This type of strategy will succeed in the long run only if the company follows its maverick strategy with an offensive strategy to retain its technological lead over the competition.[7]

6. Acquisition of companies: An alternative strategy is to acquire a whole company through takeover or a merger. Some small companies are highly creative, entrepreneurial, and strategically offensive. They do, however, have limitations regarding research and development funds, and may not be effective in production and marketing. This makes them attractive and easy targets for large companies who are less likely to create such innovation and adopt

such offensive strategies themselves. The takeover of an already established small company can be much less of a risk to a large company than trying to develop the technology itself.

7. Acquisition of personnel: Rather than acquiring a company or pursuing a licensing strategy to gain a competitor's innovations, an organization may try to "steal" the opposition's employees or personnel. This strategy is not wholly ethical, although it is a low-cost method of acquiring technology and can prove to be fruitful. A further problem is the fact that such personnel will tend to rate low on loyalty and will probably be equally likely to leave your company if they are given a better offer elsewhere.[8]

These seven strategies can be combined with the ten new technologies to multiply the economics of networks to multiply these improvement strategies, making digital technology even more valuable at a faster pace. Table F.2 provides a short-list of ten new technologies that we work with more closely to provide real-world examples of how businesses across industries are applying these strategies and technologies to release trapped value. The value potential for these technologies is somewhat astonishing. Predictions for AI, for example, suggest a doubling of the economic growth of developed countries between 2020 and 2035 (15-year period), potentially adding seven million to the US economy alone. Additionally, human genomics is already a multi-billion industry and the Internet of Things (IoT) is projected to create $14 billion in new value by 2030, thereby contributing to a 1.5% increase in real GDP growth.[9]

SYSTEMS APPROACH TO MANAGEMENT

This principle is expressed as follows: Identifying, understanding, and managing interrelated processes as a system of jobs to be done contributes to the organization's effectiveness and efficiency in achieving its objectives. As the theory goes, a system is an ordered set of ideas, principles, and theories, or a chain of operations that produce

TABLE F.2

The Impact of the 10 New Technologies

Tech #	Technology Name	Technology Description
Tech #1	Extended Reality	This technology consists of interactive experience software that combines, blends, overlays, or replaces true reality with virtual ones. This encompasses virtual reality with augmented and blended reality.
Tech #2	Cloud Computing	This consists of distributed computing models whereas a third party provides software, an IT infrastructure, a platform, or other resources virtually or at scale.
Tech #3	Edge & Fog Computing	These are methods of optimizing cloud applications by taking some portions of an application, along with its data or services, away from one or more central nodes.
Tech #4	3-D Printing	This consists of a process of additive manufacturing whereas 3-D layers are printed layer by layer, which enables rapid prototyping and innovations in materials, leading to 4-D printing.
Tech #5	Quantum Computing	Building on classical computing which runs on bits that have either a value of 1 or 0, this method uses quantum bits that can hold much more complex information, of even negative values.
Tech #6	Human Computer Interactions	This consists of sensing technologies that enable more natural reactions between humans and computers, including gesture recognition and brainwave mapping.
Tech #7	Smart Robotics	This consists of robots that combine traditional robotic capabilities with sensors, computer vision, and intelligence, which enable new capabilities, such as collaborative robotics, autonomous vehicles, or swarm robotics.
Tech #8	Blockchain Technology	This involves distributed ledgers with time-stamped verified changes. Some useful applications include asset tracking, document management, payments and smart contracts.
Tech #9	The Internet of Things (IoT)	Consists of an ecosystem of sensors and analytics that monitor condition and performance of physical assets. New applications include digital twins, smart dust sensors, and IoT-specific cybersecurity.

(Continued)

TABLE F.2 (*Continued*)

Tech #	Technology Name	Technology Description
Tech #10	Artificial Intelligence	Consists of algorithms that initiate human intelligence, reasoning and decision-making, and improve over time. New branches include Swarm AI and Bayesian logic, as well as AutoMI, which automates production of AI applications.

specific results. To be a chain of operations, the components need to work together in a somewhat routine type of a relationship. Taking a systems approach to management means (1) managing the organization as a system of processes so that all the processes fit together, (2) the inputs and outputs are connected, (3) resources feed the processes, (4) performance is monitored, (5) sensors transmit information which cause changes in performance, and (6) all parts work together to achieve the organization's objectives.

This view clearly implies that a system is a dynamic entity, and not a static state. The system is not a random collection of elements, procedures, and tasks, but a set of supportive, yet not necessarily interconnected, processes. The systems approach recognizes that the behavior of any part of a system has some effect on the behavior of the system as a whole. Even if the individual processes are performing well, the system as a whole is not necessarily performing equally well. For example, assembling the best electronic components regardless of specification may not result in a world-class computer or even one that will run, because the components may not operate together. It is the interaction between parts and in the case of a management system, between processes, and not the actions of any single part or process that determines how well a system performs.

NOTES

1 For more details, see *The Mathematical Corporation: Where Machine Intelligence and Human Ingenuity Achieve the Impossible,* by Josh Sullivan

and Angela Zutavern. Sullivan and Zutavern's extraordinary examples include the entrepreneur who upended preventive healthcare, the oceanographer who transformed fisheries management, and the pharmaceutical company that used algorithm-driven optimization to boost vaccine yields. Together they offer a profoundly optimistic vision for a dazzling new phase in business, and a playbook for how smart companies can manage the essential combination of human and machine.

2 Source: https://hbr.org/2011/04/why-most-product-launches-fail. According to a leading market research firm, about 75% of consumer packaged goods and retail products fail to earn even $7.5 million during their first year. This is in part because of the intransigence of consumer shopping habits. Consultant Jack Trout has found that American families, on average, repeatedly buy the same 150 items, which constitute as much as 85% of their household needs; it's hard to get something new on the radar.

3 FMC Technologies, Sikorsky Aircraft, Hallmark Cards, Bank of America, and Abbott Laboratories are among them.

4 Source: https://hbr.org/2011/04/why-most-product-launches-fail. According to a leading market research firm, about 75% of consumer packaged goods and retail products fail to earn even $7.5 million during their first year. This is in part because of the intransigence of consumer shopping habits. Consultant Jack Trout has found that American families, on average, repeatedly buy the same 150 items, which constitute as much as 85% of their household needs; it's hard to get something new on the radar.

5 For its biggest launch since Diet Coke, Coca-Cola identified a new market: 20- to 40-year-old men who liked the taste of Coke (but not its calories and carbs) and liked the no-calorie aspect of Diet Coke, but not its taste or the sometimes-feminine image. This drink, which had half the calories and carbs and all the taste of original Coke, was introduced in 2004 with a $50 million advertising campaign. However, the budget couldn't overcome the fact that its benefits weren't distinctive enough. Men rejected the hybrid drink, as they wanted full flavor with no calories or carbs, not half the calories and carbs. And the low-carb trend turned out to be short-lived.

6 Dutch company Philips has also pursued a strategy of licensing to good effect. Philips has a strong technology and innovation base and the company has been responsible for many of the most successful "new-to-world" products. Examples of Philips' inventions range from the cassette tape through to the laser disc. Leading consumer goods companies throughout the world, including Sony and others, have licensed Philips' technologies, and is the basic approach with licensing to the benefit of all concerned parties.

7 An example of a company pursuing a maverick strategy for a product range is Procter & Gamble's range of "Fairy" brand products. Most of the products in the "Fairy" cleaning product range are claimed to be much more effective in their cleaning properties than those of competitors. This means much less of the product is needed for each cleaning operation, and although initially more expensive, is claimed to be much better value.

8 As we can see from the wide-ranging scope of innovation strategies listed here, there are a number of different alternatives for achieving innovation objectives. Clearly, the scope of your innovation strategies has a major bearing on the focus of new product development and the means of achieving product innovation. The selection of appropriate innovation and new product development strategies will depend on many factors, including company, competitor, and customer considerations. However, a key input to innovation strategies and decisions is technology itself, and in particular the way that technology is developing and likely to change in the future. No discussion of innovation, particularly the formation of innovation strategies, would be complete, therefore, without some consideration of technological forecasting.

9 Source: *Pivot to the Future: Discovering Value and Creating Growth in a Disrupted World*, by Larry Downes, Omar Abbosh, and Paul Nunes.

1

Clauses 0, 1, 2, and 3

CLAUSE 0: INTRODUCTION

Purpose

To acquaint the reader with Innovation Management System (IMS) theory, applications, operations, and benefits. It also provides them with an understanding of the scope of ISO 56002:2019.

Overview

It clarifies the difference between a creative organization and an innovative organization. A suggested scope for an innovative organization is discussed along with the advantages of being innovative. It consists of the introduction that will help you understand and make a decision related to upgrading your IMS. We make the basic assumption that most organizations had some type of IMS in place, as most organizations want to improve their performance and customer satisfaction. Included in this chapter is information related to four clauses that are within the ISO Standard 56002:2019. They are:

0. Introduction;
1. Scope;
2. Normative references; and
3. Terms and definitions.

Benefits

This ISO Standard has been created to provide the reader with best practices that will help to increase an individual and/or organization's ability to improve its innovation and creativity.

- It provides the reader with a list of standard innovation terms and definitions.
- It provides the reader with a means to understand the breadth and depth of the IMS.

Classification of Action

This clause is written as a *Should do* activity. It provides a list of best practices, but each organization can select the clauses that they wish to include in their IMS. This clause is classified as a guidance document always.

Introduction to the IMS

The basic management structure of all organizations consists of a set of systems that define the way the organization operates. These operational systems can be formally documented systems similar to those used in large corporations and stored in corporate operating manuals; or they can be informal, as in a one-person operation where a few systems (other than financial) are normally documented.

- Definition of a system: The International Organization for Standardization (ISO) defines a system as the organizational structure, responsibilities, procedures, and resources needed to conduct a major function within an organization, or support a common business need.[*]

Systems are usually made up of many major processes that take an input, add value to it, and produce an output. These processes may or may not be interconnected, for example, the new product development process, or the supply chain management system.

The first consideration in designing a system or a process is to produce a specific desired result. As a result, in addition to the basic process flow

---

[*]©ISO. This material is excerpted from ISO 56000:2020, with permission of the American National Standards Institute (ANSI) on behalf of the International Organization for Standardization. All rights reserved.

that creates the output, the following seven factors need to be designed into all systems and/or processes:

- ways to determine what the customer wants and needs;
- ways to identify improvement opportunities;
- ways to prevent errors from occurring;
- ways to segregate good items from bad items;
- ways to correct bad items; and
- ways to prevent the errors from recurring.

Keeping this in mind, it is easy to understand how this process control perspective is readily applicable across many of the functions within an organization, such as the design of products and services, human re-sources management, marketing, sales, and invoicing. They are often embedded within their management systems (see Table 1.1. for typical embedded systems). The notion that processes and their interfaces should be subject to analysis and continuous improvement is the key conceptual basis for the ISO 9000 family, and the fundamental building block for a Quality Management System and IMS.

- Definition of an Innovation Management System (IMS): An Innovation Management System is an organizational structure, procedures, processes, and resources needed to implement quality management.

TABLE 1.1

Inputs and/or Parts Systems that Support an IMS

Personnel System
Safety System
Environmental System
Security System
Production System
Financial System
Information System
Development System
Procurement System

Let us enlarge on this definition by suggesting that an IMS is an organizational structure, procedures, processes, and resources needed to implement innovation management.

An organization's IMS impacts all areas of any business because every system, process, activity, and task have the potential of creating errors and being improved. Because of the size and complexity of the total IMS within most organizations, many of the IMS's elements have been designed into the individual systems. For example, the IMS's elements that support the financial system are designed into the financial system, and includes third-party audits. Universities have dedicated major parts of their accounting curriculum to this one small part of a total IMS. Major accounting firms like Ernst & Young LLP and Coopers & Lybrand provide third-party financial auditing services to organizations on a yearly basis. Although all areas of the business are involved in the IMS, this book simplifies its scope, by focusing on the activities that are involved in or impact the product and/or service cycle (see Figure 1.1).

Focusing this book's scope to the IMS that supports the product and/or service cycle, greatly simplifies the remainder of this book. We realize that

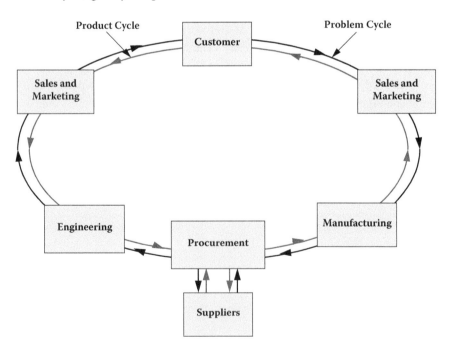

FIGURE 1.1
The Product and/or Service Cycle.

innovation/creativity should be present it every part of the organization independent of its size or product. This book also primarily focuses on mid- to large-size organizations ignoring innovative systems required to support a startup company, artists painting a landscape, individuals writing songs, etc. This also allows the book to focus on the parts of a total IMS that impact the most external customer and the products and/or services that the organization delivers to them.

Focusing this book's scope on the IMS in this manner also aligns the book with a number of national and international guidelines and/or procedures, which are used to define the elements of an IMS that a supplier/organization should have. There are many such standards that have been and still are widely used throughout the world. Today, the most well-known standards are the:

- ISO 9000 Series of International Standards (updated in 1994);
- ISO 1400 Environmental Standard; and
- QS-9000 (Automotive Industry Suppliers Standards for Chrysler, Ford, and General Motors, released in 1994).

Most of these management system standards began as procurement requirements to meet two-party contractual needs. As such, they have been written in a way that explains the type of IMS a supplier should have. For example, QS-9000 applies to all of the first-tier suppliers to Ford, GM, and Chrysler, but does not apply to the "Big Three" themselves.

We truly believe that a good IMS is a basic building block that every organization should have in place prior to starting to deliver products or services to any customer or consumer. Keeping this in mind, we are going to talk about the supplier–customer relationship with much more proactive terms, as described in Figure 1.2.

There are very few natural work teams and/or processes that don't make use of the cascading customer/supplier model.

Throughout this book, except when direct quotations are made relating to the ISO Standards, we will refer to the organization that is implementing the IMS as "the organization" or "your organization." Also, we much prefer the term "supplier" to identify the organization(s) that provides key inputs (products and/or services) that form a part, and ultimately influence the innovative output from your IMS and your organization's final product. This approach is taken because we believe

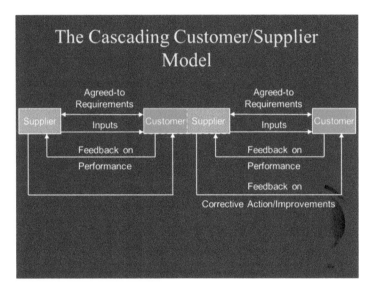

FIGURE 1.2
Supplier–Customer Relationship.

all organizations can benefit from having a formal IMS in place, not just those organizations that are involved in contracting.

Flowcharts are a useful tool to help understand IMS when installing it into an organization that has already focused on the processes and have produced a number of flowcharts.

- A supplier provides input to a process or an organization that adds value to the input.
- A customer is the organization or individual that receives the output from a process for organization.

CLAUSE 1: SCOPE

Our mission is to assist the reader on how to implement ISO Standard 56002:2019.

- Definition of scope : Scope provides guidance for the establishment, implementation, maintenance, and continuous improvement of an IMS for use in all established organizations.

Typical things that might be included in a scope statement are offerings, processes, structures, partners, collaborations, timing, and what is outside scope. In other words, scope involves the process of identifying and documenting specific goals, outcomes, milestones, tasks, costs, and timeline dates specific to the entity objectives.

This clause first defines innovation's limitations in a complete product cycle. The last part that is outside of the scope of this document is the disposal activities. Continuous improvement is the last phase covered in 56002:2019.

It clearly states that the scope of this document includes all established organizations. That means that it applies to production, service, education, finance, government, and international organizations. It doesn't make any difference if it's a temporary or startup company or a governmental organization. It's vague if it applies to individuals working for themselves like writers, gardeners, painters, and handymen, as many of them do not work in an established organization. It does definitely apply to organizations who have business lines to operate within a region/state/country/or internationally and also applies to for-profit, non-profit, and all levels of government.

It emphasizes the importance of applying the standard to users and customers plus interested parties. A second grouping of statements focuses on how the standard scope includes product, services, processes, model, and methods ranging from incremental to radical, plus all types of methods and methodologies that can have an impact upon the innovative activities.

It also points out what the scope limitations are. This working standard is only a guide and not intended to define or describe detailed activities nor does it reference or recommend any assistive tools and methodologies designed to support innovative activities. In the case of 56002:2019, it applies to the following 11 sectors: energy and utilities, manufacturing, government services, consulting, financial systems, healthcare, technology, insurance, transportation, retail, and travel services (hotels, restaurants, rental, etc.).

Benefits

It defines the type of businesses and/or organizations that the procedure is designed to provide guidance for. Many experts refer to innovation as new knowledge incorporated in products, processes, and services. It classifies innovations according to technological, market, and administrative/

organizational characteristics. Technological innovation is the knowledge of components, linkages between components, methods, processes, and techniques that go into a product or service. It may or may not require administrative innovation. It can be a product, a process, or a service. Product or service innovations should be new products or services aiming at satisfying some entity's needs. Process innovation is concerned with introducing new elements into an organization's operations such as input.[1] It provides limitation on the tools, methodology, and direction that can be applied. It defines what types of organizations including customers, users, and interested parties that the procedure is designed to satisfy.

Classification of Action

Each individual clause could be classified as *Should do, Will do,* or *Must do.* In the case of 56002:2019, the entire document is classified as *Should do.*

Summary

Clause 1 does not require the reader to take any action. The primary focus is on the depth, breadth, and limitations of the standard. To put it simply, it applies to you, your organization, or any organization that you obtain resources or services from. It also includes yourself if you are making or growing something for your personal consumption and/or your family. It doesn't matter how simple or how complex the organization is.

Because this is a guidance document, you can select parts of the document that you want to apply and the parts of the document that you don't want to apply. We suggest that you look at each of the clauses and subclauses and then decide if you want to do it in your organization. None of them are required to be included in your IMS. Don't feel it's necessary to do.

To summarize, the scope of 56002:2019 includes small, medium, and large-size organizations, both public and private, as it applies to all new or changed entity realizing or redistributing value that you or your organization is involved in.

We recommend that before you go much further. You need to stop and measure how the organization is performing today and decide on how you would want to change in the next five years.

To aid you in measuring the maturity level of your current IMS, we have created an online questionnaire that will be computer analyzed and reported immediately back to you free of charge. This report will not only measure your current status, but it will also provide you with information related to the root cause of your problem. To get this free report, go to HarringtonManagementSystems.com/IS/h102.

CLAUSE 2: NORMATIVE REFERENCES

- Definition of normative reference: A normative reference in ISO parlance is equivalent to a referenced document. It is indispensable to the application of the standard.

Without the referenced document, all the subject technical standard cannot be fully and properly utilized. For example, it could be a test method for determining a property of a specified material. In ISO Standard 56002:2019 there's only one reference document referred to. It is *ISO 56000:2020 Innovation Management – Fundamentals and Vocabulary.*

Great care should be given to ensuring that the correct level of the referenced document is the one specified in the standard. Standards continuously change, and these changes could have an impact upon how the reference is interpreted. This frequently results in the need to have multiple records of the same standard.

CLAUSE 3: TERMS AND DEFINITIONS

In 56002:2019 the terms and definitions recorded in ISO 56000:2020 are the controlling definitions. The standard contains most of the terms and definitions that are required to operate and manage an IMS. For example, below are some of the terms and definitions (in alphabetical order) that are included in the standard.

- Culture
- Deviation
- Entity

- Ideation
- Innovation

Note: there is a much more extensive list of definitions in Appendix A in this book. Many of the definitions that the authors thought were necessary to use in this book were not included in 56000:2020. Most of these additional definitions came from the International Association of Innovation Professionals (IAOIP).

It is extremely important that you refer to ISO 56000:2020 for all key definitions. The definitions used within this standard may be very different from the way you would normally use the word. We strongly recommend that if you bought *ISO Standard 56002:2019 – Innovation Management System*, you should also buy *ISO Standard 56000:2020 – Innovation Glossary*. It is absolutely essential that you have a firm understanding of how the individual terms are used in 56000:2020 to effectively use 56002:2019.

NOTE

1 See Davydenko, L. (2011). *Fundamentals Of Economic Theory: Principles, Problems, Politics Of Transformation. International Experience and Belarusian Vector Of Development*. Manual, Minsk.

2

Clause 4: Context of the Organization

PURPOSE

To consider all internal and external stakeholders when developing your Innovation Management System (IMS). In Clause 4 we discuss four major considerations. They are:

1. Defining the organization's status and key issues.
2. Identifying stakeholder needs and expectations.
3. Defining the requirements and limitations of the IMS (scope).
4. Defining the content of the IMS.

OVERVIEW

- Defining the extent that internal and external issues impact the IMS
- To understand the interest and needs of the organization's stakeholders (interested parties)
- Presenting cultural best practices
- Consider the previous three conditions to develop the scope of the IMS

BENEFITS

- Provides a systematic way to identify risk from outside sources
- Prepares you to develop a plan that considers the different cultures throughout the world

- Provides a basis for the Organizational Change Management Plan
- Provides an understanding of the stakeholders' (interested parties) desires and needs
- Provides a view of future products
- Delphi future products

CLASSIFICATION OF ACTION

This clause is written as a *Should do* activity. It provides a list of best practices, but each organization can select the clauses that they wish to include in their IMS. This clause is classified as a guidance document always.

DEFINING THE ORGANIZATION'S STATUS AND KEY ISSUES

The World's Context

In 2020, the biggest single factor driving the world's organizational context was COVID-19, the virus that spread rapidly from Wuhan, China, to the rest of the world killing many people, interrupting businesses and services in all forms, costing more jobs than any other factor that has ever occurred, and removing the individual's freedom of choice and environment. Many small businesses went bottom-up even with the national government providing emergency funds.

In many countries people are slipping back into deep levels of economic distress. It's an environment where individuals are struggling to get by with what they have, without thinking about new and exciting things. The focus for most now is trying to secure necessities that had been taken for granted like toilet paper, paper towels, etc. It's a lot like an unbelievable science fiction movie that was written in the 1980s where some monster is about to devour the earth. Many of us are beginning to wonder if these movies were science fiction movies or were they predictions of what was to come.

The Black Death, also known as the Pestilence, Great Bubonic Plague, the Great Plague or the Plague – or less commonly as the Great Mortality or the Black Plague – was one of the most devastating pandemics in human history, resulting in the deaths of an estimated 75 to 200 million people. The death rate in major cities was so high that they couldn't bury the dead and just left them laying in the streets. The disease killed so many in Europe that it created labor shortages, that increased the demand for peasant workers. It peaked in Europe from 1347 to 1351.

In 1918, the Spanish flu immediately followed World War I and was more deadly than the war itself. It is considered the deadliest influenza in history that infected 500 million people worldwide, which is about one-third of the world's population. This was a lethal disease that killed between 50 and 100 million people. This is many times more than the number who died in combat during World War I. It was an influenza virus, similar to the common seasonal flu but considerably more deadly. In those severely affected, it caused the skin to turn blue, violent coughing that sometimes tore abdominal muscles, bleeding from the mouth and nose, incontinence, and vomiting. In some cases, victims were reported to die in a matter of hours. This virus quickly spread around the world thanks to air and ocean travel, overwhelming doctors and nurses, who were often forced to erect temporary tents to deal with the sheer number of patients. It is estimated that over 500 million people were infected with the disease. Now, that sounds like what happened around the world in 2021.

For the past 25 years, we have been fighting a deadly epidemic, HIV, (Human Immunodeficiency Virus) that is mostly a sexually transmitted condition. After coming out of latency, the virus causes sufferers to develop AIDS (Acquired Immunodeficiency Syndrome), which prevents the victim's immune system from fighting disease and generally leads to death from infections or cancer. AIDS is particularly common in sub-Saharan Africa, where as many as 15% of the population are infected in some areas. Since its discovery, HIV/AIDS has caused between 25 and 30 million deaths.

Here we are today with the new virus COVID-19 that has shut down all countries leaving only emergency activities still operating and then even in a reduced, cut-back operating mode. This new virus (coronavirus disease) could be deadlier than the Black Plague if we don't get it under control. Certainly, this presents the biggest world context that all of our population faces today and the biggest challenge to government and nongovernment activities. This affects everyone – from farmers who grow food but can't find anyone to pick it, to bus drivers who acquire the disease from the passengers. It is estimated that, this condition combined with the over-abundance of oil stripped away over 30% of the world's wealth, as markets around the world have gone into a whirlpool that drained the value-added out of the marketplace.

Around the world the basic habits of its people are undergoing a massive change. Due to the combination of the online market, Amazon, and the coronavirus disease, shopping in big malls has given way to shopping on the internet because it is more effective, safe, and affordable. The need for large massive educational facilities is rapidly disappearing as home education becomes more and more popular. The virus is proving that online training and education can effectively be distributed to hundreds of students by a single teacher. There is a growing belief that learned knowledge is much more effective than thought knowledge.

The European Context

Europe, as a whole, has been a strong proponent of IMS standards from the beginning. As experience with ISO 9000 has shown, Europeans are generally more comfortable than North Americans with standards and conformance assessment schemes. Of the companies now certified/registered to ISO 9000 worldwide, the largest number by far is in Europe. North America was relatively slow to accept certification/registration. The argument against registration is, who's going to pay for it? The answer is the customer, of course. A guidance standard that defined the best practices allows the organization to select the real value-added innovative management system in order to optimize competitiveness. As a result, 56002:2019 standards has been released as a guidance standard. Every organization should be looking into it to determine what real value-added content each of the clauses provide, selecting the ones that give them a unique innovative management system and makes the output the best value to their stakeholders. It's like the old saying

"Tell me I have to do something and I will do it begrudgingly. If I want to do something, I'll do it enthusiastically."

Europe was somewhat in advance in the development of management system standards. In fact, several of the European countries generated internal national standards for IMS. They included items like innovation organization and personnel, innovation effects, innovation objectives and targets, innovation management program, operational control, management records, innovation management audits, and innovation management reviews. Many of these innovation management standards were based on ISO 9001.

The requirement for an innovation effects register (i.e., a list of the significant innovation effects, direct and indirect, of the activities, products, and services of the organization upon the IMS) was a major objective of some of the countries participating on ISO Technical Committee (TC) 279, the Innovation Management Systems standard. So far, the concept of a mandatory standard has been rejected by TC 279. The present IMS standard is a voluntary standard. As such, it does not define or set specific innovation performance criteria, objectives, indicators, targets, or timetables for a business or organization. The single level of performance specified is to consider the best practices documented in the 56000:2020 series and implement the ones that provide the best overall value to the stakeholders.

Since these are defined according to a company's own performance objectives, which may be minimal, there is no guarantee that they will be meaningful to society-at-large or part of a broader sustainability strategy. A similar civil proposal for ISO 14000 environmental standards was rejected by its technical committee. According to the British Federation of Small Businesses, these reservations arise from experience in implementing the BS 5750 environmental management systems specification and include claims of disproportionately high implementation and registration costs.

Now there are many other international contexts that need to be included in your evaluation, for example, things like what countries will go to war, changes in weather patterns, foreign competition, etc.

The North American Context

One of the most common indicators of innovation within a country or an organization is their patent record. For many generations, the US has been the world leader in creativity and innovation. Steel, railroading,

TABLE 2.1

STEM Graduates

The Countries with the Most STEM Graduates	
China	4,700,000
India	2,600,000
United States	568,000
Russia	561,000
Iran	335,00
Indonesia	206,00
Japan	195,000

agriculture, computers, software, etc. are places where the US excels and outpaces the rest the world, but that is changing drastically. There has been a drastic shift in the university educational system away from hard engineering science to softer more financial rewarding career paths like MBAs, lawyers, etc. Table 2.1 shows the number of graduates in science, technology, engineering, and mathematics (STEM) in 2016.

Table 2.2 shows the projected millions (m) of graduates in STEM in 2030.

TABLE 2.2

Projected STEM Graduates in 2030

China	37.0 m
India	26.7 m
United States	4.3 m
Russia	4.4 m
Indonesia	3.7 m
Saudia Arabia	3.0 m
Mexico	2.2 m
Brazil	2.0 m
Japan	1.9 m
Germany	1.4 m
UK	1.4 m
France	0.8 m
Canada	0.8 m
Rest of the world	11.6 m

Source: OECD 2015 education indicators.

Table 2.2 visually shows the problem we are facing today with both China and India graduating more students into the science fields than the United States. Today the combination of universities and colleges in China and India produce 11 STEM scientific focus graduates to one graduate in the United States. How can the United States hope to maintain its present stature in innovation when China and India are both growing their technical capabilities much faster than we are?

If you look to the future, the United States will drop from number 3 on the list to number 4 as Russia starts graduating more science-oriented individuals. In fourth place, the United States will be just a little bit ahead of the number of scientific individuals graduating from universities in Indonesia.

The trend to sell off major parts of US companies' products and technologies was originally based upon low cost labor. Today an equally important consideration is the abundance of engineering and scientific support. IBM selling its PC products business to a Chinese company is an excellent example of one of our leading innovative companies moving out of the engineering field and into the consulting field. While originally China focused on manufacturing someone else's product, the present governmental trend is to establish brand-name products that are re-cognized throughout the world. Good Baby, the Chinese company that manufactures children's products, and presently produces well over 80% of the world market on children car seats, is a good example of a company focused on brand recognition. In China, technology has been set by the government as a key building block in the future. The government is pouring large amounts of money into development activities. For example, artificial intelligence (AI) is be giving a high priority rating and heavily supported by government funding. They openly discuss their objective of taking the AI development away from Silicon Valley and having it recognized as one of China's strong areas.

As bad as this picture looks, the United States is even worse than Europe. The European patent office recorded 127,608 approved patents in 2018, while China recorded 432,147 approved patents.

In North America, Canada was much more active in the development of IMS standards than the US. They have continued to maintain a strong leadership position in TC 279 since it was founded, and they have had a major impact on the content in 56002:2019.

Initially the US representative to TC 279 was the American Society for Quality (ASQ). Around 2019, the ASQ decided not to support the ISO efforts to prepare an IMS standard. For approximately one year, ISO TC 279 functioned without United States formal representation. The International Organization for Innovation Professionals (IAOIP) headed by Brett Trusko accepted the responsibility for representing the United States. Immediately, US activities came back to life in time to have some impact upon the final version of 56002:2019 – The Innovation Management System ISO standard. Since that time, US participation in TC 279 has grown to the point that it has more people on subcommittees than any other country. Together Leo Colombo, Frank Voehl, and Richard Fernandez have re-established the United States as a leader in the innovation community.

Historically, North America has not been as receptive to international standards as has Europe or other parts of the world. This is changing slowly. Recent surveys indicate that there is considerable interest in the ISO 56000:2020 series in North America, but many companies are approaching the innovation standard cautiously. This is largely the result of fear that if they became mandatory documents requiring certification/registration, it would lead to higher product costs and increased bureaucracy. Companies are assessing their current systems using ISO 56000:2020 as the benchmark. They are finding out that almost every organization, private or governmental, are in compliance with some parts of ISO 56002:2019, but fewer of them are in compliance with all of the statements within 56002:2019. With 56002:2019 being a guideline-only document, almost every organization is in compliance with it. So, there is little value in the statements that an organization is in compliance with the ISO 56002:2019 Innovation Management System standard. They see that it could open the door to everyone claiming that they have an innovative organization, because they are in compliance with the ISO standard. Many organizations are waiting to see what happens in Europe and other parts of the world to determine when market and business factors make it beneficial for them to become in compliance; in addition, today there is no agreed-to definition of what not being in compliance is. For example, one of our clients has to be certified to four different quality standards in order to remain in business – biomedical, aerospace, automotive, and ISO 9000. This has become a nightmare in separate record-keeping, unproductive effort, and increased costs.

It could be even worse with IMS, as it would be necessary to have different standards for different type products and different standards for the maturity of the organization. Many organizations are waiting to see what happens in Europe and other parts of the world to determine if the market and business factors would make it beneficial for them to become in compliance with a standard that has no agreed-to definition of what not being in compliance means. Many organizations feel that the innovation standard could follow the same pattern if it became a mandatory document. We believe that the correct approach is to use 56002:2019 as a list of best practices that provide a guide to increasing value to the stakeholders with a particular emphasis on the employees, customer, and investors.

Since the recent change of ISO 9000, a number of organizations have decided not to remain registered, but continue to maintain the system. They require their employees to audit the system resulting in decreased cost and a decrease in interruptions and executive-devoted time. Organizations more interested in domestic markets are waiting to see what their customers are going to require related to the ISO 56000:2020 series. Will ISO 56002:2019 be driven down through the supply chain like ISO 9000 was? Will TC 279 develop a new document that is mandatory and can be used by registers to certified innovative management systems? Parties in the know have indicated that is a real possibility.

In the early part of 1995, the US Technical Advisory Group (TAG) team began to work with the American National Standards Institute (ANSI) to pursue synchronization of ISO 14000. Three organizations were assigned to work together to define ANSI's position. These groups were American Society for Testing and Materials (ASTM), American Society for Quality Control (ASQC), and National Sanitization Foundation (NSF) International. As a result, at a meeting held on September 14–15, 1995, ISO 14000 was adopted verbatim as an American National Standard. This is the way it looks like 56000:2020 will follow in the United States.

As a result of a trade agreement that lowered the tariff barriers between Mexico, United States, and Canada, Mexico finds itself in an excellent position to increase the living standards of its people if it can produce high quality innovative products without increasing costs or pollution. As a result, Mexican organizations are embracing ISO 9000 (Quality

Management System) enthusiastically and need to embrace ISO 56002:2019. Unfortunately, over 90% of the industrial organizations in Mexico are extremely small with fewer than 15 employees. There is little chance that these small companies would become registered to ISO 56002:2019 as they are primarily producers of domestic products or components that are delivered to the other 10% of the industrial organizations.

It is unfortunate, but many organizations in Mexico have had negative experiences with ISO 9000. Many executives feel that it greatly increases the bureaucracy within the organization, and they are concerned that conformance to ISO 56002:2019 will make the system even more complex and bureaucratic.

The Asian Context

Innovation and technology are but two flowers that flourish on the same vine. Both of their buds have swollen to the point that they are about ready to explode in Asia and when they do, they will shower their seeds throughout the world. Often, we can use history to predict the future. If you look at modern civilization and technology, it started in China and then progressed west with Alexander the Great's Empire systematically moving it west into Egypt. There, it flared for a while until power and progress moved it west again into Greece. From Greece, the power and technology center of activity moved west again into Rome. From Rome it moved west to Great Britain and the great British Empire. From Great Britain it moved west again to the New England states. It then moved westward into Ohio. From that point it slowly crept westward across the United States until the technology and the power that goes along with it is located in California. But in the 1970s it moved again westward to Japan. Today, Japan is giving up its throne as a leader in technology and production as the US and Japan both have moved westward again back to China.

Technology evolution has always moved westward creating new wealth, new standards of living, and new opportunities in the areas that finds a home for it. Surely, the flower buds that represent technology and innovation are thriving in China and India and are soon to break open into unsurpassed glory and beauty. Truly, China and India are now in the process of positioning themselves as the world leader in innovation and technology. If we are not very careful, the United States would be just another colony under the China's direct and indirect control. Our trade balance continues to worsen with both of these countries draining more and more of United States wealth out of the country and transferring it to Asia.

IDENTIFYING STAKEHOLDER NEEDS AND EXPECTATIONS

- Definition of interested party: ISO 56000:2020 defines interested party as a person or organization that can affect, be affected by, or perceive itself to be affected by a decision or activity·
  - Note 1 to entry: This constitutes one of the common terms and core definitions of the high level structure for ISO management system standards.*

There is nothing wrong with this definition, but in the most cases we focus our IMS design on the needs, requirements, applications, and regulations of the following six interested parties – employees, customers, investors, management, governmental bodies, and suppliers. Even with just a list of six, there is a long-time delay and extra costs involved just to understand each of their needs, expectation, and applications. As a result, we recommend that you collect no information that you don't plan on using in some way.

There are a number of ways that you can go about collecting this information. Some of them are:

- Customer surveys
- Customer roundtables
- Employee opinion surveys
- Focus groups
- Internal estimates
- Personal interviews

- Question and answer activities
- Lost customer interviews

Often when you ask a group of people what they need and expect, we get a variety of answers. For example, 45% of them want to run faster, 30% want increased functions, and 25% want it to be simpler to use. Now what are your external customers really thinking?

- 55% of them are thinking – it's going to be more expensive.
- 25% think – it's going to be more complicated.
- 20% of them think – it's will be less reliable.
- And a large percentage of them are thinking – all of the above.

Just to meet the perceived needs of one of the stakeholders (the external customer) the new product has to be less expensive, more functional, simpler to use, and more reliable.

Now to make it more complex, the interested parties' needs and expectations frequently vary from region to region and again vary based upon age. Think how complicated the matrix would be if you just collected this type of information on the six interested parties (stakeholders).

But that is just the start of the complexity in using the interested parties' needs and expectations in driving the innovation process within your organization. You can collect a lot of data, but it isn't the amount of data that you have, it's a confidence level you have in the data. If the sample size of the information that is collected is too small, it becomes questionable information to base your decisions on. Accuracy of the projections is the absolute crucial part of determining product size, shape, or function. When doing a business case analysis, all of your estimates should have a confidence level associated with each one. For example, the following is this statement that we made about what your customer is thinking.

- 55% of them are thinking – it's going to be more expensive.
- For example, the statement should read if you're using it in a business case analysis "55% plus 10% minus 15% of them are thinking, it's going to be more expensive."

It is also important that each of these estimates should be based upon worst case, best case, and projected actual. For example: the car will sell for $24,000 (worst case), the car will sell for $32,000 (best case), and projected actual is $28,495. To make this analysis even more complex, different interested parties often have conflicting needs and requirements. The investor wants the price to be high so that the dividends are bigger and the stock market value of their company is higher. On the other hand, the customer wants the price to be as low as possible. It is important to realize that the sales price is based upon market price; it not based upon the costs to provide the output. Employees want a shorter work week, more time to do each assignment, and increased salary with more holidays. That increases the cost of the car, which is a negative value to the external customer and it reduces profit, which is a negative value for the investors that is important.

A method that is often used is to have the part of the organization that is in the closest contact with the interested party prepare their estimate of the assigned parties' needs and expectations. For example, marketing should prepare the initial product specification defining the customers' wants and needs related to function, design, and shape. They should also provide estimates on projected sales at a specific price if performance parameters are met. The problem with this is the customer/consumer only knows his needs and requirements based upon the present methodology. In an innovative company, the development group should have a much better understanding of the technology trends and be in a better position to predict what the customer will want in the future. The customers' inputs are usually based upon obvious improvements or minor improvements. They have little or no insight into what can be available in the future. Manufacturing engineering and product engineering can provide estimates related to production costs and cycle times. Personnel can provide input based upon opinion surveys related to changes in the way employees are treated. Research and development can provide estimates related to technology improvement that should be included in the design. Research and development and marketing can provide inputs related to future competitive activities.

The lack of good long-range improvement plans has cost the U.S. government trillions of dollars and will cost them trillions more over the next 4 years.

H. James Harrington

DEFINING THE REQUIREMENTS AND LIMITATIONS OF YOUR IMS

Defining the requirements and limitations of the IMS is often referred to as defining the scope of the IMS. In fact, Subclause 4.3 refers to it as scope.*

Scope in a specific program, project, or product. It's a lot like the organization's mission and objectives statements as it defines what activities are assigned to the specific program, project, or product. It defines start and end dates plus the items that enter the entity and those items that leave the entity.

- What is included in the entity.
- What is not included.
- What are the outputs are from the entity.
- What are the inputs to the entity.
- What parts of the organization are involved in the entity.

Strict adherence to the scope specification will help reduce overruns and expansions to the program.

Liliya Yaushevs, a certified Six Sigma consultant, points out, "The project scope document should include all the important information about what's included and excluded in the project. The key elements should include, but not be limited to:

- Objectives
- Deliverables
- Milestones
- Requirements
- Assumptions
- Risks
- Review and Approval"

In many cases, we will need to box-in the systems and related processes that are involved in the entity. This is often much more difficult than you would first consider. Like any system, we should start off with defining the beginning boundaries and resources that enter the systems. We would then define the end boundaries where the output from the system is delivered to another source outside of the systems, often referred to as the customer. That gives us our beginning and ending boundaries, but that is not enough. Resources are often entering the system and being set up at many places between the beginning and ending boundaries. These entry points make up the upper boundary. Likewise, outputs are leaving the system at many different points between the beginning and ending boundaries. These are particularly important trigger points that are drivers of other parts of the organization. These outputs are what is known as the lower boundaries. Now that we have constructed a box-in entity with beginning, ending, upper, and lower boundaries, they fit together to define what resources the system will be using and what value the system will out putting. Figure 2.1 is a view of the box in a very simple system.

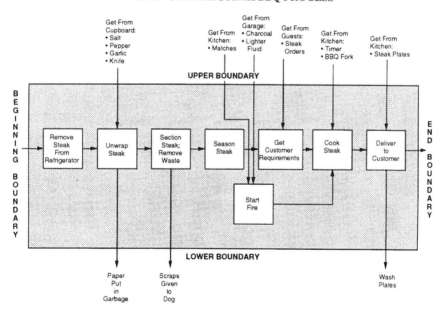

FIGURE 2.1
A Simple Boxed-in System.

DEFINING THE CONTENT OF THE IMS

- Definition of culture: Culture is defined as your background, your history, your heritage, your religion, and your beliefs.
- Definition of personality: Personality is defined as an individual or group's impact on other individuals or groups.

Everyone is talking about the need for a cultural change, but we believe that focusing on it is the wrong answer to today's problems, and does not prepare most organizations in the developed world to survive in the 21st century. Culture is defined as your background, your history, your heritage, your religion, your beliefs. Most organizations want to hold on to their culture and in fact, are worried about losing it. America should be proud of its culture. It is a culture rich in imagination, hard work, caring, risk taking and accomplishment. It is a culture that made the United States the richest, most progressive, most powerful, and most productive nation in the world. Organizations in Asia and Europe also have national cultures that they want to hold on to. And let's not forget the organizations in South America and Africa. Our culture is not the problem. It is the personality of today's population that is the problem. We talk about "workaholics" like work is the worst four-letter word in the English language. People work overtime begrudgingly if they are notified 72 hours in advance, and if not, they refuse. It is the personality of today's work force and our children that needs to be changed. Personality is defined as an individual or group's impact on other individuals or groups. We need to change the personality of our people before we lose the culture that our forefathers worked so hard to create. It is the personality of our key managers that dictates the personality of the total organization. When a new CEO is appointed, the total organization adapts to his or her personality.

> If the new CEO is a basketball fan, everyone knows last night's basketball scores.
>
> *H. James Harrington*

We cannot go back to what we used to do for this old world has changed. The amount of information available to the individual doubles every five years. According to Richard Worman in "Information Anxiety," the weekday edition of the *New York Times* contains more information than the average person was likely to come across in a lifetime in 17th century England.

How do we create a change in the personality of our people? We do that by changing the environment that they live in. Our personality is molded by an ongoing series of environmental impacts that we are subjected to. It starts at birth and ends with our last heartbeat. The biggest impact occurs during the formative years of a child's life – the period before they enter school (a time when more and more of our children are not spending the amount of time they need with their parents, due to the two-salary families and the single-parent family environment we are subjecting them to). Our children do not understand quality time. Around the world people frowned on China's approach to one child per family. This resulted in a significant improvement in the family bond and the attention paid to the children. I believe that this change had a very significant impact upon child mortality rate. In China the child mortality rate fell from 118.4 deaths per 1,000 live births in 1969 to 8.6 deaths per 1,000 live births in 2018. They need full-time parents to help them mold their personality, but that subject is outside the scope of this document.

Let's focus on what we can do to influence and change the environment that impacts the personality of today's work force. What the organization needs is to develop a plan that will change the environmental factors that impact the personality and behavioral patterns of the employees, placing special emphasis on the management team. If we sustain a positive change in the personality of the organization for a long enough period of time (about 5 years), we will change the organization's culture.

We have done a lot of work with executive teams to change their behavioral patterns. The average executive makes between 50 and 80 behavioral errors per week. Correcting these behavioral problems can do more to improve the organization's performance than any Six Sigma program can.

CULTURE CHANGE MANAGEMENT (CCM)

So far in this book and in most other literature related to change management, the focus has been on project-related organization. But the really successful organizations have been able to harmonize their Organizational Change Management (OCM) project-related change activities to complement and strengthen their day-to-day management of change. We will call this close harmony between the three parts of the change concept – projects, process, and daily management – Culture Change Management (CCM). This CCM is taking place today in your organization. You may not realize it. You may not recognize it. And probably you are not managing it, but it is taking place (both positively and negatively) in the day-to-day activities within your organization, and at every level in the organization. It means driving a change in the culture within your organization.

There are five principles for conditions involving transformational change. They are:

1. Use community resources to publicize the intervention and increase accessibility.
2. Develop communication strategies which are sensitive to language.
3. Work with cultural or religious values.
4. Identify and address barriers to access and participation.
5. Accommodate varying degrees of cultural identification.

Each of these five principles plays a key role in developing your cultural change strategy. Look at each one to be sure you understand its impact upon your specific culture change and addresses the positive and negative impact it can have on making an effective IMS.

There are six elements for driving a change culture associated with our CCM model, as shown in Figure 2.2.

1. Understand the five principles for conditions involving transformational change.
2. Mobilize commitment to change through a joint diagnosis of business problems.

Culture Change Management (CCM) Model

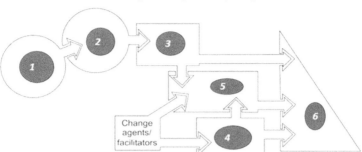

Key Components:

① Understand Conditions for Transformational Change

② Mobilize Commitment to Change

③ Develop a Shared Vision & Plan to Create a Resilient Culture

④ Foster Consensus on the *Desired Future State*

⑤ Spread and Institutionalize Revitalization

⑥ Monitor and Adjust Change Path Strategies

FIGURE 2.2

The Harrington–Voehl Culture Change Management Model.

Source: ©Strategy Associates 2015, All Rights Reserved.

3. Develop a shared vision of how to organize and manage for competitiveness, and a plan for dealing with resistance to change.

4. Implement a process for fostering consensus on the desired future state and the competence and cohesion to move it along.

5. Spread and institutionalize revitalization through formal policies, systems, and structures with a culture of assessment.

6. Monitor and adjust strategies in response to problems in the various change paths.

The above Figure 2.2[1] depicts the six elements of the model according to the usual sequence in the implementation process. We contend that in many cases, most efforts in the management of change do not achieve a positive impact on the organization's culture. Our research indicates that most organization's culture is spiraling downward. Based upon our personal observations as consultants who have looked at many organizations and have been in high executive positions within organizations, we can easily see the negative trends that have developed within the culture for most organizations. These negative trends in culture are not solely driven by business decisions and, in fact, they are often more driven by outside factors that the organization has no control over. Accordingly, it is imperative that leaders understand the conditions for transformational change in terms of the five main principles.[2]

Using the Culture Change Models

The CCM framework has identified a number of outcomes that may need to be generated by the end of each phase of the lifecycle. Of necessity, these outcomes may be a robust combination of technical information, culture change objectives and constraints. Models and prototypes will help to analyze and present some of the required technical information for culture change to succeed in manageable increments, and to test the developing models or prototypes. Context diagrams of the whole solution area (the big picture) at early stages in the lifecycle are invaluable as a guide to the scope and dependencies within the solution space and as an unambiguous communication of these elements to the stakeholders within and outside the development effort.[3]

The Context Diagram shows the system under consideration as a single high-level process and then shows the relationship that the system has with other external entities (systems, organizational groups, external data stores, etc.). Another name for a Context Diagram is a Context-Level Data-Flow Diagram or a Level-0 Data Flow Diagram. Since a Context Diagram is a specialized version of Data-Flow Diagram (DFD), understanding a bit about data-flow diagrams can be helpful. A Data-Flow Diagram is a graphical visualization of the movement of data through an information system. The DFDs are one of the three essential components of the structured-systems analysis and design method (SSADM).

A Context Diagram is process centric and depicts four main components.

- Processes (circle)
- External entities (rectangle)
- Data stores (two horizontal, parallel lines or sometimes and ellipse)
- Data flows (curved or straight line with arrowhead indicating flow direction)

A sample Context Diagram is shown in Figure 2.3.

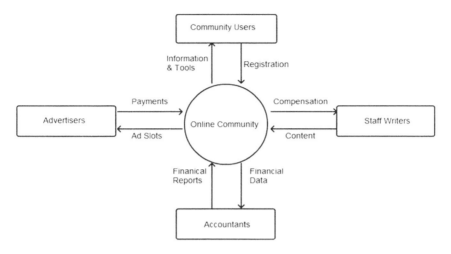

FIGURE 2.3
A Sample Context Diagram.

As shown in Figure 2.3, the best context diagrams are used to display how a system interoperates at a very high level, or how systems operate and interact logically. The system Context Diagram is a necessary tool in developing a baseline interaction between systems and actors, actors and a system, or systems and systems.

A culture model tells us about the values and norms within a group or an organization, regardless of the type or complexity. It identifies what is important to the organization and its leaders, as well as how people approach work and each other; how "we do things around here." For example, one culture may value stability and proper order. In this case, clearly defined processes will be very important and there will be a strong expectation of conformance rather than of innovation and creativity, which can often be a problem when trying to change the culture toward more creativity. The Schneider Culture Model[4] defines four distinct cultures:

- *Collaboration* culture is about working together.
- *Control* culture is about getting and keeping control.
- *Competence* culture is about being the best.
- *Cultivation* culture is about learning and growing with a sense of purpose.

The diagram shown in Figure 2.4 summarizes the Schneider Culture Model. Each of the four cultures are depicted – one in each quadrant. Each has a name, a "descriptive quote," a picture, and some words that characterize that quadrant. Please take a moment to read through the diagram and get a sense of the model and where your company fits.

An important aspect of the Schneider model is the axes that indicate the focus of an organization:

- Horizontal axis: People Oriented (Personal) vs. Organization Oriented (Impersonal)
- Vertical axis: Actuality Oriented (Reality) vs. Possibility Oriented

This provides a way to see relationships between the cultures. For example, Control culture is more compatible with Collaboration or Competence cultures than with Cultivation culture. In many cases, Cultivation culture is the opposite of Control culture in that, learning and growing are opposite of security and structure. Similarly, Collaboration is often seen as the opposite of Competence.

All models are wrong, some are useful.

George Box, statistician

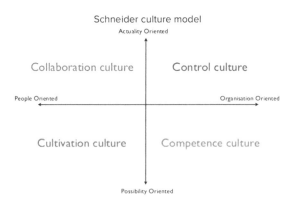

FIGURE 2.4
Schneider Culture Model.

Reference: The Reengineering: A Plan for Your Current Culture Work by William E. Schneider (Apr 1994). © 2013 Scrum WithStyle scrumwithstyle.com

All models are an approximation of reality and it is important to remember that we are ignoring minor discrepancies so that we can perform analysis and have meaningful discourse. Also, we may wish to consider other models such as Spiral Dynamics if we wanted to understand cultural evolution.[5] In the Schneider model, no one culture type is considered better than another. Please refer to the book for details on the strengths and weaknesses of each. Depending on the type of work, one type of culture may be a better fit.

Companies typically have a dominant culture with aspects from other cultures. This is fine as long as those aspects serve the dominant culture. Different departments or groups (e.g., development vs. operations) may have different cultures. Differences can lead to conflict.

Examples of Culture Change Measures

This is the measure of value of human needs and motivations being delivered from and to the business, i.e., when the customer is able to start earning value or reducing cost from the deliverables of the employee efforts and vice versa, as shown in Figure 2.5. For example, when a new business process is implemented or when a new service is launched on the market.

The power and impact of an organization's culture is often only felt when it is challenged. For example, when you merge two organizations requiring different teams of people to work together, or when you seek to

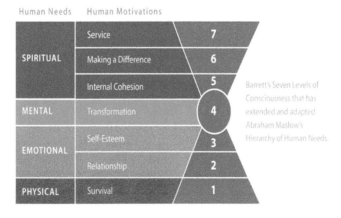

FIGURE 2.5
Barrett's Seven Levels of Consciousness.

lift business performance with your existing work force requiring a change in how the work is done. The measurement of both human needs and human motivations is shown in Barrett's diagram.

Figure 2.5 shows an extension of Maslow's Hierarchy of Needs as applied to culture change. Barrett realized that with some minor modifications Abraham Maslow's Hierarchy of Needs could be turned into a model for mapping the evolution of consciousness in individuals, and all forms of human group structures – organizations, communities, nations, etc.

CCM Summary

We agree with all the work that the CCM gurus have publicized and promoted for the past 25 years related to the importance of preparing the individuals that are affected by the output from a project to accept and embrace the project output. But we feel too little emphasis has been placed on the importance of how the content of these change initiatives impact the organization's culture, and how the day-to-day decisions made by managers, that does not trigger a project, impacts the culture and performance of the organization. We believe that improving the resiliency factor within the culture of the organization has a bigger impact upon the ability for the organization to change and operate in a turbulent economy that exists today than changing the degree of acceptance of individual project outputs. Project Change Managment (PCM) has a relatively short time and little impact upon how the organization functions.

In the more successful organizations, cultures act as re-enforcers for productive behavior in that they assist employees in coping with the environmental uncertainties and in coordinating their activities. According to Wilkins, Dyer, and Burrell, cultural roadmaps are made up of general and specific frames of reference that allow individuals to define situations they encounter and develop the appropriate response.[6] Mottoes, Visions, and Mission Statements add to an organizations ability to shape its own culture. For example, in 1912 the following words were inscribed on the walls of the New York City Post Office: "Neither snow nor rain nor gloom of night stays these couriers from the swift completion of their appointed rounds." Although this pledge was never intended to be the official motto of the US Post Office, such is the power of words to shape belief that millions of Americans still take this pledge to be the motto of the Postal Service and accept the words with an almost sacred trust.[7]

People need to be both empowered and motivated in order for real change to take place. That is, you need to achieve a situation where all of management and staff are both able and willing to change, as outlined in the checklist below:

- A cultural audit will in itself facilitate change – "if you measure it, you change it." A very powerful form of measurement is to obtain customer feedback on the service provided – this provides a significant motivation for change across all levels of management and staff.
- The behaviors and attitudes in the department often reflect those exhibited in the management team. Undertake some management team building and it will have an exciting positive impact throughout the whole organization.
- Changing people in influential positions can have an effect on the culture, but their personalities and approach need to be "different" to the existing culture. They also need to to be encouraged to bring in a fresh approach, or else it might be their behavior that changes (by conforming) rather than the culture.
- A well-designed organizational change can also change the culture. But beware – as Caesar first observed, reorganization can simply be a substitute for achievement.
- A "bottom up" program is more pragmatic – trying to change the culture in a few parts of the organization and hoping it will spread out from there. These are generally cheap programs, but not that effective.
- A well-designed mission, vision, or set of objectives will also facilitate change. Having "a mission" is not good enough – it has to be a "motivating mission" that inspires people and makes them feel good about coming to work.

Finally, we covered the following major considerations involved in changing an organization's culture:

- Before an organization can change its culture, it must first understand the current culture, or the way things are now.

- Once you understand your current organizational culture, your organization must then decide where it wants to go, define its strategic direction, and decide what the organizational culture should look like to support success. What vision does the organization have for its future and how must the culture change to support the accomplishment of that vision?
- Next, the management team needs to answer questions such as:
  - What are the most important values you would like to see represented in your organizational culture?
  - Are these values compatible with your current organizational culture? Do they exist now? If not, why not?
- However, knowing what the desired organizational culture looks like is not enough. Organizations must create change management plans to ensure that the desired organizational culture becomes a reality. In reality, the individuals in the organization must decide to change their behavior to create the desired organizational culture. This is often regarded as the hardest step in CCM, and the most rewarding.
- But even that is not enough, the cultural impact must be considered in every decision and action that is considered for implementation. It doesn't matter how small or how big that decision is. The cumulative impact on the culture of many small decisions/actions can often have a bigger impact upon the organization's culture than a reorganization has on it.

In the final analysis: there are lots of resources out there on leading culture change. But none of these will likely help unless you are truly willing to ask yourself these four fundamental questions (Beer, Eisenstat and Spector, 1990):

1. Do we know how to lead culture change?
2. Have we developed the skills to put that knowledge into action?
3. Are there any hidden conflicts that stop us from using what we know?
4. Are there unwritten rules in our culture that inhibit our well-intended plans?

Cultural Change Management changes the way the organization operates, reacts and functions. Project Change Management improves the way affected parties except an individual change.

H. James Harrington

The ability for an organization to accept change is driven by the cumulative effect of the decisions that are made and the ability to reduce learning tension, not on the individual change initiatives themselves.

COLLABORATION

- Definition of collaboration: Collaboration is a working practice whereby individuals work together to a common purpose to achieve business benefit. Collaboration enables individuals to work together to achieve a defined and common business purpose.

There are four basic types of collaborations being used today. They are:

- Alliances
- Portfolios
- Networks
- Ecosystems

Alliances collaboration is the most common way to establish long-term cooperation for innovation between two or more organizations with some specific common interest. Strategic alliances are usually formal documents where independent entities agree to combine resources temporarily in an effort to reach their strategic goals. This usually results in the sharing of current information and knowledge with the hopes of creating new and more profitable future knowledge. A good example was the information technology alliance between Apple, IBM, and Microsoft in the 1970s and 1980s.

Portfolio collaborations were created so that firms could benefit from a collaboration agreement for longer periods of time and across different entities. This growing interdependencies between independent organizations is becoming more popular. The basic concept behind port-folio collaboration is the legal authority to transfer best practices between independent firms without being considered a monopoly or price-fixing. Often this type of arrangement is led by a focus firm frequently called an ego firm that manages the knowledge flow between the independent firms. Often this results in joint patents being issued the two independent orga-nizations. This approach is often used by pharmaceutical organizations.

In effect, portfolio management was all about extracting best practices from alliance experiences and then spreading these internally. In this process a so-called ego firm (or focal firm) established agreements with independent companies but then managed the knowledge flows through specific functions.

Network collaboration is the third type of innovation collaboration. It included organizations that were willing to share research and devel-opment knowledge and goals related to their key entities. A typical ex-ample would be the collaboration between KLM and Northwest airlines in the early 1990s. This approach became popular in the 1990s and still exist to some degree. It was the next step in the collaboration metho-dology from alliances and portfolios collaboration.

Ecosystems are the most advanced approach to collaboration that brings about a cooperative working environment between different en-tities. Ecosystems are defined as: "relatively self-contained, self-adjusting systems of resource-integrating actors connected by shared institutional arrangements and mutual value creation through service exchange."

Within an ecosystem shared vision, shared enterprise, serving each other, helping each other create value, committing to each other, and pursuing jointly formulated strategies and goals hence becomes the norm.

Collaboration is not for everyone. Before making a commitment to a collaboration approach, carefully review the benefits you will gain from the collaboration and the potential risks that are involved in the free exchange of proprietary information. It is not unusual for one member of a cooperation becoming a competitor of another member of the collaboration. Be sure to clearly define the positive and negative impact that the cooperation could be to your organization. Ask yourself if a sophisticated exchange of knowledge is in the best interest of the orga-nization's strategic goals.

SUMMARY

In Clause 4 of this book we discussed four major considerations. They are:

- Defining the organization's status and key issues.
- Identifying stakeholders' needs and expectations.
- Defining the extent and limitations of IMS (scope).
- Defining the content of IMS.

In IMS they use the "contexts" extensively during this section. To alleviate any potential confusion, see definition of "context of the organization" below:

- Definition: Context of the organization is the combination of internal and external issues that can have an effect on an *organization's* approach to developing and achieving its *objectives*.
  - Note 1 to entry: In English, this concept is often referred to by other terms such as "business environment", "organizational environment" or "ecosystem of an organization".
  [Source: ISO 9000:2015, 3.2.2, modified by removing the original Notes 1, 2 and 4 to entry.]*

Most of the items that are discussed in Clause 4 are basic items that apply to most of the systems that are embedded into most organizations. The exception to this is technology advancements that are applied only to a few parts of the organization. Even when they only apply to the continuous evolution-type improvements within an already established product. For example, the cultural aspect that supports the innovation cycle are the same that support the personnel systems.

If you consider the innovation cycle starting with marketing, development engineering, product engineering, manufacturing engineering, quality engineering, manufacturing, procurement, and sales, it would be very undesirable and costly to have a separate culture for the innovative activities within the organizations that differs from the rest of the operations culture.

---

*©ISO. This material is excerpted from ISO 56000:2020, with permission of the American National Standards Institute (ANSI) on behalf of the International Organization for Standardization. All rights reserved.

The only exception to this would be when management establishes an organization that is allowed to take on a different set of principles and operating procedures. For example, you may build typewriters in one plant and manufacture computer chips in another location, or you might be like Ernst & Young where one group does management consulting and the other group does financial audits. There may be a need for a very different culture in research and development than there is in finance. In any case, management should try to establish an IMS that is the same as possible throughout the organization. Failure to do so can cause conflict, greed, envy, and resentment between different parts of the organization. I have seen situations where resentments were high in an organization because the development function allowed their employees to work one day a week on anything they would like to work and the manufacturing people weren't given this option. This resulted in comments like, "How come research is allowed to work for one day a week and get paid for five days?" We would suggest that Subclauses 4.1, 4.3, and 4.4 be viewed from a total organization's viewpoint, not just the innovation cycle.

Organizational change has been recognized as a building block for organizational effectiveness and survival. Creativity is "the cornerstone of organizational change, the foundation of innovation, and a key to organizational effectiveness" (Gilson, Mathieu, Shalley, & Ruddy, 2005, p. 521). As part of organizational change, creativity and innovation are closely related processes in organizations; what is more, they are part of almost the same process (Anderson, Potočnik, & Zhou, 2014).

We need to face it. Today is very different than yesterday and tomorrow will even be more different than today was. From our point of view the world has never been in such a dynamic state of change and fluctuation. The behavioral patterns that made countries and organizations great will not work in tomorrow's environment. Here in the United States we may be faced with as much as 18% unemployment as companies around the world will be hesitant in bringing surplus employees back into the work force.

In the 1990s, the business theme was, "Small is beautiful." This drove a breaking up of many of the big and powerful organizations. Countries broke up into smaller countries, believing that if anything happened to them, their Big Brothers would come in and take care of the intruders. There was a strong belief that small companies move faster, accomplish more, and are more loyal to their leaders.

Today the theme of business has changed to "Big is better." Big organizations are buying up their small competitors making them bigger and bigger. This also allows them to eliminate duplication of effort which was the basic concept in growing larger organizations. This growing bigger often results in increasing productivity which often results in increased unemployment.

The theme of today is everyone should go to college and everyone should have a job that they love. This leads to a mindset that everyone wants to be a white-collar worker sitting in their office giving instructions to other people while they drink their coffee. It can be a good objective for some, but if everyone is a manager who are they going to give instructions to? A second problem is, many of our people love their jobs so much they don't have time to love their spouses and their children. The lack of parental guidance and love forces their children to turn to technology for the satisfaction they should be getting from the parents. To offset the lack of attention and love they should be getting from their parents, children turn to electronic games and phones as their way of connecting with the real world. But in real life, their success is measured by what they accomplish, not the number of monsters they kill. My granddaughter, who is 11 years old, makes play dates with two friends from 9:30 AM to 11 AM just like an adult would set up a meeting in the business atmosphere. Somehow, I feel that children should be allowed to play together without being forced into a schedule.

Yes, tomorrow is a new day and we have a chance to turn it into a blue-ribbon day or a funeral. It really is a time for major change in our behavioral patterns in our personal and business life.

It is absolutely imperative that at the very start of an upgrade to your IMS you have an excellent understanding of the inhibitors and advantages related to the external conditions and the internal culture and handicaps. But that is far from enough to have a successfully implemented IMS. You need to have a comprehensive understanding of the needs and requirements from all relative interested parties. We need to wrap them altogether to develop an active efficient project management plan that includes a detailed risk assessment accompanied by a mitigation plan. Tomorrow will require you to be more creative and more innovative than you ever have been before. The time to start is now.

We need TIME – Total Improvement Management Excellence in both the private and public life.

H. James Harrington

NOTES

1 Figure 2.2 was first created by Frank Voehl and Bill Hayes for a handbook and software program about BPM (Business Process Management), which included a component on change management, and is adapted by Voehl for use in this CCM book.
2 These five conditions are a blend of many experts and authors over the years, representing many types of industries. For example, in particular, we like the thinking of Jared Roy Endicott, whose five principles are: Have a good reason, the Vision Thing, the Flywheel effect, Direct and Honest Communication, and Establish Trust.
3 A Context Diagram (and a Data Flow Diagram for that matter) provides no information about the timing, sequencing, or synchronization of processes such as which processes occur in sequence or in parallel. Therefore it should not be confused with a flowchart or process flow which can show these things.
4 See http://www.methodsandtools.com/archive/agileculture.php. The Schneider book is called *The Reengineering Alternative* and it was first published in 2001. The premise is that very business has its own particular kind of corporate culture. Before you sink a lot money, time, and effort into a reengineering/ culture change initiative, you will need to know if and how your organization would benefit from such a program. *The Reengineering Alternative* explains how companies can develop effective culture change improvement plans based not on some cookie-cutter notion of change management, but upon that organization's unique strengths and corporate objectives. This book will be especially valuable to managers who recognize the need for organizational change, but either haven't found an appropriate improvement program or can't fit an outside program into their own particular budget.
5 Don Edward Beck, Christopher C. Cowan, *Spiral Dynamics: Mastering Values, Leadership, and Change.*
6 In *The Words We Live By*, Brian Burrell, a lecturer in mathematics at the University of Massachusetts at Amherst, turns his father's passion for words into a spirited study of the ideals and principles recorded in America's key texts. While Brian Burrell was growing up, his father began collecting mottoes, oaths, and creeds from around the country in a notebook titled "The Words People Live By," which takes its reader on a tour of America through the phrases of belief, duty, and community that offer ready-made opinions and profess values for everyday life in the United States.
7 CCM has a much bigger impact upon the way the organization operates and its attitude related to embracing and accepting change initiatives. It brings about a basic change in the attitude and the way the organization operates on a day-to-day basis. CCM also has a major impact upon the content of the individual change initiatives and management decisions. Comparing the results between CCM and Organizational (Project) Change Management, the later has a relatively minor impact upon how the organization brings about fundamental changes in the way it reacts.

3

Clause 5: Leadership

PURPOSE

In IMS they use the word "context" extensively during this section.

- Definition of context: ISO 56000:2020 defines context as the combination of internal and external issues that can have an effect on the organization's approach to developing and achieving its objectives. It is also sometimes called an organizational environment.[*]
- Definition of leadership: Leadership is a process of social influence, which maximizes the efforts of others, towards the achievement of a goal.

    Note: Notice key elements of this definition. Leadership stems from social influence, not authority or power. Leadership requires others, and that implies they don't need to be "direct reports." Leadership is not defined in ISO 56000:2020.

Most of the items that are discussed in Clause 4 are basic items that apply to most of the systems that are embedded in most organizations. The exception to this are technology advancements that are applied only to a few parts of the organization even when they only apply to the continuous evolution-type improvements within an already established product. For example, the cultural aspect that supports the innovation cycle are the same that support the personnel systems.

If you consider the innovation cycle starting with marketing, development engineering, product engineering, manufacturing engineering,

---

quality engineering, manufacturing, procurement, and sales, it would be very undesirable and costly to have a separate culture for the innovative activities within the organizations that differs from the rest of the operations culture. The only exception to this would be when management establishes an organization that is allowed to take on a different set of principles and operating procedures. For example, you may build typewriters in one plant and manufacture computer chips in another location. Or there may be a very different culture in research and development than there is in finance. We suggest that Subclauses 4.1, 4.3, and 4.4 be viewed from a total organization's viewpoint, not just the innovation cycle.

The purpose of this chapter is to provide a general framework for the role of leadership to enhance the IMS. It discusses the components of leadership behavior that inspires people to engage in innovation activities and programs and describes actions leaders should take to support the IMS. Examples of actions are the communication and awareness campaign leaders should engage in, executive presence, and the structure that top management should provide to create an alignment and coherence in the functioning of the IMS. Clause 5 consists of the following Subclauses:

- Leadership and commitment
- Innovation policy
- Innovation responsibilities

OVERVIEW

This chapter focuses on the leadership behavior that supports an Innovation Management System (IMS). The chapter shows you how to create a vision, how to craft an innovation strategy, how to communicate it to employees, and how to set an innovation policy that clarifies roles and responsibilities.

BENEFITS

At the end of this chapter, you will learn the criticality of leadership commitment to the effectiveness of an IMS. You will also learn how to create an innovation strategy, how to establish an innovation policy, and how to communicate it to your organization.

CLASSIFICATION OF ACTIONS

There are clauses of this chapter that are written as a *Must do* action, like the vision, the strategy, and the policy. Other actions you can choose to delay at a later time based on the specifics of your organization.

SUBCLAUSE 5.1: LEADERSHIP BEHAVIOR THAT DRIVES INNOVATION

Top management should demonstrate leadership and commitment with respect to the innovation management system.[*]

This clause addresses the role of top management in the design and implementation of the IMS. It defines the role of top management around three key areas:

- Top management engagement and the role of leadership in setting the innovation vision and defining the innovation strategy.
- The role of top management in designing the innovation policy and communicating it to the rest of the organization.
- The role of top management in defining and assigning roles and responsibilities on who should do what during the implementation of the IMS.

---

[*]©ISO. This material is excerpted from ISO 56002:2019, with permission of the American National Standards Institute (ANSI) on behalf of the International Organization for Standardization. All rights reserved.

Leadership's role in fostering innovation and cultivating a culture of creativity and change is crucial to the success of the implementation of your IMS. Without an explicit engagement from top leadership and a clear direction from senior executives on what innovation means for the company, your IMS will not be effective. ISO 56002:2019 is very clear on the issue of leadership engagement and the fact that ISO 56002:2019 clustered the questions of innovation strategy, innovation vision, and innovation policy under the leadership clause, speaks volume to the importance of leadership commitment to the success of innovation in general and to the IMS in particular.

This Subclause of ISO 56002:2019 addresses seven key points. These are the pillars of your leadership commitment.

1. Leadership commitment in driving innovation (Subclause 5.1).
2. Value realization as a core concept to your IMS (Subclause 5.1.2).
3. Innovation vision as a guide to people's behavior (Subclause 5.1.3).
4. Innovation strategy (Subclause 5.1.4).
5. Innovation policy in setting rules and procedures (Subclause 5.2).
6. Communicating the innovation policy (Subclause 5.2.2).
7. Roles and responsibilities: Defining reports and clarifying line of authorities in your IMS (Subclause 5.3).[*]

Leadership commitment and engagement in driving innovation is of paramount importance to the success of your IMS. Regardless of how good your strategy and your vision are, and how much resources you pour into the IMS, it is the top management leadership engagement that conditions the success or the failure of your IMS.

According to a study conducted by Jack Zenger (2015), leadership behavior is important to innovation because it provides clarity on the direction of the organization. It inspires trust and helps employees build connections with different management levels in charge of the IMS. Commitment from top leadership affects perception and shapes the mindset. It creates a safer environment for people to think differently, try

---

[*]©ISO. This material is excerpted from ISO 56002:2019, with permission of the American National Standards Institute (ANSI) on behalf of the International Organization for Standardization. All rights reserved.

new ways of doing things, and take risks. Zenger points to the following leadership behaviors:

- Innovative leaders provide a vision that projects the organization into the future.
- Innovative leaders establish trust and provide the safety needed for creative minds to flourish.
- Innovative leaders challenge the status quo by pushing the envelope higher to drive change.
- Innovative leaders are fast in responding to crises and move swiftly to seize on new opportunities.
- Innovative leaders are driven by data, facts, and knowledge, and use scientific research methods in their decision-making process.
- Innovative leaders value teamwork and collaboration and put their own self-interest aside.
- Innovative leaders value diversity and recognize that the difference is what sparks creative moments.
- Innovative leaders are experts in what they do and are curious about technological breakthroughs

These types of leadership behaviors, when present in your organization, can be your best ally in implementing ISO 56002:2019 and establishing the IMS. The impact of these behaviors on the implementation of your IMS can be summarized in three important outcomes:

- When leadership is committed to innovation, IMS implementation becomes a high priority on the management agenda. Your IMS becomes part of the strategic planning and strategic management of all management layers of the organization.
- When leadership is engaged, accountability becomes important and that would drive interest in tracking progress and measuring behavior.
- And finally, leadership presence drives culture change. People's perception of innovation changes. A new cultural transformation emerges to shape the mindset of the organization.

ISO 56002:2019 outlines eleven actions that leadership needs to take in order to ensure a good implementation of the standard (items a through k).

Of these eleven items, there are some items that are critical and have to be put in place as early as possible. These are *Must do* recommendations. They are accountability and consistency (clauses a and b), culture (clause c), structure and processes (clauses d and e), outcomes (clause g), and evaluation (clause j). These are *Must-do* activities and are needed for the early installation of your IMS.

The other clauses may not be needed in the beginning, as we do not see them as critical to early IMS installation. Although it would be nice to have them, the second set of recommendations can be delayed. We will devote a clause to them at the end of this chapter. These will be nice-to-have recommendations.

Accountability and Consistency

Top leadership must show their commitment to IMS and take responsibility over the functioning, effectiveness, efficiency, and outcomes of the IMS. This is what ISO 56002:2019 recommends. Accountability starts with a commitment taken by senior leadership to be personally responsible for the implementation of the IMS as well as its effectiveness in achieving goals. An attitude of "The Buck Stops Here" is a must-have attitude that fosters culture of accountability and teaches employees and young innovators about authentic leadership. A healthy practice is also to hold managers, responsible for different parts of the IMS, accountable of consequences of not achieving the goals or not meeting the expectations set by the IMS. It is a good practice to have all managers sign an IMS pledge in which they pledge their engagement in making the IMS a successful system, while using available metrics and measurements tools to monitor their contribution.

Culture

The second action that must be taken to show leadership commitment to innovation is the leadership engagement in shaping an innovative culture. Culture is the hidden operating system that runs your organizational social fabric. Unless you change that operating system, innovation will not flourish. Generally speaking, there are three cultural barriers that inhibit innovation and innovative thinking. These barriers are fear, the absence of reward, and a disengaged leadership.

Fear

Fear is the enemy of innovative thinking and creativity. In organizations where there are harsh consequences for trying out new things and unconventional ways of doing things, innovation will stifle. There is a reason for start-ups to beat older companies on innovation. Start-ups companies are more tolerant of mistakes and provide a wider margin of error to their employees, while established companies tend to narrow the margins of error. Our recommendation is that leadership needs to empower their employees to take risks and inspire employees to "ask for forgiveness, not for permission" in order to help them take initiatives. When employees feel that they are free to try out options, and that they are backed by top leadership, their mindset changes.

The Absence of Reward

When employees come up with new ideas and new suggestions and they see no tangible or intangible rewards, their excitement and engagement turns off; worse in some cases, they lose the change momentum and become themselves an obstacle to change. So establish a reward system that differentiates innovators and those who support innovation by recognizing them as a role model. While for some the reward may be tangible; for others, the reward could be intangible. Recognition, time off, trips, or a dinner with the CEO can be a rewarding experience.

Disengaged Leadership

The last critical factor in creating a culture of innovation is the need to establish a role model for young entrepreneurs, new recruits, and independent thinkers. The leadership model is extremely important in motivating employees and engaging ambitious ones. When young innovators join a company, they look up to senior execs for examples. If your senior execs are disengaged, absent, or inaccessible, young innovators are left without a model. Help your senior leadership practice an open-door policy so they can meet, coach, mentor, and empower your innovators.

Structure, Resources, and Processes

The third must-have component of your IMS is the need to establish a structure, provide resources, and define processes. When employees spend a lot of time figuring out how to submit an idea or develop a prototype, this could be a drag on your innovation capability. Leadership commitment to innovation is materialized by putting in place the structure and the process needed for innovators to engage. These structures and processes could be an idea management platform that allows innovators to submit and track their ideas, or an accelerator facility that helps them develop a prototype. It could be also a budget that allows them to run testing outside of the facility or rewarding an exceptional innovator to help employees overcome funding constraints.

Outcomes

The fourth must-have component of your leadership engagement is the commitment the executive team shows to results and outcomes. It is nice to have a functioning IMS; but if the IMS does not produce results and lead to tangible outcomes, then leadership has to take action. Outcomes should be linked to the initial strategic objective so you can track and measure them. An innovation outcome could be a better service, an improved interface, time saved, better productivity, better market presence, or a new product or service that differentiates the offer.

Evaluation and Improvement

The final must-have variable in leadership commitment is the engagement of leadership towards IMS improvement and assessment. Leadership needs to review the IMS frequently in order to evaluate its effectiveness, its efficiencies, and its results. The assessment must be done internally at least twice a year and externally by an outside assessor at least once a year. Leadership needs to be involved in the assessment by reviewing and acting upon the assessment reports, the assessment recommendations, and the millstone improvements to underscore their interest and their engagement in the IMS.

The second category of actions that leadership needs to take is as important as the previous one. However, and depending on the specifics of your circumstances, they may not be critical during early installation. We call them "should-have" or "nice-to-have" actions because they do not impact the effectiveness during the early adoption. You can always implement them during the next improvement cycle. These are the action listed in Clauses d, f, h i, and k of Subclause 5.1.1 of ISO 56002:2019. Let us briefly explain them.

Integration of the IMS into the Existing Systems

Leadership needs to make sure that the IMS is fully integrated with other management systems such as human resources, logistics, supply chain, finance, customer service, sales, marketing, and analytics.

Awareness

Leadership needs to ensure that people know about how innovation works inside the organization and how the innovation strategy affects the success of the organization. They need also to make sure that people understand why the organization invests in innovation.

Talent Support

Top leadership needs to engage in actions that support the development of talents and encouraging them to engage with the IMS.

Innovator Support

Top leadership needs to engage in recognizing and supporting innovators, and people who contribute to the suggestions and the promotion of new ideas in the organization.

Line Supervisor Support

Top management needs to support lower-level management and line supervisors, especially those who are at the bottom of the pyramid.

BOX 3.1 FIVE QUESTIONS THAT HELPS GAUGE YOUR LEADERSHIP ENGAGEMENT

How do I know that leadership is truly engaged in supporting and promoting my IMS? If you want to check whether your top management is truly engaged in supporting and developing your IMS, ask the following five questions:

1. What actions or steps our top leadership has been involved with to define innovation and develop a common language and framework around innovation?
2. Have we defined the level of leadership that owns innovation strategy?
3. To what extent is our top leadership engaged in leading our innovation portfolio?
4. What actions or steps have our top leadership taken to drive engagement around innovation?
5. How and to what extent is our top leadership engaged in creating and fostering a culture of innovation?

Subclause 5.1.2: Value Realization

Top management should demonstrate leadership and commitment with respect to value realization.*

In addition to the leadership behavior outlined earlier, ISO 56002:2019 addresses another equally important component: Subclause 5.1.2 is devoted to the value realization.

Value realization is different from value creation. While value creation refers to the effort you make in order to improve a process inside your department or within your team, value realization speaks to the impact of these improvements on your customers. It is one thing for you to make improvements internally that impresses your management; it is another thing to show how these improvements affect growth and realize value for your shareholders. As well argued by John Catalfamo from

---

*©ISO. This material is excerpted from ISO 56002:2019, with permission of the American National Standards Institute (ANSI) on behalf of the International Organization for Standardization. All rights reserved.

Salesforce's Innovation and Transformation Center, value realization is achieved only when the change you make affects the entire organization. Segmented or isolated change initiatives that have minimal effects on the customer and your growth are not considered as innovation initiatives that realize value, even though they may create value. A change initiative may create some value for your team and your department, but unless the initiative has a measurable impact on your customers and the entire organization, it is not a value realization. When managers launch innovative initiatives to improve their work and team processes and think of it as value realization, they make a conceptual mistake.

So, what is value realization then, and how does ISO 56002:2019 define it? ISO 56002:2019 builds the concept of value realization around two main ideas: Customer insights and customer needs on one hand, and risk tolerance on the other hand (Clause a, b, and c, Subclause 5.1.2).

Customer Insight and Customer Needs/Wants

Innovation is triggered by an opportunity. There are four types of opportunities. They are:

- The identification of a problem that is detracting the value of an entity.
- The identification of something that is needed.
- The identification of something that is wanted.
- The identification of something that would be wanted if it was available.

It is important to understand that most of today's innovation is the result of defining an entity that is not needed, but wanted by a potential customer. For example, I want Lobster Newburg for supper tonight, but I need a vegetable and salad. I need a car to take me to the doctor and the grocery store, but I don't need the Buick, Cadillac, or Lincoln town car that sits in my garage, but I want them. Many individuals in the United States have everything they need but want to buy something new, brighter, and shinier if it's only to keep pace with their friends. Throughout this book, as we talk about customer needs, we are defining needs as needs/wants.

Innovation starts with a need, and a need is better understood through customer insights. Without an intimate knowledge about your customers, you will not be able to innovate or improve their experience. So, you need to collect data on your customer behavior, using a variety of sources that are available to you. Here are the five questions you need to ask about your customer's purchase decision making:

1. How do my customers identify my products and how do they fulfill their needs? (need recognition)
2. How do they search for information to find my product? (information search)
3. How do they evaluate alternatives and how do they choose my product over a different product from a competitor? (evaluation of alternatives)
4. How do they make the final purchase decision? (purchase decision)
5. What do they do after they buy my product? (post-purchase decision)

When you use and exploit the purchase history of your customer, understanding their reviews of your product, their complaints, the defects, and rejected products, and how your customer come into contact with your products, you will have a better understanding of your customer's decision-making process.

More importantly, you need to take advantage of the new technologies in order to understand better, and in a real time, your customer experience. Recent breakthroughs in exponential technologies, such as artificial intelligence (AI) and machine learning (ML) bring tremendous value to the way we understand customer decision making. While in the past, data was generated from secondary and primary sources, AI and ML now can help you understand your customer needs and wants in real-time. The importance of AI in helping you understand your customer is that it can provide actionable insights by feeding real-time data into your Customer Relationship Management (CRM) and other decision-making platforms.

You can improve your customer experience (CX) by taking the following steps:

- Craft a customer experience strategy and appoint a CX leader who will work with the customer relations or your marketing leader.
- Understand your customer journey and experience by mapping out your customer touchpoints, how and where your customers interact with your brand.
- Walking through the customer touchpoints to gain specific knowledge of the customer experience.

- Deploy AI and ML technologies to collect and understand better your customers. You may have a wealth of data, such as information coming from your sales, social media, net promoter score, but the AI solution will provide you with real-time insights on how your customers interact with your brand.
- Use AI technologies to simplify your understanding of how your customers get to your brand. Often customers get to your brand by accident or take different and non-obvious paths. AI-based tools, such as facial scanning and text analytics, will allow you to turn your unstructured data into a real-time insight into the identities and the emotions behind the buying impulses of your customer.

Risk Tolerance and Risk Appetite

The second idea around which ISO 56002:2019 defines value realization is the notion of risk tolerance and risk appetite. The fundamental dilemma you will struggle with is how to balance innovation and risk. Innovation is an inherently risky activity. When you launch a new product or service, you still are not sure how successful the product or the service will be. You can learn from failure and improve your innovation process from previous product launches, but if the failure is too costly to the organization, this could affect your innovation capability. People will retrench and innovation gets stigmatized.

This is why your top leadership needs to articulate clearly the organization's view on risk appetite and risk tolerance. In other words, how much risk we are willing to take to develop a product x (risk appetite); and how much consequence can we accept in case of a product failure (risk tolerance). This will help you develop an innovation risk management strategy. Here are a few suggestions on how to articulate the risk management strategy:

- Engage your leadership to clearly define their risk appetite (what they are willing to take) and risk tolerance (the consequences they are willing to suffer) about innovative products and growth.
- Use a heat map to help those involved in innovation understand the different levels of risk and what is acceptable to the organization. A typical heatmap would have on the X-axis the different levels of risks, such as extreme risk, major risk, moderate risk, minimum risk, and insignificant risk, while on the Y axis the heatmap will have the

likelihood of event occurrences, such as remote event, unlikely event, possible event, probable event, and highly probable event.
• Work with your risk management department to train your innovators to understand and learn about how to balance innovation with risk, how to fail fast, and how to use minimum viable product process to accelerate their learning.

Normally when we are working with risk analysis, we consider five severity and five likelihood relevant factors (see Figure 3.1).

5x5 RISK MATRIX

LIKELIHOOD ↓ / SEVERITY →	1	2	3	4	5
1	LOW 1	LOW 2	LOW 3	MEDIUM 4	MEDIUM 5
2	LOW 2	MEDIUM 4	MEDIUM 6	HIGH 8	HIGH 10
3	LOW 3	MEDIUM 6	HIGH 9	HIGH 12	EXTREME 15
4	MEDIUM 4	HIGH 8	HIGH 12	HIGH 16	EXTREME 20
5	MEDIUM 5	HIGH 10	EXTREME 15	EXTREME 20	EXTREME 25

FIGURE 3.1
The 5×5 Risk Matrix That Combines Likelihood with Severity.
(*Source*: Smartsheet Corporate Website)

- Severity: The impact of a risk and the negative consequences that would result. The following are five severity levels:
  - **Insignificant:** Risks that bring no real negative consequences
  - **Minor:** Risks that have a small potential for negative consequences
  - **Moderate:** Risks that could potentially bring negative consequences
  - **Critical:** Risks with substantial negative consequences that will seriously impact the success of the organization or entity
  - **Catastrophic:** Risks with extreme negative consequences that would impact daily operations of the organization. These are the highest-priority risks to address.

- Likelihood: The probability of the risk occurring. The following are the five likelihood levels:
  - **Unlikely:** Almost no probability of occurring
  - **Seldom:** Risks that are relatively uncommon
  - **Occasional:** Risks that are more typical
  - **Likely:** Risks that are highly likely to occur
  - **Definite:** Risks that are almost certain to manifest

BOX 3.2   ARTIFICIAL INTELLIGENCE (AI) AND CUSTOMER INSIGHT

The deployment of new technologies in recent years by leading firms such as Amazon, Alphabet (the parent company of Google and other subsidiaries), and Facebook provides a new break-through in the way we understand and manage the customer decision-making process. Artificial intelligence (AI) based tech-nologies help you develop a better insight on how customers connect with the product and why they make the purchase decision. In an article by Alison DeNisco Rayome published in *TechRepublic* (2017), it was found that 91% of world-leading brand recognition companies use AI to increase customer satisfaction and guide their decision about customer analytics. A study conducted by Forrester Research in 2019 on how technology is changing the face of customer experience defines four new technologies that are changing the way customer insights is being used. These technologies are:

- **Facial Scanning, Speech Analytics, and Text Analytics:**
These applications provide insights into customer sense.
These technologies use unstructured data to analyze feeling,
sentiment, and context behind the buying behavior in order to
contextualize motives and intent.
- **Machine Learning:** These are algorithms that create predictive models of future behavior based on current and past
behavior. ML identifies patterns that help you predict your
customer's next move so you can customize the offer.
- **Deep Learning:** This technology is a more complex version of
ML. It mimics the human brain and uses an unsupervised approach to process large amounts of data to sort out and predict
behavior. DL is used by large online companies to improve
searches, train models on images, and improve predictability.
- **Natural Language Processing:** This is an AI-based technology that is used as an interface between the machine and
the human. Companies use it as bots to chat with customers.

BOX 3.3   FIVE QUESTIONS TO ASK TO DEFINE VALUE REALIZATION AND CUSTOMER INSIGHT

1. Have we defined a clear process to capture customer insight
and what technology have we deployed to engage with our
customers?
2. What other market research tools and/or analytics are being
deployed to engage with the customer? Do marketing and
R&D share information about customer insights?
3. Have we exploited all insights and understood our customer
emotions, needs, and changing identities?
4. To what extent have we involved users and other stakeholders
in developing, testing, and experimenting with new products
and prototypes?
5. Have we defined our risk appetite and risk tolerance? Have we
taught our innovators these concepts so they can learn what is
acceptable and what is not acceptable by the organization?

Subclause 5.1.3: Innovation Vision

Top management should establish, implement and maintain an innovation vision.[*]

Subclause 5.1.3 of ISO 56002:2019 addresses innovation vision. Establishing an IMS requires that you come up with a blueprint plan that shows interested parties and stakeholders how you will achieve your innovation goals. The importance of this blueprint plan is that it helps you create a mental framework that provides clarity of direction to your employees and management.

ISO 56002:2019 provides a great description of the attributes of the vision statement and provides specific steps on how to craft a vision that guides your innovation intent. Generally speaking, a vision statement, according to ISO 56002:2019, needs to have two essential components.

- First, it has to address the future of the company. Being a future-oriented organization is a critical step that helps change employees' mindset and influence their behavior. Often in organizations, and specifically in old organizations, there is a resistance to looking into the future. The company's leadership tends to be stuck in the past; however successful it might have been for the organization. Innovation is about the future. In fact, Section 0.2, Innovation Management Principles, of ISO 56002:2019 makes it clear that for innovation to be successful, leaders have to be forward-thinking, curious, constantly challenging the *status quo*, and projecting themselves and the organization into the future.
- Second, the vision has to be consciously ambitious. Often, companies, especially the successful ones, get used to the success and start taking customers for granted. Employees in these organizations start to fall into the trap of a self-imposed boundary driven framework that they cannot question because they are not challenged enough. Challenge your employees to think critically about the way business is conducted. Help them become better employees by offering them networking, training, and development opportunities so they can see a new future. And finally, be more

---

open to criticism specifically the one coming from lower ranks on the way business is being conducted.

But practically speaking, how do you develop an innovation vision? Lisa Bodell (2014) with Forbes offers three practical steps that help get off the ground:

1. Start by defining where you want the organization to be five to ten years from now. You can start this exercise by asking the following questions, according to Lisa Bodell:
   - Who are the best companies that you have in your mind from your industry?
   - What characterizes success in your industry?
   - How does the future look in your industry?
2. Define your opportunities by asking your management to describe what success looks like for them. Helping them articulate what innovation means for them.
3. Use distinctive language. Thompson et al. (2020) provide the following tips on how to word a vision statement:
   - Be graphic (don't be vague or incomplete).
   - Be forward-looking and directional (don't dwell on the present).
   - Keep the statement focused (don't use overly broad language).
   - Be sure the journey is feasible (don't be generic; indicate why the direction and path).
   - Make good business sense (don't rely on superlatives).

BOX 3.4 HOW TO COMMUNICATE A VISION STATEMENT

Communicating a vision to employees and to your outside audience is a critical step in rallying people around your innovation effort. Once you created your innovation vision and put it in a statement, it is critical that you invest time and effort to communicate it to your stakeholders. Clauses d, e, f of Subclause 5.1.3 recommend that you document the innovation vision so it can inspire your internal and external audiences.

Below are a few examples of a Vision Statement that are truly inspirational. While these are not innovation statements per se, they provide a good example of how a well-crafted Vision Statement can be inspirational.

- Tesla: *"To accelerate the world's transition to sustainable energy."*
- Nike: *"Bring inspiration and innovation to every athlete in the world. If you have a body, you are an athlete."*
- Shopify: *"Make commerce better for everyone, so businesses can focus on what they do best: building and selling their products."*
- Disney: *"To make people happy."*

BOX 3.5   FIVE QUESTIONS TO ASK TO TEST YOUR VISION OF INNOVATION

To help your company develop an innovation vision, ask the following five questions:

1. Have we clearly articulated our vision, and have we defined our aspiration and intent?
2. What do we want to be in the future and how should we challenge the status quo?
3. To what extent has the vision been communicated to all stakeholders internally and externally?
4. To what extent and in what way are employees able to align their behavior with the vision?
5. In what ways does the vision help structure organization behavior?

Here are four vision statements from leading companies. When you look carefully at these statements, you realize that they are concise, to the point, and carry a powerful message that engages employees and makes customers believe or become curious about their product.

- **Glaxo, Smith, Kline:** *"To improve the quality of human life by enabling people to do more, feel better, and live longer."*
- **3M:** *"To be the most innovative enterprise in the world."*
- **Disney Corporation:** *"To use our imagination to bring happiness to millions of people."*
- **Merck:** *"We are in the business of preserving and improving human life."*

Subclause 5.1.4: Innovation Strategy

Top management should establish, implement, and maintain an innovation strategy, or several innovation strategies, if appropriate.*

In Subclause 5.1.4, ISO 56002:2019 addresses innovation strategy. In addition to the Vision Statement, ISO 56002:2019 suggests also that leadership crafts an innovation strategy with the following components.

- A statement on how innovation is aligned with the corporate strategy.
- The roles, authorities, and people involved in innovation with some details on how they interact with each other, and a description of their responsibilities.
- The process that supports and allocates resources to innovation, activities, R&D, and other programs that are directly or indirectly linked to your innovation output.

How Do You Create an Innovation Strategy?

At its core, innovation is about solving problems. When you think of your innovation strategy, think of it as a framework that helps your employees find solutions to the challenges your customers face. Framework and strategies are different from one company to another and from one sector to another, so it is important that you review and revise those frameworks and strategies as frequently as possible. Locking yourself into one type of solution or one type of framework, or one type of strategy, damages creativity and the ability of your organization to innovate.

Next, we will explain the steps you need to create an innovation strategy. We will first explain the different categories and types of innovation, then we will discuss how you analyze the organizational context analysis, and finally how you conduct a strengths, weaknesses, opportunities, and threats (SWOT) analysis.

Understand the Difference between Innovation Category and Innovation Types

In innovation strategy, we make the distinction between two concepts: innovation categories and innovation types.

Innovation Categories

There are four categories of innovation strategy:

- **Product or Service Innovation**

  In this category, the output of innovation is what matters. This could be a tangible product, like an iPhone or an electric car, or an intangible product like a service. An example of a service innovation is a new government policy aiming at engaging people in solving a social problem. Other examples of service innovation could be a website or a platform such as Facebook, LinkedIn, or Netflix.

- **Business Model Innovation**

  In business model innovation you are looking at new ways of doing things. Rather than focusing on a particular product or services in business model innovation, you are changing the way you run the business. In this category of innovation, your goal is to rethink the entire way of creating value and the means by which you get this new value to your customers. In a business model innovation, you can either focus on your current market or venture out to a new and or adjacent market. A good example of a business model innovation is the business model created by Apple. By integrating its products (computers, iPhones, Apple Watch, Apple TV) with its services such as iTunes and Apple Store, Apple created an ecosystem in which integration, complementarity, and synergy add value to the customer and to the company.

- **Technology Innovation**

  Technology has been a major driver of innovation. Technology helps an organization speed up processes, automate traditional tasks, organize data, boost productivity, and streamline operations. When technology innovation targets an end-user, this can be a game-changer like in the case of personal computers, cell phones, and iPad.

- **Market Innovation**

    In market innovation, also called architectural innovation, you can either focus on existing markets by sustaining the product and services you are offering to your current market, or take the same product, service, or technology and apply it to a different market. The goal, when you apply your current solution to a different market, is to capture a new value, disrupt the target market, or simply create an entirely new market.

Types of Innovation: The Innovation Matrix

In creating an innovation strategy, it is helpful that you ask yourself two questions:

- What will be the impact of my innovation on the market? (market impact)
- How old or new is the technology I am using, or what I will be producing? (technology newness)

The answer to these two questions provides you with a two-by-two matrix that helps you understand the types of innovation strategy you should be in. The following are the four type of innovation strategies.

Incremental Innovation

Incremental innovation is the basis of innovation (lower left quadrant, see Figure 3.2). It has a low impact on the market and uses current known technology (low on the newness of technology). It is what most companies do. New additions to products or services, new improvements and alterations to existing products and services to make the output more desirable to customers, is a form of incremental innovation that progressively improves the product and makes it attractive to customers.

You can think of incremental innovation as an improvement that has some level of risk, involves uncertainty, and is the result of experimentation. This makes incremental innovation different from normal continual improvement that you are engaged in. A good example of incremental innovation is a new feature, or a new design, that the auto industry introduces when they introduce a new series or a new model of cars.

Radical Innovation

Also called breakthrough innovation, this type of innovation strategy introduces a completely new technology that will radically change the way business is conducted without too much impact on the market (bottom right quadrant, see Figure 3.2). Because the technology is new, adoption is slow and, therefore, the impact on the market is weak at the beginning. A good example of a radical innovation is artificial intelligence and blockchain technologies. These are two new technologies that are radically changing the way we do business, but their market impact still has not transformed the economy. Over time, and when the new technology is widely accepted, radical innovation tends to transform markets and behavior. It is characterized by high risk, low adoption in the beginning, with high transformative effect in the long term.

Disruptive Innovation

Disruptive innovation is a type of innovation that slowly transforms current behavior by displacing current products and services (top right quadrant, see Figure 3.2). Disruptive innovation is high on market impact and high on technology newness. While in theory, all innovations have certain levels of disruptions, disruptive innovation, explained by late Clayton Christensen (Christensen et al., 2018), happens when a new entrant, often from a smaller organization with limited resources, provides a better solution to customers at the lower end. By doing so, the new entrant disrupts current incumbents and more established organizations. A good example of a disruptive innovation is the impact of digital maps had on the industry of traditional printed maps.

Architectural Innovation

In architectural innovation, the organization is applying existing learning and existing technologies and processes to new or existing markets (top left quadrant, see Figure 3.2). The goal is to capture new value from a new market or an adjacent market. Architectural innovation involves low risk because the organization has already, presumably, established itself in its current market. Architectural innovation is high market impact low on technology newness. A good example of architectural innovation is how Nike moves from one sport to another sport using the proven success in its current market.

Types of Innovation: The Innovation Matrix

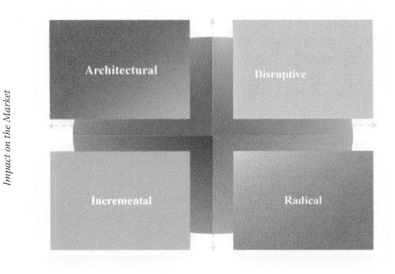

Technology newness

FIGURE 3.2
Types of Innovation Matrix.

Understanding the Context of the Organization

Once you have decided what category of innovation you want to be in and what type of innovation strategy you want to pursue, ISO 56002:2019 recommends in its Subclause 5.1.4.2 that you run an analysis of your context. In the context analysis, you need to address three dimensions:

- *The general environment*
  In the general environment, your goal is to understand the demographic segment, the economic segment such as supply and demand, interest rates, and other macro and micro-economic trends. You will need also to understand the social and cultural dimensions of your customer, as well as as well as the value system that is driving customer behavior.
- *The industry environment*
  In the industry environment, you will conduct an industry analysis about the forces that shape your industry, the level of competition,

the suppliers and buyers' power, the threat of product substitute, as well as the intensity of competition between rivals. In the industry segment, pay particular attention to technology trends like in the case of exponential technologies. A good framework to industry analysis is Porter's 5 Forces model in which you analyze the competition, the potential threat of new entrants, the power of suppliers, the power of customers, and the threat of substitute products.

- *The global environment*

  In the global environment, you need to look particularly at emerging markets and the type of innovation developed in these countries.

Once you conduct the context analysis, ask yourself the following questions:

- What are our future goals and how do our goals compare with the competition?
- What is our attitude towards risk and are there any opportunities or any unmet needs that we can exploit?
- Is our current strategy working or do we need to aggressively be innovative to seize on new opportunities?

SWOT Analysis

Another important step in crafting the innovation strategy is to conduct a SWOT analysis. In the SWOT analysis, you look at the strength, the weaknesses, the opportunities, and the threats. Let us take a quick look at explaining this framework.

1. **Strength**

   Start by listing the strengths of your organization. A strength of an organization can be a resource, a process, a capability, capital equipment, a financial position, talents, management systems, or a patent.

2. **Weaknesses**

   In weaknesses, you are listing what you think are limitations on your ability to innovate. Innovation weaknesses can relate to:
   - Lack of infrastructure such as labs,
   - Location disadvantage, like being in a geographical area that has

    limited access to research institutions or industry networking capabilities,
- Lack of innovative and creative employees,
- Limited incentives to engage people in the innovation and creative process,
- Risk aversion culture that does not support change and experimentation, and
- Lack of supporting leadership to innovate.

3. **Opportunities**

   In looking at opportunities, focus on market and industry trends that you can seize on and take advantage of. Opportunities may be related to changes in demographics, changes in the regulatory environment, technological disruptions, or economic changes like changing interest rates.

4. **Threat**

   In the threat section, list situations and factors that may hinder your ability to innovate, or more importantly, may affect the overall performance of the organization. Examples of threats could be inflation rates, rise in interest rates, geopolitical threats that may affect the ability of the organization to function, a new substitute product that is priced lower than your product, or a new competitor who just moved to your market.

Once you conduct the SWOT analysis, you need to link the different categories of the analysis and reflect on the meaning of connections between the four categories of the SWOT analysis. A good way to reflect on these connections is by asking the following four questions:

1. How can we use our strengths to take advantage of an opportunity?
2. How can we use our strength to neutralize a threat?
3. What can we do to overcome weakness by taking advantage of an opportunity?
4. What can we do to minimize a weakness so we can overcome a threat?

Finally, it is very important to understand that the success of an innovation strategy is in its execution. When you establish a strategic framework, make sure that:

- People understand that the implementation of the strategy should involve everyone in the organization, not just management and top leadership.
- Your strategy is an operations-driven strategy so people can relate to it.
- You explain to those involved in the execution that the implementation requires determination, commitment, and an agile mindset that improves from failure.

BOX 3.6   FIVE QUESTIONS TO ASK ABOUT INNOVATION STRATEGY

1. Have we defined our innovation strategy and how it fits into our overall corporate strategy?
2. How often and to what extent does our strategy get revisited and updated to reflect the external environment and market evolution?
3. Have we clearly spelled out structure and governance processes to support our innovation activities?
4. Have we defined who owns different innovation activities and programs and how these programs actively support our innovation strategy?
5. Have we established metrics to measure our innovation programs, activities, and outcomes?

Subclause 5.2.1: Innovation Policy

Top management should establish, implement, and maintain an innovation policy.*

In addition to the innovation vision, the innovation vision statement, and the innovation strategy, ISO 56002:2019 also suggests that you craft an innovation policy (Subclause 5.2.1). The innovation policy is a document that describes the commitment and engagement of the company to

---

*©ISO. This material is excerpted from ISO 56002:2019, with permission of the American National Standards Institute (ANSI) on behalf of the International Organization for Standardization. All rights reserved.

innovation. If the innovation strategy helps your organization and your people understand why they needed to embark on the innovation journey, an innovation policy is the mental template that glues innovation parts together and spells out the position of the organization vis-à-vis innovation. It serves as a template that defines who is doing what while helping employees understand how innovation works and the people in charge of it. It is a set of principles, procedures, rules, and guidelines that govern the behavior of people and link different parts of the IMS together.

When writing your innovation policy, ISO 56002:2019 suggests that you take a look at the Innovation Management Principles (IMP). These principles are the foundation of any IMS. They are a core belief and they are not negotiable. They are meant to help you define your innovation philosophy and are listed under Subclause 0.2 of ISO 56002:2019. They address issues like the purpose of the IMS, the need to future-oriented leadership, the management of uncertainty, and the need to be adaptable. In the policy, you can also provide a description of the role of management, how different units or departments interact with each other, how people are rewarded, how people are recruited, how labs or incubators are integrated, how partnerships are run, how intellectual property is managed, and all and any part, procedure, or a process that interfaces with the IMS.

When crafting your innovation policy, make sure it has the following:

- A statement or a description of why your organization should engage in innovation.
- A description of the end result and the purpose you hope to achieve by committing to establishing an IMS.
- A description that shows the alignment between innovation activities and innovation output, and how the IMS integrates these two ends.
- A commitment to learning and continual improvement of the IMS so that it is constantly up-to-date.
- A commitment and a description of the Innovation Management Principles.

Finally, the innovation policy should also be part of the documentation that a company is required to produce to comply with different frameworks of business excellence (see Figure 3.3).

Sample Innovation Policy

Innovation at XYZ is a central pillar to performance. It is a fundamental concept that drives our achievements and guides our actions. We believe that innovation is what helps our organization achieve its strategic goals in providing products and services that meet or exceed the expectations of our customers. This policy defines:

- The role of innovation in our organization
- People in charge of innovation
- Structure and units in charge of innovation
- The process of innovation
- Different procedures on how to run an innovation innovative

FIGURE 3.3
Sample Innovation Policy.

Communicating the Innovation Policy

Once you complete the drafting of your innovation policy, you should build a communication plan to explain the policy and share it with employees and management. In creating your innovation policy communication plan, clarity of the ideas to be communicated and consistency in the way you communicate them is a key ingredient to success. The clarity of ideas helps you alleviate confusion about what an IMS is and why you need one, while consistency helps you overcome resistance and manage psychological and bureaucracies' barriers that impede the implementation of any policy. We will address the communication framework in Clause 7 – Support.

BOX 3.7 FIVE QUESTIONS TO ASK ABOUT INNOVATION POLICY

1. Have we set an innovation policy that defines the roles and responsibilities?
2. Does our innovation policy define structure and processes, and are these structures and processes well explained to all levels of employees?

3. Does our innovation policy define ownership and sponsorship of different innovation programs and activities?
4. Have we defined a process for funding and staffing innovation projects, as well as killing failed ideas?
5. Have we set rewards and recognition mechanisms to foster innovation?

SUBCLAUSE 5.3: DEFINING ROLES AND ESTABLISHING RESPONSIBILITIES

*Top management should ensure that the responsibilities and authorities for relevant roles are assigned, communicated, and understood within the organization.**

In this clause, ISO 56002:2019 suggests that top management should assign roles and responsibilities for managing innovation and establishing the IMS according to ISO standard. Depending on the company's size and the specific circumstances of your organization, roles, and responsibilities can be assigned either to all leaders or to a specific leader within a specific function.

While ISO 56002:2019 does not provide a prescriptive description of the nature of the role and the responsibility, in practice, innovation has been managed by what we refer to in the field as Chief Innovation Officer (CINO). A relatively new term and a new position, CINO was first coined in 1999 by Miller and Morris in their book *Fourth Generation R&D* (Miller and Morris, 1999). However, it is only in the past few years that the term has become widely used and accepted. As a position, CINO refers to the person who is in charge of driving innovation programs and activities and managing processes and innovation governance structures. He or she is an ecosystem builder and enabler in charge of spurring innovation.

As a first step to installing ISO 56002:2019, you can assign the implementation of the standard and the establishment of the IMS to a

---

*©ISO. This material is excerpted from ISO 56002:2019, with permission of the American National Standards Institute (ANSI) on behalf of the International Organization for Standardization. All rights reserved.

CINO, who will oversee the initial implementation and the management of the innovation system. When selecting your CINO, look for people who have the following leadership traits:

- **People Skills:** Someone with excellent team management skills who is able to work with and through people.
- **A Visionary Leader:** Someone who can see disruptive threats and trends in the industry and is able to link them to what the company does.
- **A Change Manager:** Someone who can lead people through transitions taking advantage of their people and technical skills to help people overcome resistance.
- **An Idea Manager:** Someone who can foster idea generation and link them to the core business.

Opportunity Center

Some companies are bringing together their suggestion department, change management, human resources, and innovation management activities to form a new department called "Opportunity Center" that serves as the foundation for the change and improvement activities within the organization. At first, this may seem like a strange combination of responsibilities, but when you think about it, all of these functions are focused on developing the employee's capabilities. The Opportunity Center focuses on developing increased creativity and innovation throughout the organization. It will help any employee document a concept or idea and help sell the concepts that meet the organization's requirements to become a project. It also aids the employees in presenting it to the proper management level. Often the Opportunity Center helps teams develop their value proposition.

4

Clause 6: Planning

PURPOSE

To provide guidance for organizations that are setting up an IMS. This clause is directed at accomplishing two objectives. First, it defines what is required to plan for installing or upgrading an IMS; and second, it defines how individual projects/programs will be processed through the IMS. The major purpose of this clause is to determine if an initiative will become part of the organization's portfolio and thus have resources committed to it or to drop the initiative.

> A final reminder: The ISO Standards 56002:2019 and this book were written to provide guidance for midsize and large organizations. To try to apply some of the standard and the tools, methodologies, and some of the culture building recommendations suggested in this book to a small startup company could easily burn-up (use up) resources which could be used much more effectively doing other activities. After all, it is not the IMS that is important; it is how it can be used to be of more value to you, your organization, and other stakeholders.
>
> *H. James Harrington*

OVERVIEW

This chapter focuses on the process of developing a plan that will be used for assigning resources (e.g., employees, money, space, and management resources). It addresses establishing a plan to develop, install, and evaluate an IMS. It also provides guidance on planning for the activities that could be used in processing an innovative improvement through the Innovation Systems Cycle (ISC). It consists of four subclauses. They are:

- Subclause 6.1 Actions to address opportunities and risks
- Subclause 6.2 Innovation objectives and planning to achieve them
- Subclause 6.3 Organizational structure
- Subclause 6.4 Innovation portfolios*

BENEFITS

This chapter provides the content, the structure, and the timeline for establishing the improved IMS. It includes major milestones required to maintain the project/program schedules and costs. It separates and removes marginal projects from the projects with a high probability of being successful.

CLASSIFICATION OF ACTION

This clause is written as a *Should do* type activity. It provides a list of best practices but leaves the discretion for using them up to the individual organization. It is classified as a guidance document only.

INTRODUCTION

The Five Negative P's are Poor Planning Produces Poor Performing.

H. James Harrington

---

*©ISO. This material is excerpted from ISO 56002:2019, with permission of the American National Standards Institute (ANSI) on behalf of the International Organization for Standardization. All rights reserved.

We like to start our efforts to improve an organization's IMS by defining, Who do we want to believe that the organization is innovative? Check the following boxes indicating which groups of people you want to believe that the organization is innovative.

1. ☐ No one
2. ☐ Everyone
3. ☐ Your customer/users
4. ☐ Your potential customers/users
5. ☐ Your employees
6. ☐ Your Board of Directors
7. ☐ Your investors
8. ☐ The stockbrokers
9. ☐ Your family
10. ☐ All interested parties

It's easy to see that depending upon what group of individuals you want to influence, you will need specific strategies directed at that group. For example, if your primary focus is on your current customer/users, your IMS focus should be on improving the innovation of your product development and after-sales service organizations. If it is high priority for your employees to think that the organization is innovative, work on improving your reputation and you need to focus on the innovative styles of managing the organization. (Example: transferring workload from Asia to the United States). If your focus is on your potential customer/consumers, you need to focus on your innovative approaches used by your sales and marketing team and developing more innovative products and services. If your focus is on your investors, take action that could result in increased profits thereby increasing stock value and dividends. (For example, removing waste from your processes and transferring work from high-cost labor markets to low-cost legal markets.)

The planning system is a very comprehensive look at the ISC designed to ensure that when it is used, it would be used effectively, efficiently, and still be adaptable to meet individual performance needs. Its subclauses address the following:

- Subclause 6.1 How you go about addressing opportunities and risk?
- Subclause 6.2 Setting and achieving objectives

- Subclause 6.3 Organizing to support the IMS
- Subclause 6.4 Project and portfolio management of the IMS projects and programs.

- Definition of clause: A clause is a unit of grammatical organization below the sentence in rank and in traditional grammar said to consist of a subject and predicate.

From the titles of the individual clauses you can readily see that the Standards groups are using planning in a much more comprehensive way than it is normally used. It's assuming that the activities in Clause 4 have identified or should identify improvement opportunities and the risks associated with new and present outputs. This requires that the organization have effective failure-analysis laboratories and research and development centers that are not understaffed or overcommitted. It also requires that you have accurate value proposition's estimating system. It emphasizes having a staff of individuals who use project management methodologies and manage portfolios of projects effectively.

Although this document is written like its output will be a standalone system, which it can be, we believe that a more effective way is to integrate IMS into the total operating procedures processes and procedures manual as innovation should be supported by the total organization.

A great deal of effort is required for the total organization to identify improvement opportunities and risks. This clause requires the user to consider the information collected related to Subclause 4.1. In addition, it requires that the information gained in performing Subclause 4.2 is used to determine opportunities and risks to be considered. It would require a great deal less effort if it was confined to products only, but innovation as defined by ISO includes product, process, people, and management. That means we should look at it from all four perspectives.

This large database collected in Clause 4.0 serves as the foundation that the innovation plan depends upon. It should also define any parts of the organization that are not considered as candidates for innovation activities. The data collected and analyzed needs to be documented and provided to the IMS design team.

To effectively manage the innovative organization or any organization, you need to have a firmly based information reservoir so that the annual project plan and the strategic long-range plan are based upon reality and availability of resources. Basically, you need to have excellent information related to the following three items in order to prepare the annual operating plan that supports a long-range strategic plan including upgraded IMS. For example, you need

1. Operation cost for present products and facilities modified to the next two years projected schedule and cost increases
2. The work breakdown structure for all of the projects/programs that will be operational during the next two years
3. Contingency resources set aside for unexpected risks, problems, and opportunities

We will start this clause by discussing what planning is and how management is used in an IMS. Here are some important definitions. (Note: the definition of innovation has radically changed for the better since we first completed this clause of the book.)

- Definition of Innovation Management System (IMS): ISO 56000:2020 defines IMS as a management system with regard to innovation.
  - Note 1 to entry: An innovation management system can be part of a general or integrated management system of an organization.[*]
- Definition of innovation management: ISO 56000:2020 defines innovation management as management with regard to innovation.
  - Note 1 to entry: Innovation management can include establishing an innovation vision, innovation strategy, innovation policy and innovation objectives and organizational structures and innovation processes to achieve those objectives through

planning, support, operations, performance evaluation, and improvement.*

- Note 2 entry: We prefer the definition of innovation management as the handling of all the activities needed to innovate, such as creating ideas, developing, prioritizing, and implementing them, as well as putting them into practice.

- Definition of planning: ISO 56000:2020 did not provide a definition of planning. As a result, the one that we will use is the following: Planning is thinking about the activities required to achieve a desired goal.

  Planning involves the creation and maintenance of a plan. An important, albeit often ignored, aspect of planning is the relationship it holds to forecasting. Planning combines forecasting with preparation of scenarios and how to react to them. Planning is preparing a sequence of action steps to achieve some specific goal. A plan is like a map. When following a plan, a person can see how much they have progressed toward their project goal and how far they are from their destination.

  Planning is the fundamental management function, which involves deciding beforehand what is to be done, when is it to be done, how it is to be done, and who is going to do it. It is an intellectual process that lays down an organization's objectives and develops various courses of action.

- Definition of forecasting: Forecasting is predicting what the future will look like.

- Definition of goal: A goal is a desired result that a person or a system envisions, plans, and commits to achieve: a personal or organizational desired end-point in some sort of targeted development. Many people endeavor to reach goals within a finite time by setting deadlines. A specific result that a person or system aims to achieve within a time frame and with available resources (*Reference Business Dictionary*).

- Definition of interested party: ISO 56000:2020 defines interested party as a person or organization that can affect, be affected by, or perceive itself as being affected by a decision or activity.
  - Note 1 to entry: This constitutes one of the common terms and core definitions of the high level structure for ISO management system standards.*
- Definition of decision: A decision is a specific result that a person or system aims to achieve within a time frame and with available resources.
- Definition of objective: ISO 56000:2020 defines objective as result to be achieved.
  - Note 1 to entry: An objective can be strategic, tactical, or operational.
  - Note 2 to entry: Objectives can relate to different disciplines (such as financial, health and safety, and environmental goals) and can apply at different levels (such as strategic, organization-wide, project, product, initiative and process).
  - Note 3 to entry: An objective can be expressed in other ways, e.g., as an intended outcome, a purpose, an operational criterion, as an innovation objective, or by the use of other words with similar meaning (e.g., aim, goal, or target).
  - Note 4 to entry: In the context of innovation management systems, innovation objectives are set by the organization consistent with the innovation strategy and the innovation policy, to achieve specific results.
  - Note 5 to entry: This constitutes one of the common terms and core definitions of the high level structure for ISO management system standards. The original definition has been modified by adding "initiative" to Note 2 to entry and "innovation strategy" to Note 4 to entry.*

In general, objectives are more specific and easier to measure than goals. Objectives are basic tools that underlie all planning and strategic activities. They serve as the basis for creating policy and evaluating performance. Some examples of business objectives include minimizing expenses, expanding internationally, or making a profit (source http://www.businessdictionary.com).

Note: It is important to understand that ISO 56000:2020 uses objectives rather than goals. This requires a greater depth of specific in defining future performance for the IMS.

In Appendix A we provide a list of definitions from the book *The Innovation Tools Handbook – Evolutionary and Improvement Tools Every Innovator Must Know* published by CRC Press (2016) plus input from the International Association of Innovation Professionals (IAOIP) with some additional definitions used in this book. We have also included all definitions from ISO 56000:2000 that we have inserted in this book.

Realization of Value

One of the innovation management principles is realization of value. Value is recognized from the timely implementation, adoption, and resulting impact of new and improved solutions for all involved stakeholders.

With value realization being a key focus of an IMS, it suggests that planning for the implementation of an IMS must include adequate planning that considers not only the opportunities but also the risks involved. In addition, innovation objectives should be developed along with supporting plans to achieve those objectives. These plans need to be:

- In alignment with the strategy of the organization
- Defined with specific deliverables and expected results
- Properly resourced
- Adequately monitored and adjusted over time to assure completion
- Fit within either existing supportive organizational structures or within new structures that are specifically designated for the purpose of supporting the IMS

In most companies there are a number of operational and strategic plans in existence at the same time. One of the major problems that face an organization is to keep the total organization's planning commitments in harmony with one another. Typical examples of individual plans are:

1. Strategic planning
2. Human resource planning
3. Controlling
4. Succession planning
5. Production schedule playing
6. New product development plan
7. Sales planning
8. Acquisitions planning
9. Quality improvement planning
10. Field support planning
11. Innovation planning

There are four different types of documents. They are:

1. It **should/could** be done plan – Dreaming planning
2. It **will** be done plan – Wishful thinking planning
3. It will be done **if necessary** plan – Exception planning
4. I **(John Jackson) will do** a specific activity by January 16, 2021 – Ownership planning

ISO 56002:2019 is a *should* be done document – Dreaming planning. In discussions with the authors of ISO 56002:2019, the recommendations were best practices and should be taken very seriously. When you have a guidance document, the organization selects the parts of the document that will provide value added to the organization and/or its stakeholders. It's always better to do what you want to do, rather than do what you have to do. If your customer or the government tells the executive team that they have to have a meeting, they often will do it halfheartedly hoping it will get over fast and they can get onto something that's meaningful. This is the very reason that so many of the quality initiatives were unsuccessful and had little or no impact on the bottom line. The guide-type document along with this supporting plan documentation allows the organization to distribute their resources to the areas that provide maximum value added. In Subclause 5.1.2 of ISO 56002:2019 it suggests that the planning process focuses on value realization for the organization and all of their interested parties.

THE FOUR MAJOR TYPES OF PLANS

- Definition of Organizational Master Plan (OMP): The Organizational Master Plan is the combination of the business plan, strategic business plan, the strategic improvement plan, and the annual operating plan.

As previously pointed out, there are numerous plans going on at the same time in an organization. They can be condensed down into four major types of planning that make up the OMP (see Figure 4.1). They are:

- The Business Plan
- The Strategic Business Plan
- The Strategic Improvement Plan
- The Annual Operating Plan

These four different but related types of plans often overlap in some areas. They are:

- Business Plan – This plan's primary use is to inform potential investors about the organization. It provides input into the Strategic Business Plan and the Strategic Improvement Plan.
- Strategic Business Plan and the Strategic Improvement Plan – Together these two plans make up the Strategic Plan. Its focus is on the future. They are used to set direction, not to tell the organization how to do it. The Strategic Business and the Strategic Improvement Plans should go through a major update every one to three years and be reviewed every year.
- Annual Operating Plan – This plan's focus is on the current/present short-range activities. It covers the tasks that are scheduled to be done and when they will be done. The Annual Operating Plan should be redone at least once a year and reviewed once a month plus whenever a major tollgate is schedule.

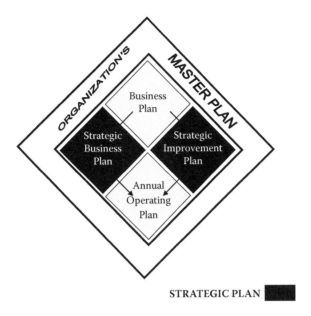

FIGURE 4.1
The Organizational Master Plan.

Yes, an OMP is the heart of the transformation. But the heart needs veins to pump life-giving blood throughout the organization. Without this, the heart is of no value and when one of these major veins gets clogged, the body stops functioning. This is true of OMP; it serves as the pump that provides the direction, and it is the way that direction is implemented that makes the organization a success or a failure.

THE PLANNING PROCESS

Your organization's plan should provide answers to three action areas. It should set direction. It should define expectations. It should define the actions that are required to meet the expectations within the culture of the company (see Figure 4.2).

The best practice model for planning unites the plan with the organization starting with its vision all the way through to the individual's performance plan (see Figure 4.3).

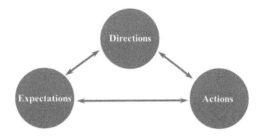

FIGURE 4.2
Three Purposes of Planning.

> One of my favorite sayings is – The best time to stop a project that will fail is before you start it.
>
> *H. James Harrington*

Now tollgates are frequently used in support of major projects/programs and new products. It often is not necessary to use tollgates on entities that are slight evolutionary improvements of an output that is being delivered today. Tollgates are often applied to entities that have significant impact upon one or more stakeholders.

- Definition of entity: ISO 56000:2020 defines entity as anything perceivable or conceivable. Some examples would be product,

Best Practice Business Planning Elements and Timing

PURPOSE	11 OUTPUTS	TIME FRAME
Direction	Visions	10 - 20 years
	Mission	Open-ended
	Values	Open-ended
	Strategic focus	5 years
	Critical success factors	3 years
Expectations	Business Objectives	5-10 years
(measurements)	Performance Goals	1-5 years
Actions	Strategies	1-5 years
	Tactics	1-3 years
	Budgets	1-3 years
	Performance Plans	3-12 months

FIGURE 4.3
The Best Practices Planning.

service, process, model (e.g., an organizational, business, operational or value realization model), method (e.g., a marketing or management method) or a combination thereof.
- Note 1 to entry: Entities can be material (e.g., an engine), immaterial (e.g., a project plan) or imagined (e.g., the future state of the organization).*

PREREQUISITE CULTURAL DOCUMENTATION

The IMS cannot exist by itself. It has to fit in homogeneously with the organization's culture and the other stakeholders' needs. The basic starting point in developing an improved IMS is a set of documents that define the direction and culture of the organization. Typically these documents are

- Vision of the organization
- Mission of the organization
- Organizational values
- Strategic focus
- Critical success factors
- Performance goals

Often, an organization focused on improving their IMS will feel it is necessary to have a specific phrase, clause, or document related to each of these directional documents. Often, adding a word or two to a sentence that is already there provides the desired results with less interruption to the organization. (For example, the old statement: "Quality is our top priority." The new statement "Quality and innovation are our top priorities.")

MARKET FOCUS

A clear market focus provides an organization and its people with an opportunity to accomplish great things through understanding the customer's needs better than its competitors (Source: Harrington and James, 1994). This understanding then provides the foundation for the development of superior products and services. Knowing who you're serving is the first step in developing a good business plan and achieving the ultimate business results that the winners in business experience. The losers more often are so unfocused that they cannot serve anyone well with the demands on their limited resources. The really successful organizations will understand markets in terms of what actual customers want and will pay for it, thus reaching a level of understanding few others achieve. As one leading computer manufacturer said, "We feel that one of our significant competitive advantages over other companies is our ability to better understand and anticipate customer needs, whether it's through our sales force or through superior market/customer research." You certainly couldn't argue with their results!

SETTING DIRECTION

The principle role of top management is to set the direction for the organization. This can best be accomplished and communicated to the stakeholders through the business plan. The outputs that are used to provide this direction are:

Vision of the Organization – A vision statement gives a picture of an organization in the future. It is normally inspirational and provides a framework for strategic planning. It is usually prepared by top management and is directed at what the organization's output will be like and/or how it will be used 10–20 years in the future.

Mission – A mission statement articulates an organization's fundamental purpose. The mission is the stated reason for the existence of the organization. It is usually prepared by the chief executive officer and seldom changes – normally only when the organization decides to pursue a completely new market.

Values – The basic beliefs that the organization is founded upon and the principles that make up its culture are often called values. These are prepared by top management. They are rarely changed, because they must be statements that the stakeholders can depend on as being sacred to the organization.

Strategic Focus – These are the key factors that will set the organization apart from its competitors over the next five years. This list is defined by top and middle-level management.

Critical Success Factors – These are the key things that the organization must do exceptionally well to overcome today's problems and roadblocks to meeting the vision statements.

VISION OF THE ORGANIZATION

What's the difference between a *vision* and a *mission* for an organization? Many organizations go through an agonizing process of trying to determine the distinction between the two. By "vision," we mean a view of what the business will be like 10–20 years from now. It could be as simple as "an affordable, easy-to-use personal computer on everyone's desk" or "news available immediately from anywhere in the world." The winners tend to be able to express an energizing picture of the future in terms of market presence and customer benefits. The losers tend to lack any vision and exist from day to day reacting to the market and the leads of other competitors. One of the most clear vision statements was articulated by President John F. Kennedy in 1961 when he said: "We will send a man to the moon within this decade and bring him back safe." This was short, pithy, and inspirational, and was intended to be uplifting.

MISSION

The mission statement is essential to linking the organization with its vision of the future. Some organizations call this their *purpose statement*, or the central reason why they are in business. A good mission statement will require leadership and should be internally oriented to inspire employees and externally focused with customers in mind.

Organizations whose employees understand the corporate mission clearly enjoy a 29% greater return than other companies, according to a study conducted by Watson Wyatt. In the United States, 75% of the employees do not think their company's mission statement reflects the way they do business (Workplace 2000 Employee Insight Survey).

Winners make their missions short, clear, and compelling, while losers will have missions focused on shareholder value or some other non-customer, noncompetitive emphasis. In addition, winners embody a strong leadership emphasis in their planning, as reported in a study of almost 300 companies in Ernst & Young's "American Competitiveness Study." This emphasis on being a leader is essential to both the development of strategy and to motivating the organization's people, customers and suppliers by focusing on being a winner and not a follower.

Here are a few examples of mission statements:

- **UNEP**: To provide leadership and encourage partnership in caring for the environment by inspiring, informing, and enabling nations and peoples to improve their quality of life without compromising that of future generations.
- **World Bank**: Our mission is to help developing countries and their people reach the (Millennium Development) goals by working with our partners to alleviate poverty. To do that we concentrate on building the climate for investment, jobs and sustainable growth, so that economies will grow, and by investing in and empowering poor people to participate in development.
- **Boeing:** Our long-range mission is to be the number one aerospace company in the world, and among the premier industrial firms, as measured by quality, profitability and growth.
- **Wal-Mart:** To give ordinary people the chance to buy the same thing as rich people.
- **McDonalds:** To satisfy the world's appetite for good food, well-served, at a price people can afford.

Mission statements are mainly for internal consumption – a way to engage employees and other stakeholders. Vision statements are inspirational. Value statements cannot be inspirational. They must be thoroughly realistic.

VALUES

Values can be defined as the deeply ingrained operating rules or guiding principles of an organization. Some may see them as the specific cultural attributes that drive behavior. The winning organizations set out to create a specific culture and operating style to further define their strategic change and focus.

Unlike mission statements, which are primarily for internal consumption, value statements cannot be inspirational. They must be realistic.

Merck's value statement is brief and powerful: "To preserve and improve human life."

Owens/Corning Fiberglas uses "guiding principles" in place of "values." Their guiding principles are:

- Customers are the focus of everything we do.
- People are the source of our competitive strength.
- Involvement and teamwork is our method of operation.
- Continuous improvement is essential to our success.
- Open, two-way communication is essential to the improvement process and our mission.
- Suppliers are team members.
- Profitability is the ultimate measure of our efficiency in serving our customer's needs.

Now let's take a look at Corning Fiberglas guiding principles and see that we could easily slip in the emphasis on innovation. They have one statement that states "Continuous improvement is essential to our success." They could reword this statement to say, "Continuous improvement and innovation is essential to our success." Often you do not have to make major changes to communicate to the stakeholders the emphasis you're placing on innovation. The word "innovation" should be inserted in just the right place to communicate the importance of innovation which will have in rewriting the major communication document.

Call them basic beliefs, guiding principles, or operating rules. Call them what you will. The important thing is that they must be defined, and the organization must live up to them, for they surely are the "Stakeholders' Bill of Rights."

In contrast, losing organizations tend not to have explicit values or to have "hollow" values, or perfectly stated values that no one operates by.

We believe that every manager should have a documented set of values that they post in the office. It is important that they communicate to their employees the things that are important to the manager as an individual. A copy of H.J. Harrington's value statements can be found in Appendix C of this document. Of course, individual values should not conflict with the organization's values or you're working for the wrong organization. Taking it one step further, Harrington has encouraged his employees to develop their own set of values to help them live a better life.

STRATEGIC FOCUS

Organizations which have been successful in part due to good planning know that they must provide their employees with a road map to help translate the vision and mission into "things people can do." The next most critical element of what is in a good business plan is the strategic focus of the organization in terms of "how" it will compete. The key factors that organizations need to compete are defined as follows:

- Core competencies – The technologies and production skills that underlie an organization's products or services (e.g., Sony's skill at miniaturization).
- Core capabilities – The business processes that visibly provide value to the customer (e.g., Honda's dealer management processes).
- Strategic excellence positions – Unique and distinctive capabilities that are valued by the customer and provide a basis for competitive advantage (e.g., Avon's distribution system).

These leading definitions are actually quite compatible, and debate over which is proper is not time particularly well spent for most organizations. Regardless of the definitions applied, what is common among all the successful organizations is their ability to identify those four or five key areas of strategic focus that are characterized by the following:

- Customers value the benefits that the focus provides.
- Concentration of resources toward being the absolute best in your chosen areas of emphasis will enable you to excel.
- Excellence in these areas will be difficult for competitors to imitate.
- These areas of focus are your organization's capabilities or what you're really good at, not outcome measures like market share, profit margin, etc.

The clarity provided by having a few key goals to focus on can help set the foundation for dramatic improvements in business results. For example, years ago Hewlett-Packard established the lowering of their product failure rate as one of their key business goals. They also coupled this goal with a very clear objective or measurement, with the specific target being a ten-fold improvement in results. Their continuing success in a number of rapidly changing markets speaks for itself.

CRITICAL SUCCESS FACTORS – OBSTACLES TO SUCCESS

Planning with a leadership emphasis requires a focus much beyond where you are today. Pushing your vision into the future often requires "thinking out of the box" or an unconstrained strategic perspective. The winning planning processes link this back into today's reality, by specifically focusing on the obstacles to success or things that would prevent the implementation the plan. These obstacles can range from the lack of sufficient funding to excessive organizational layers. The point here is to better link the vision to today's starting reality, and being honest enough to highlight and correct the obstacles. This often creates several additional strategies to be incorporated into the plan. Winning organizations will attack this with a positive attitude, while losers will use it to tell themselves they can't do anything about it. Many organizations will translate the obstacles to success (things in your control which prevent you from successfully implementing the plan) into critical success factors (things that you must do right in order to succeed). This positive transition can help set the proper winning tone on the challenges of moving forward.

PERFORMANCE GOALS

Performance goals can take the form of short- and long-range targets that support the business objectives. They should be quantifiable, measurable, and time-related. (Example: Increase sales at a minimum rate of X% per year from 1995 to 2010, with an average annual growth rate of Y%.) A typical long-range performance goal would be to decrease the cost of maintaining customer purchased equipment at a minimum rate of 10% per year for the next five years; or to correct 99.7% of all customer problems with one service call per customer over the next 24 months. Each year, a set of short-range goals should be generated by first-line and middle management, directly tied into their budgets. These goals should be reviewed and approved by top management to be sure they support the business objectives and are aggressive enough.

Note: Goals have two key ingredients. First, they specifically state the target for improvement; and second, they give the time interval in which the improvement will be accomplished.

THE PLANNING ACTIVITY

ISO 56002:2019 provides guidance in how to develop and install a functioning IMS. This is very different than the activity of cycling an entity through the IMS. In the case of establishing an IMS within an organization, it needs to be treated like a project or program that is impacting culture and operating mode of most, if not all, of the employees.

Consistency between the changes in the culture is assessed on the following dimensions:

- Management processes
- Motivation
- Decision-making
- Performance appraisal
- Leadership
- Teamwork

- Business
- Structure
- Change implementation

Strength of the existing culture is assessed on the following dimensions:

- History
- Common beliefs, behaviors, and assumptions
- Shared beliefs, behaviors, and assumptions patterns
- Consistency of behavior and beliefs
- Consistence of assumptions with belief and behavior patterns
- Clear and constant signals about beliefs, behaviors, and assumptions
- Location of operations
- Strength and duration of leadership
- Suitability of membership
- Consistently communicated and rewarded beliefs, behaviors, and assumptions

(Source: *Project Change Management* published by McGraw-Hill)

THE TWO DRIVERS OF INNOVATION

There are two basic drivers of innovation: they are culture and technology. Culture can be subdivided into two major headings – structure and people. Technology also can be divided into two major headings – technology and task (see Figure 4.4). The least stressful upon the organization is when the interface is between technology and task only. This provides a smooth direct two-way communication and operating condition. This Task Affected condition is called a first order magnitude complexity. This provides an active two-way communication and operational system that usually can be implemented with minimum resistance. This could be a representation of a new cell phone with a larger screen that can be processed through the same production facility without major changes in the equipment that is used. (Minimal training required for the experienced employee.)

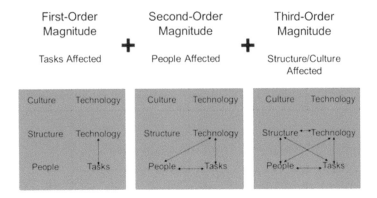

FIGURE 4.4

The Magnitude of Driven Change.

Source: O'Hara Watson & Kavan

We will create a second order magnitude complexity called People Affected condition. In this case, we added one more major heading called "people." Figure 4.4 illustrates how the complexity of sensibly installing the project has increased by 300%. In these cases, the increased resistance has a major negative impact as we try to integrate people into the total system.

In the third order magnitude complexity we've added structure/culture to the system which greatly increases the entities' risk of failure if you don't implement a very effective organizational change management (OCM) initiative. Unfortunately, when we're talking about innovation and installing an IMS, we are operating at the third order magnitude, which usually requires a very comprehensive change management initiative be implemented early in the project.

THE BASIC STRATEGIC PLANNING PROCESS

Every effort should be made to have the IMS improvement plan be in line with the organization's strategic business plan. The point I am making here is that, in for-profit organizations the basic management responsibility is to manage the organization not manage the innovation process. Certainly, innovation is a key element in the business, but it is not the total picture. This is particularly true when you remember that more than 95% of the patentable ideas are evolutionary-type improvements. Although we like to talk about the discovery (wow-type) innovations, very few organizations will ever reach that level of innovation.

WHAT MAKES ORGANIZATIONS INNOVATIVE?

Now that we have defined a standard planning process, we will need to divide it down into tasks that should be considered as part of your detailed plan. Some examples of typical tasks include:

- Task 1: Assign a study individual/team to investigate what makes organizations innovative as viewed by the stakeholders and potential customers.
- Task 2: Collect and research data to understand the assignment.
- Task 3: Prepare a mission statement and have it approved by the appropriate management.
- Task 4: Assign IMS development team and prepare team charter.
- Task 5: Review the mission, strategies, policies, long-term vision, and value statements.
- Task 6: Evaluate the maturity level of your present IMS.
- Task 7: Define the short-term vision.
- Task 8: Define the strategic scope and timeframe.
- Task 9: Define the assumptions.

This detailed information is particularly useful when you are preparing a work breakdown structure.

- Definition of team charter: A team charter is a management-written commitment or contract stating the purpose and objectives of an assignment. It stipulates resources, performance targets, participants, and review authorities.

  The team charter is prepared prior to assigning a team leader or members and takes into consideration the project's effect on innovation, quality, cost, schedule, and customer satisfaction. It also documents approval to fund the project. This document is based on the best information management has available at the time and is often adjusted as more data becomes available.

- Definition of work breakdown structure (WBS): A work breakdown structure is a hierarchical decomposition of the total scope of work to be carried out by the project team to accomplish the project objectives and create the required deliverables.

- Definition of team objectives: Team objectives are closely aligned with the charter, the objectives specifying a team's direction over a period of time. A typical project objective would be to develop and implement changes that reduce customer complaints related to the product delivery process by at least 50% within 120 days.

- Definition of team project plan: A team project plan is a document formally approved by management used to guide the project execution and control. Plans primarily develop assumptions and decisions, facilitate communication among stakeholders, and record approved scope, cost, and schedule baseline.

  A project plan can be a summary or a detailed report. The project plan is used to provide a visual timeline of the strategies that the team will use to meet the charter requirements, the team's project objectives, and the team's project goals.

PROJECT MANAGEMENT

Your organization may or may not use professional project managers to manage your projects/programs/entities, but the project management concepts and activities apply to all projects that are critical to the organization and/or use a great deal of resource. One of the very first things that should be done is to establish an integrated project management plan for each entity that includes the following sub-elements. (Source: *Effective Portfolio Management Systems* published by CRC Press.)

The body of knowledge for project management falls under two headings (see Figure 4.5).

- The five Knowledge Domains (Process Groups)
  1. Initiating the Project
  2. Planning the Project
  3. Executing the Project
  4. Monitoring and Controlling the Project
  5. Closing the Project

- The ten Knowledge Areas
  1. Integration Management
  2. Scope Management
  3. TIME Management
  4. Cost Management
  5. Quality Management
  6. Human Resource Management
  7. Communications Management
  8. Risk Management
  9. Procurement Managment
  10. Stakeholder Management

Each of these Knowledge areas provide insight into project management as noted below (see Figure 4.6):

1. Project Integration Management: Answers the question, where does this portfolio intersect with its sub-programs and projects, or with other portfolios? (critical to understand and minimize cross-portfolio impacts)
2. Project Scope Management: The scope of the portfolio as outlined in the Business Case
3. Project Time Management: Outlined in the Work Breakdown Structure (see next clause)
4. Project Cost Management (as outlined in the Value Proposition and Business Case)
5. Project Quality Management: Essential to establish how project performance will be measured and evaluated

6. Project Human Resource Management: Consider use of the Critical Resource Chain method (A framework of critical resource chain in project scheduling to maximize and integrate constrained resources within a tight schedule)

7. Project Communications Management (For more information see Chapter 5 of the book *Practical Applications Of Change Management Within Portfolio Management* published by Taylor & Francis)

8. Project Risk Management: Consider the processes outlined in the PMI (Practice Standard for Project Risk Management), which outlines risk identification, risk quantification, risk response development, and risk response control

9. Project Procurement Management: This may be handled by a dedicated procurement department within the organization, or within the province of the Project Management Office on a dedicated or as-needed basis for individual portfolios, programs, and projects

10. Project Stakeholder Management: This knowledge area takes into consideration all of the individuals interested in the outcome of the innovation.

11. Project Change Management: We believe that this technology should be added to the knowledge areas.

12. Project Information Management (see Technology Resource Management Process; Sample Documentation). We believe that this item should be added to the knowledge areas.

Note: We believe that Project Change Management and Project Information Management should be added to make a total of 12 knowledge areas.

5 Knowledge Domains (Process Groups)	10 Knowledge Areas	
I. Initiating the Project II. Planning the Project III. Executing the Project IV. Monitoring and Controlling the Project V. Closing the Project	• Integration Management • Scope Management • Schedule Management • Cost Management • Quality Management	• Project Resource Management • Communications Management • Risk Management • Procurement Management • Stakeholder Management

FIGURE 4.5
Project Management Body of Knowledge.

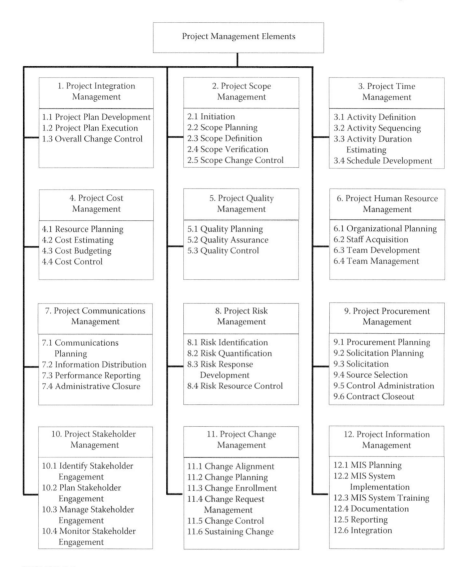

FIGURE 4.6
The 12 Knowledge Areas.

WAYS TO IMPLEMENT AN IMS PLANNING ACTIVITY

There are many different ways to implement an IMS planning activity. We find that flowcharting current and future processes is a very effective to aid in design development, and implementation of an IMS. We have seen it as small as three phases and as large as over 200 tasks in a work breakdown structure. The "planned-for tasks" is one of the many ways that we have found to be a comprehensive, efficient, and effective way of managing the project. In this model we made the assumption that there was some level of resources within the organization that were not already committed and could be used in a discretionary activity. We also made the assumption that the organization wanted to use these discretionary resources in a way that provided real positive value to the organization and the Board of Directors was open to considering different alternative ways to invest discretionary resources.

Let me reiterate again, a very small portion of the approved innovative activities need to have a complete project management approach applied to the development of the concept and its implementation. Entities that have a high return on investment, require a lot of resources, and have a high risk associated with it requires a comprehensive plan are innovations that should be considered for the project management methodology. But those innovative ideas that are classified as continuous improvement entities may require little or no improvement in the way their IMS is operating. Usually for these minor entity improvements setting up a complete control system and including them in the portfolio management system is not justified based upon the amount of resources that are required and the degree of value-added to the stakeholders.

DEVELOP AN AS/IS MODEL OF THE PRESENT IMS

It is not practical to begin any type of improvement effort without determining the As/Is operating model of the present organization's performance. You would not start a trip to New York City without knowing if you are currently in Boston, Buffalo, or the Bronx. In looking at any improvement effort you have to understand where you are. Next you have to decide where you want to go. Then and only then can you look at the improvement methodology to determine if it is the right thing for you. We all know of European companies that look at the United States' successful innovative products and then decide that they will come out with a competitive alternative that they can sell for less because they did not have to invest in the development cycle. It is helpful to know the customer's acceptance level of the entity and its value added before proceeding with well-intentioned interventions. Your doctor would not prescribe surgery without first giving you a thorough physical check-up. Obtaining valid information about the health of the organization's performance with regard to innovation and the factors that affect performance is a sound place to start.

To answer the question, "How are we doing?" we explore a variety of assessment tools and methods that offer tips to help you succeed. You can use off-the-shelf surveys, create one from scratch, conduct in person assessments, or take advantage of online tools to survey people at random. For example, you might gather the executive team for a two-hour meeting to get a quick snapshot of their perspective on innovation. You could have them consider their organization's effectiveness in executing foundational innovation tasks.

1. Strategizing: Setting direction and priorities for innovation
2. Exploring: Uncovering unmet needs and significant opportunities
3. Generating: Creating many high potential ideas
4. Optimizing: Iterating and improving the value of ideas
5. Selecting: Making good choices among new ideas
6. Developing: Designing, building, and testing operational improvements as well as new products and services
7. Implementing: Delivering innovative solutions on time and within budget
8. Commercializing: Launching and scaling up new businesses or offerings
9. Competing: Beating the competition with new or enhanced offerings
10. Profiting: Generating sufficient returns from operational improvements as well as new offerings

The process is straightforward. Ask each leader to write on a Post-it note their "effectiveness" rating (very low 1/10 very high) for the organization. The notes are collected and posted for all the leaders to see how the group evaluated the innovation tasks. Each task is discussed and then the group is asked to step back and consider the overall picture and the implications on their output and their IMS. Through this process, they discover what their colleagues think about the enterprise's innovation strengths and weakness as well as where they have consensus and where their opinions differ. The exercise also raises questions about what they don't know. Self-discovery is the best discovery, and this two-hour meeting may prove to be a tipping point for the leadership team and your innovation improvement effort. Activities like these offer helpful insights and often provoke leaders into action, one of which is to authorize the innovation team to conduct a more comprehensive assessment of the organization.

This is particularly important because one of the major mistakes many organizations make is to believe that the executive team has an accurate understanding of the problems the workforce is facing. We often discover the executive team has a more positive view of the organization's operations and innovation practices than their employees. This dynamic surfaces when we ask individuals taking one of our organizational surveys to list the top ten activities needing the most improvement within the company and then to list the activities that need the least improvement. Typically, the survey is completed by the executive team and a sample of management and employees. One of the questions that is evaluated is, "How much trust and confidence do you have in the upper management team?" Almost without exception, this question is rated on the executive's list between #9 and #10 indicating that there is little need of improving. The view of the organization often is based upon the position within the organization the individual is holding. We are not surprised to find out that the subject is rated as one of the top #10 needs-improvement for middle management and employees. It is absolutely essential that any assessment of an organization collects information related to the needs, expectations, and desires of the executive team, middle management, and the employees and oh yes, the board of directors.

Once this is done, the stakeholders are in a position to compare the organization's strengths and weaknesses as viewed from these three separate levels. (**Note**: It is a rare organization where a single survey and/or assessment is adequate to characterize the culture of the organization and identify opportunities for major improvement.) This chapter will show you how to overcome issues like "executive team bias" as well as introduce a set of innovation assessments and question formats for your consideration.

Types of As/Is Assessments

1. Innovation Fitness Survey – This survey takes a systems' perspective to gather employee views on the key innovation factors driving the organization's overall innovation performance.
2. Is-Should Be Analysis – Focus groups are run for stakeholders at all levels (e.g., employees, first-line managers, middle managers, executives, and key staff personnel) and the results are analyzed related to where the organization is today, where it should be in three years, and how important is it to reaching the objectives.
3. The 7S Survey – This survey is directed at management and explores the organization's hard elements (i.e., strategy, structure, systems) and soft elements (i.e., shared values, skills, staff, style). The model is based upon James M. Higgins' theory that for an organization to perform well, these seven elements need to be aligned and mutually reinforcing.
4. Historical Trend Analysis – Past performance is an effective way of projecting future performance. An individual's attitude is usually based upon their past experience in implementing changes within the organization. The survey is designed to define potential roadblocks to the change in an innovative culture.
5. Customer Focus Groups – These focus groups are designed to develop an understanding of how the organization's innovation activity is perceived by the customer. The data is used to identify the customer's perception of the organization and how the organization's innovative reputation can be improved.

> As much as we would like to think innovation is a process, in truth it is not; it's an attitude of self fulfillment.
>
> *H. James Harrington*

6. Magazine Innovation Analysis – A number of major magazines (e.g., *Fortune, Fast Company*) have developed comprehensive strategies for rating and then ranking the innovation level of the top organizations

7. Total Innovative Management Excellence Top 100 companies ratings – If you're not in the top 100 most innovative companies, the rankings can provide an excellent target goal for the organization. The strategies and analysis can be applied to your organization, providing deep insight and a path toward improved innovation.

8. General Employee Opinion Surveys – One benefit of conducting an employee opinion survey is that it provides feedback on a wide variety of management issues. From an innovation standpoint, it allows the questions targeting innovation to be intermixed with other probing questions on different topics eliminating a tendency to provide positive feedback on any single issue. We have seen instances when a survey directed toward innovation got an overall rating of 82% above average. When it was mixed in with an employee opinion survey, the innovation rating was only 46% above average.

9. Do It Yourself (DIY) Survey – Creating your own online innovation survey allows for easy targeting and tailoring of questions, provides cost savings, and is convenient in terms of distribution and gaining audience participation.

The surveys have their differences, but they are all tools intended to help you efficiently and effectively collect high-quality data about your current innovation capabilities, generate actionable insights, and develop a sound strategy for moving forward. Examine the surveys carefully and take time to think about how you might apply them to your situation. You may use all or part of the surveys, or find another one better suited to your needs, or create a customized assessment tool from scratch. Constructing your own survey has now become much easier with the growth of online survey providers like QuestionPro.

The individual to whom the executive team has assigned the responsibility for coordinating the design and implementation of the upgraded IMS should form an Innovative Systems Team (IST) made up of individuals who represent each function within the organization whose output impacts the organization's innovation. Typical functions that would be represented on this team are procurement, sales, product engineering, research and development, manufacturing, after sales service, manufacturing engineering, and quality assurance.

The IST will be trained to understand the concepts contained within ISO 56002:2019 – IMS. The team will then do a detailed analysis that compares the present IMS with the required outline in the standard. This analysis will be supported with estimates of the effort required to upgrade each element of the IMS to the standards requirements. The IMS should not be limited to the items defined in the particular IMS standard that is being used. Additional processes that are of specific interest to the organization should be considered at this time; remember that ISO 56000:2020 series sets only the minimum requirements in using the ISO 56000:2020 documents. We believe that most organizations are not satisfied at just meeting minimum requires but want to excel in their industry.

The IST will define the IMS documentation structure and which documents will be included in the innovation manual or the supporting operating procedure. We prefer that the operating procedures related to innovation be included in the organization operating manual rather than in a separate document set. By including these procedures within the organization's operating manual, you leave the impression that is part of the normal operating procedures of the organization rather than something special that is an added-on activity. Basically, the IMS documentation strategy is divided into four levels. They are:

- Strategic level – Innovation manual (usually part of the organization's operating procedures manual)
- Tactical level – Procedures
- Operational level – Work instructions
- Historical level – Innovation data and records

The IST should also develop a set of measurements that will be used to define the effects that the upgraded IMS has on the organization and how this effort will be measured.

Within most organization changing, the IMS had a significant impact on the emotion of most employees. As a result, the OCM plan should be prepared to help the organization internalize the changes to the IMS. The importance of an effective OCM plan in support of any major revision to the IMS cannot be over emphasized. It is important to note that part of the assessment effort that takes place in an earlier phase should be directed at identifying the level of resistance to a change that the IMS will encounter. The OCM plan is designed to minimize this resistance and its impact.

Analyzing the true value of innovation entity is one we always struggle with. Innovation entity is one that is a new or changed entity, realizing or redistributing value to the organization and its interested parties. Value is defined as financial or nonfinancial resources or advantages that you can create, realize, acquire, redistribute, share, lose, or destroy. Value is relative to and determined by the perception of the organization and interested parties. Interested parties is defined as persons or organizations that can affect, be affected by, or proceed itself being affected by a decision or activity. Many people in initially reading ISO 56000:2020 are left with the impression that an innovative entity needs to provide positive value to the organization and its interested parties. I personally like to think of an innovative initiative providing combined positive value when the impact on the organization and its interested parties are combined. Unfortunately for many innovation initiatives, the initiative has a negative impact on one stakeholder while having a positive impact on another stakeholder. (Example: in company X the work being done by a ten-person product engineering department is being transferred to a subcontractor in India. This certainly is classified as an innovative entity as it should have a very positive added value to the organization as costs are reduced. But it would have a very negative impact on the ten development engineers who are laid off. The organization could save $200,000 in development engineering added value.)

Now the second part of the equation has a very different value content. What is the negative value as it relates to the other interested parties (employees, employees family, small businesses in the area, lost the revenue, etc.)? We have seen conditions where individuals who were laid off lost their homes and were not able to afford sending a child to college and that was only part of the negative impact. It is extremely difficult to quantify the impact upon interested parties when we implement an innovative entity. Most organizations that we have dealt with do not take this negative impact into consideration when they define value-added.

A MAJOR IMS DESIGN ERROR

Often the IST sets about developing an IMS that is in line with the organization and its interested parties' needs and expectations. This is a very complex job when you plan on developing an IMS that meets everyone's needs and desires. We often find that a more organized approach is to select what the primary parties are interested in and focus the initial system design to meet the needs and requirements of these parties. In a typical organization, these primary parties would be the investors, executive management, employees, customers/consumers, and suppliers. Some organizations shorten this primary parties list down to investors, employees, and customers. The other interested parties' interfacing activities and information transfer can be easily added when you complete the initial system design for the primary interested parties.

TOP FIVE POSITIVE/NEGATIVE INNOVATION CHANGE IMPACTS

In order to understand the complexity of trying to satisfy all stakeholders/interested parties, we need to understand each stakeholder's priorities. The following are lists of six of the interested parties and their top five priorities, and top five negative change impacts.

List 1.1 – Investors Measure of the Improvement in Priority Order

1. Return on investment
2. Stock prices
3. Return on assets
4. Market share
5. Successful new products

List 1.1.1 – Investors Measure of Negative Change Impacts in Priority Order

1. Reduce stock prices
2. Reduce dividends

   3. Lower profit levels

   4. Reduce market share

   5. Failure of new products

List 1.2 – Management Measure of the Improvement in Priority Order

   1. Return on assets

   2. Value-added per employee

   3. Stock prices

   4. Market share

   5. Reduced operating expenses

List 1.2.1 – Management Measure of Negative Change Impacts in Priority Order

   1. Increased operating costs

   2. Reduce market share

   3. Lower customer satisfaction levels

   4. Failure of new products

   5. Reduce sales volume

List 1.3 – External Customer Measure of the Improvement in Priority Order

   1. Reduce costs

   2. New or expanded capabilities

   3. Improved performance/reliability

   4. Ease to use

   5. Improved responsiveness

List 1.3.1 – External Customer Measure of Negative Change Impacts in Priority Order

   1. Increase purchase costs

   2. Decreased reliability

   3. Fewer capabilities than competition

   4. Poor customer service

   5. Increased difficulty to use

List 1.4 – Their Employees Measure of the Improvement in Priority Order

1. Increase job security
2. Increased compensation
3. Improved personal growth potential
4. Improve job satisfaction
5. Improve management

List 1.4.1 – Employee Measure of Negative Change Impacts in Priority Order

1. Layoffs
2. Decreased benefits
3. Salaries not keeping pace with cost-of-living
4. Poor management
5. Decreased skills required to do the job (boarding work)

List 1.5 – Suppliers Measure of the Improvement in Priority Order

1. Increased return on investment (supplier)
2. Improved communications/fewer interfaces
3. Simplify requirements/fewer changes
4. Long-term contracts
5. Longer cycle times

List 1.5.1 – Suppliers Measure of Negative Change Impacts in Priority Order

1. Loss of contract
2. Shorter order cycles
3. Increased competition
4. Imposing new standards
5. Longer Accounts Payable cycle times

List 1.6. – Community Measure of the Improvement in Priority Order

1. Increasing employment of people
2. Increased tax base

3. Reduce pollution
4. Support of community activities
5. Safety for employees

List 1.6.1 – Community Measure of Negative Change Impacts in Priority Order

1. Moving work overseas
2. Decreasing the number of employees
3. Decreased facility resulting in lower taxes
4. Unsafe working conditions
5. Increase pollution of the environment (increase in toxic gases and materials)

If your organization is meeting with government standards for air pollution and it finds it can reduce pollution value by an additional 10% by putting in an additional filtering module that costs $40,000 to install and $5,000 a month to operate. Does it have a positive or negative value-added impact upon the stakeholders and how did you calculate it? Would you implement the additional filtering system or not if you were the CEO?

If the city is asking everyone to conserve on water because there is a water shortage, would you install a new sprinkler system that turned on based upon the moisture in the soil rather than the time of the day? Cost to put in the new watering system would be $850. It will reduce you water consumption by 0.5% the cost of your water bill which on average is $10 per month. Would you put in the new watering system? If you did, how do you calculate the innovation value?

This opens up all sorts of interesting questions. How do I combine financial and emotional negative and positive values together? Do I consider all of the interested parties or just major impacted ones? Can I get by just estimating the impact or do I have to have measurable data to back up the projection? Do I consider the IMS as a total in calculating value or do I look at individual parts/activities to determine which ones are positive contributors and which ones are lost value contributors? How will I know if the proposed IMS is value added or value lost? What is the negative impact upon an employee who has been laid off? What is the negative impact upon the community for an employee who is laid off? How much will it cost to replace an employee who is laid off or quits? How do I optimize the innovative performance of the IMS? Where should the products enter the S-curve? Do I need to implement all of the standard requirements or just the ones that provide the best return on investment? Well, those are some of my questions; I'm sure you have more.

It is our recommendation that you focus your attention on the combined value added of each major 56002:2019 IMS clause in preparing your planning and analysis. Limit your analysis to the impact upon customers, organization, stockholders (owners), suppliers, and employees, and then determine what impact you want to have on the other interested parties and the specific activities to your IMS. What is the value added if you install an innovation policy? Be sure you take into consideration all the time and effort that went into preparing the policy, getting approval, communicating it to your employees, your employees' time in understanding the requirements, and the policy's impact upon the individual's innovation. What would be the impact on the organization if you didn't develop the innovation policy?

SUBCLAUSE 6.1: ADDRESSING OPPORTUNITIES AND RISK (OPPORTUNITY ANALYSIS)

The opportunity analysis is the "filler" of the value proposition. If you don't do an opportunity analysis, it is easy to work on the wrong opportunities, ones that will fail in the long run and cost the organization resources. This is a time when the Opportunity Center can really contribute in a significant way to the success of the innovation or invention. By creating a formal opportunity analysis process, the project will be mandated to go through a stage gate assuring all involved that the project is not being pushed forward because of a short sighted analysis (the cool factor), or because it is the pet project of a senior manager or key customer, who doesn't actually suffer any risk if the concept fails (based upon the book by Harrington and Trusko, 2014).

If done well, the Opportunity Analysis is the strategy the organization uses to assess the potential for a change or enhancement that has the potential to positively affect an entire generation of revenue.

Opportunities can vary from a small change within a current business model that leads to greater efficiency or reduced costs, to the launch of a new business or product line that will affect the organization in profound ways. Either way, including something in between, undergoing an opportunity analysis helps to provide an understanding of what effects, positive and negative, are likely to take place if a particular approach is implemented.

With any opportunity analysis, several key questions must be answered in order for the analysis to be effective and accurate. This analysis falls into three main questions:

1. What are the benefits of implementing the opportunity?
2. What adverse effects might occur when the change takes place?
3. How will the change affect the overall business and is the business prepared to accept those changes?

Value Proposition Cycle

The data collection process is one of the most important process in a value proposition cycle. It's a process where the individual or team that is preparing the value proposition defines what data needs to be collected in order to do the evaluation and then collects this data. It is important to understand that the individual or group that is preparing the value proposition will rely heavily upon their best judgment and the input that they have received from sources like a benchmarking study, the research paper, and random idea/concept documentation submitted to them as inputs to the data collection process. Based upon our experience, there is a wide range of ideas/concepts that have value propositions prepared for them. Frequently, ideas/concepts that enter into the value proposition's cycle are rejected early in the cycle, because they do not meet the ground rules required to expend the effort necessary to prepare the value proposition. The amount and type of information needed to prepare the value proposition will vary based upon a number of factors. For example, very different types of information are necessary to prepare a value proposition for a new product that is required for a process or procedure change. Concepts/ideas that impact large portions of the organization and/or the organization's culture require a more intensive analysis than ones that have a very limited impact on just a few people in the organization.

It is also important to remember those value propositions that will have a significant impact upon the organization will be subjected to a more extensive analysis. In addition, a business case will need to be prepared for each of these value propositions and it will need to be approved for further investigation by the executive team.

The following is a description of the eleven tasks that make up the data collection process activities related to the present system. The team will need to do an extremely good job here as this will be the data that the project improvements will be based upon. Many of the more experienced innovators require that the current process and future process data is collected in parallel in order to get a more accurate picture of the comparison between the two.

- Task 1 – Assign value proposition preparation team and familiarize them with the proposed project management documents.
- Task 2 – Review project plan to define status and major issues.
- Task 3 – Does the proposal meet the ground rules to prepare a value proposition?
- Task 4 – Review goals and objectives and defining measurements that will be needed to validate that they were successfully met.
- Task 5 – Review the data and how it was obtained during the current state assessment.
- Task 6 – Collect current and old improvement proposals and re-lated project files.
- Task 7 – Define what data is available in the present database and what additional data has to be generated to validate the success of the project.
- Task 8 – Define how and the quantity of the special control data will be needed.
- Task 9 – Set up the special control data collection stations in the present system and operate them to ensure they are working effectively.
- Task 10 – Make arrangements to have the special control data re-lated to the current system collected. The person responsible for the data collection should review the results on a regular basis to be sure things are working correctly.
- Task 11 – Collect present system required data.

Risk Analysis

The biggest single problem most organizations have in their planning operation is their inability to accurately estimate the amount of resources required to develop and implement an innovation entity (cycle time, people power, facility, etc.). All too often, the organization is militarized by the new opportunities to the point that they are grossly underfunded and go through many cycles of increased scope. In many companies in their enthusiasm to take advantage of an opportunity, they will combine their value proposition and the business case analysis. This is a major error organizations make during the concept development activities. The value proposition should always be done first as it tells the organization different winning or losing propositions. The business case analysis is designed to determine what projects provide the most overall value-added to the organization and establish them as part of the portfolio of projects that is activated within the organization.

This clause makes the basic assumption that the processes defined in Subclause 4.1 and Subclause 4.2 will provide the organization's opportunities and risks considerations. Often additional opportunities and risks are identified and submitted for evaluation. Each opportunity and risk is then evaluated to determine if it is in line with the organization's mission, goals, values, and strategic plan. Those opportunities and risks that meet the initial screening will advance to Subclause 6.2 – Innovation objectives and planning to achieve them. This brings out a good point that should be emphasized. The clauses in 56002:2019 are not written so that they would be implemented in sequence as they are interrelated and interdependent.

Figure 4.7 provides a simple approach to defining the magnitude of a risk related to a specific entity.

To use the Risk Analysis Square, you will need to evaluate each risk to determine if it is:

- Acceptable risk
- Unacceptable risk

In addition, you will have to evaluate each risk to determine if it is:

- Likely to occur
- Unlikely to occur
- Very likely to occur

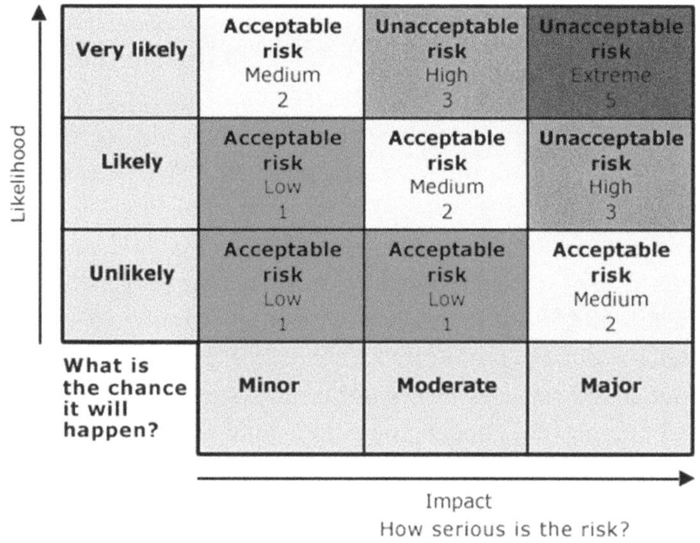

FIGURE 4.7
Risk Analysis Square.

Using the guidance provided by the Risk Analysis Square, you can gain some insight into the need for a mitigation plan. We like to use the following:

1. If it is an activity related to the customer/user, the employee, or high amount of financial investment in the entity, we would suggest that you develop mitigation plans for all the ones rated as a medium acceptable risk, and unacceptable risk.
2. For the other interested parties whose entities are rated as an un-acceptable risk, they should have mitigation plans prepared for them. The ones rated as medium acceptable risk may or may not have mitigation plans related to them. Like all guidance formulas the final decision rests in the IMS.

For each of the risks, the level of risk will be defined and its impact will be quantified. The risks that meet unacceptable risk criteria will have mitigation plans prepared for them as well as measurable objectives re-lated to implementing the mitigation plan. The considerations and ob-jectives related for each of the opportunities and risks should be documented and retained. The opportunities and objectives that do not warrant further consideration will be discarded from further processing.

We don't have time in this book to take you through a complete risk analysis cycle. As innovators, it is important that you are very familiar with the techniques and tools used to perform a risk analysis. The following is just a quick understanding of what a risk analysis entails.

- Definition of risk analysis: Risk analysis is the process of analyzing, determining, and defining the risk of danger to government agencies, not-for-profit organizations, for-profit organizations both product and service type organization. It can be used for a project, a total organization, a state, or even a total nation.

  There are two parts to risk. Each of them is required to perform a meaningful risk analysis. They are
  - The chances of something unpleasant happening.
  - The consequences – negative ones – if it does.

After estimating the probability of a particular adverse event happening, you then need to estimate the cost to correct the occurrence. These two estimates are multiplied together to have a value for the risk:

Risk Value = Probability of Adverse Event × Cost of Event

Innovation Planning to Achieve Objectives

For each of the opportunities, the impact of using IMS will be defined. Measurable objectives related to the specific opportunity will be developed. If it cannot be measured, you have to question is it worthwhile doing.

Although Subclause 6.2 only addresses entity objectives, we feel it is important to also consider and document the entity goals that should be conformed to.

Subclause 6.2.1 in 56002:2019 relates only to objectives; in our discussion we're going to include goals. This subclause should consist of two parts – entity objectives and entity performance goals. The words *objectives and goals* seem to have different meanings to different organizations. Some organizations believe that you use objectives and develop goals to support the objectives as measurements along the way. Other organizations look at goals as a higher-level measurement of objectives and the milestones along the way to meet the goals. Let's define objectives and goals based upon *Merriam–Webster's College Dictionary:*

- Objectives: are something toward which effort is directed; an aim or end of action
- Goals: the end toward which effort is directed; the terminal point of a race

In this discussion, entity objectives are the higher-level conditions and entity performance goals which are the milestones that are used to measure progress toward the entity objectives. In this case, objectives are not qualified but are quantifiable. For example, to grow with the industry can be quantified and is a good objective. If the industry grows at a rate of 15% in a given year, the organization should grow at least 15% during the same year. This is a good example of qualified goal.

A very famous example of objectives was issued in the 1960s when John F. Kennedy set an objective to put a man on the moon and bring him back safely by the end of the decade. He didn't know how it would be done or could it be done or how much it would cost. He knew there were a lot of problems that needed to be solved – technical, financial, and political. He just set the objective and defined the end date and then he left it up to others to define intermediate goals and strategies. He stepped back and got out of the way so that others could do their thing, but he never lost interest or stopped following the project.

Objectives set by management define what and when major accomplishments should be achieved. Once that is done, management should get out of their employees' way so they can get the job done. Don't think that you need to have all of the answers in advance of the setting the entity objectives.

Entity Performance Goals

Entity performance goals have two key elements:

- Specifically state the target for improvement
- Give the time interval in which the improvements should be accomplished

It is important to understand that the customer usually does not realize what they will need or want in the future. Customers' input is critical for short-term planning. As the customers' input usually reflects the current needs, even when you asked them to define their future needs, they will have a limited view of how technology will be changing over time.

Entity objectives and performance goals should be in line with your mission and visions. Then you need to develop goals that are in line with and support each objective. Goals should be measurable, quantifiable, and support your objectives. Think about achieving them in a short time frame. Effective goals must state how much of what kind of performance is to be accomplished, the deadline for accomplishing the goal, and who will be responsible for accomplishing it. Make sure both your goals and objectives build on your strengths and shore up your weaknesses, opportunities, and recognize your thoughts.

> No matter how careful you plan your goals, they may never be more than pipedreams unless you pursue them with gusto.
>
> *W. Clement Stone, author*

Goals and Objectives Planning

Subclause 6.2.2 does not clearly define that the team is responsible for developing an action plan to take advantage of the opportunity. This is probably the most important innovative task that the team will be expected to be involved in. The absence of guidance on how to take advantage of an opportunity in the Standard is probably based upon the large number of methodologies available to analyze a situation and define what action needs to be taken to meet the improvement opportunity objectives. The only improvement cycle that was mentioned in ISO 56002:2019 series was Plan-Do-Check-Act.

- Definition of Plan-Do-Check-Act: The Plan-Do-Check-Act (PDCA) cycle is a very simple approach to project management that can be used effectively on non-complex programs and for implementing corrective action.

Note: Often it is incorrectly called "The Deming Cycle." It was actually designed by Walter A. Shewhart and first published in his book, *Statistical Method from the Viewpoint of Quality Control.*[1]

The Shewhart Cycle has been used in many ways. ISO technical committee 279 designed ISO 56002:2019 around the Shewhart Cycle. The environmental group that designed ISO 14001 built it around the Shewhart Cycle (see Figure 4.8).

While the original Shewhart Cycle begins with the "planning" phase, the ISO 56002:2019 pattern begins by setting directions to the organizations and then progresses through the rest of the PDCA Cycle. The following is a list of all the ISO 14001 clauses that apply to each of the five categories.

- **Direct**
  - 4.1.0 General
  - 4.2.0 Environmental Policy

- **Plan**
  - 4.3.0 Planning
  - 4.3.1 Environmental Aspects
  - 4.3.2 Legal and Other Requirements
  - 4.3.3 Objectives and Targets
  - 4.3.4 Environmental Management Programs

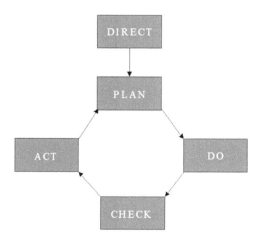

FIGURE 4.8
PDCA Pattern.

- **Do**
  - 4.4.0 Implementation and Operation
  - 4.4.1 Structure and Responsibility
  - 4.4.2 Training, Awareness, and Competence
  - 4.4.3 Communication
  - 4.4.4 Environnemental Management System Documentation
  - 4.4.5 Document Control
  - 4.4.6 Operational Control
  - 4.4.7 Emergency Preparedness and Response

- **Check**
  - 4.5.0 Checking and Corrective Action
  - 4.5.1 Monitoring and Measurement
  - 4.5.2 Nonconformance and Corrective and Preventive Action
  - 4.5.3 Records
  - 4.5.4 Environmental Management System Audit

- **Act**
  - 4.6.0 Management Review

Use of a Project Charter

Those opportunities and/or risks whose objectives justify further consideration will have a project charter related to the opportunity and/or risk prepared. The project charter will cover activities up to the point that the project becomes part of the organization's portfolio of projects. At that time, the complete project plan should be prepared for all major improvement opportunities. For those projects that use a very small part of the resources and are completed in a relative short time, in most cases simply a mission statement that includes the project's goals will be satisfactory. A project charter contains the following information.

- The project's mission
- The name of the project
- A list of the key measurements and innovation objectives.
- How and when the results will be measured
- How progress would be evaluated

- A list of alternative improvement action that were considered
- Prioritization considerations and results
- Timetable for performing the analysis
- Tollgate timing
- Return on investment estimate
- A list of individuals both internally and externally will be involved in developing the action plan and the amount of time they will be required to devote to the project
- A list of the parts of the organization that is impacted
- A list of potential change management issues

The project charter is a living and changing document that is changed to reflect new information as it becomes available. The initial project charter should be approved by the appropriate higher-level management as well as any major changes that affect completion dates, cost, or objectives.

SUBCLAUSE 6.3: ORGANIZATIONAL STRUCTURES

This clause focuses on what top management should be doing to make the organizational structure more innovatively oriented. It focusses is on how the organization should be structured to support the innovation initiative considering the other activities that are presently going on within the organization. It also is sensitive to when a new organization needs to be formed to support the new initiative. Top management will also be involved in changing the culture within the organization to be more risk oriented and to treat failure as a learning experience rather than unsatisfactory performance. They are responsible for modifying performance requirements and the rewards and recognition system to reflect the desired culture.

SUBCLAUSE 6.4: INNOVATION PORTFOLIOS

- Definition of innovation portfolios: A portfolio is a centralized collection of independent projects or programs that are grouped together to facilitate their prioritization, effective management, and resource optimization in order to meet strategic organizational objectives

Organizational Portfolio Development Cycle

This book is designed to take the reader through the complete project/ program management cycle from the submittal of the proposed project/ programs to the management of their implementation (Source: Christopher et al., 2017). To accomplish this, an effective, proven Organizational Portfolio Management (OPM) System is defined. This is not the only Organizational Portfolio Management System that can be used, but it is one that we know is both efficient and effective. The four phases of this approach are as follows:

- Phase I. Develop the organizational portfolio by selecting the right mix of projects/programs that will make up the organizational portfolio based upon the resource limitations that are present and the risks involved that are related to the individual projects and programs. Figure 4.9 is a box flowchart that represents the process flow for Phase I.

The cycle starts with information related to all of the proposed projects/ programs and all the currently active projects/programs being provided to a Portfolio Development Team. The Portfolio Development Team analyzes and evaluates each of these to determine the value added they represent to the organization, risks related, and resources required compared to resources available to determine which project/program should be rejected and which project/program should be recommended to the Executive Team to have resources applied to them. The Executive Team analyzes the recommendations made by the Portfolio Development Team and make decisions on whether the project/programs will be approved, rejected, or put on hold. Often some of the proposed projects/programs that do not require additional resources as they are already part of the function's normal activities and budget. Continuous improvement initiatives usually fall into this classification as continuous improvement should be part of every individual organization's charter. The approved projects/programs are grouped into manageable groups of Organizational Portfolio Management.

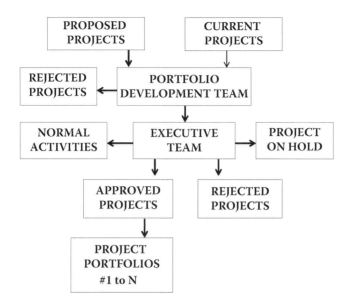

FIGURE 4.9
Organizational Portfolio Development Cycle.

- Phase II. Create the OPM System Implementation Plan. This phase develops a plan for establishing and managing the OPM System to minimize the resources consumed, cycle time to complete the projects, and increase the ability that the projects will meet their projected value-added content to the organization.
- Phase III. Implement the OPM System. This phase focuses on the complexity of managing an organizational portfolio and keeping them aligned with the organization's vision goals and objectives. It requires the development of an effective rewards and recognition system that supports the changes brought about by the IMS project/program. It focuses attention on the needs for training the individuals that are impacted by the project/program prior to its implementation.
- Phase IV. Practical applications of Project Change Management within the OPM System. This phase focuses on the difficulties and how to overcome them related to the continuous changing environment and project requirements that are encountered as projects are developed and implemented in today's demanding conditions.

Before we get into some detailed discussion related to each of these four phases, there are some additional definitions that need to be provided. They are primarily related to the OPM System structure.

- **Advocate** – the individual or group that wants to achieve a change but lacks the power to sanction it.
- **Change Agent** – the individual or group responsible for facilitating the implementation of the change.
- **Impacted Individuals** – these are the individuals whose activities will be directly affected by the output from the project/program when the project/program is completed.
- **Initiating Sponsor** – the individual or group with the power to initiate or to legitimize proposed project or program related to all of the affected people in the organization.
- **Sponsor**- the individual or group with the power to sanction or legitimize projects.
- **Sustaining Sponsor** – the individual or group that can use their logistics, their economic and/or political proximity to the individuals affected by the change to convince them that they should support, help implement and comply with the project/ program.

It's important to realize that each project and/or activity is in competition with all the other projects and or activities within the organization as it relates to the distribution of resources and the possibility to be part of the strategic plan.

The Performance Development Cycle starts with the submission of a Value Proposition.

- Definition of Value Proposition: A value proposition is an analysis and quantified review of the benefits, cost, and value that an organization can deliver to customers and other concerned groups within and outside of the organization. It is also a position in a value where Value = Benefits minus Cost (cost includes risk). Approved value propositions should result in resources being approved only till the time that the business case analysis is complete.

Both the value proposition and the business case analysis are key toll-gates that management should critically evaluate to determine if the project should be continued or dropped based upon value-added to the customer, consumer, investor, and employees.

A preliminary innovation team should prepare a value proposition using the objective set for the project. If the value proposition gets approved by management a formal innovation team should be established to support the initiative. The value proposition document should include formularies on how the impact of the innovation process will be measured. This is just a rough estimate of the innovation's impact but the preliminary innovation team members should take time to make it as accurate as possible based upon their knowledge they have or can collect plus the key measurements related to the opportunity.

The team members are the heart of the IMS strategy. The idea of "participative management" is based on allowing employees to help management make better decisions. The whole concept of "synergy" is based on two heads being better than one. If the team leader is not available to guide the team, the team members should assume responsibility for completing the task. Some specific characteristics that a team member should have are:

- Willingness to express opinions or feelings
- Active participation
- Listening intensively
- Thinking creatively
- Avoiding disruptive communication
- Be protective of the rights of the other members of the team
- Be responsible for meeting the goals and objectives of the team

A careful mixture of backgrounds, education, cultures, and work experience has proven to be very important selecting the members of the team.

A typical value proposition would include the following:

- Title and the names of the originators of the proposed change
- Table of contents
- Executive overview

1. Description of the proposed change
2. Description of the AS/IS state
3. Value added content that the proposed change would bring about
4. Overall cost and time frame to implement the change
5. Other solutions that were considered and why they were not chosen
6. Risk and obstacles related to the change
7. Recommendations

- List of the key people associated with the value proposition (executive sponsor, individuals recommending the change, individuals that created the value proposition)
- Financial calculations
- Details related to other value added results. (Example: cycle time reduction, stock reduction, improved customer satisfaction, reduced defect levels, increase market share, etc.)
- List of risks and exposures
- List of assumptions
- Other solutions that were considered and why they were not chosen
- Implementation plan
- Three-year projection of the situation if the proposed change is not approved
- The Net Value added when the cost (money and other resources) related to installation of the Change is subtracted from the Value Added content
- Detailed recommendations
- References

It is imperative that the value proposition considers the initiative's impact upon the total organization.

Often there is a general feeling that the preliminary innovation team felt the data they collected does not justify approving the initiative. In reality, their job is to separate the good initiatives from the potentially bad initiatives. Remember the following: "The best time to stop an initiative is before it is started."

- Definition of Business Case: A business case captures the reason for initializing a project or program. It is most often presented in a well-structured written document, but, in some cases, also may be in the form of a short verbal agreement or presentation.

The logic of the business case is: whatever resources, such as money or effort are consumed they should be in support of a specific business need or opportunity where it provides the greatest short-term and long-term value to the organization. For major initiatives like establishing an IMS, a business case analysis may also be required. In these cases, the value proposition is usually prepared before the improvement action plans are developed and their concepts are validated.

Another concept that is critical to the success of an IMS is the creation and management of innovation portfolios. Similar to the planning these need to be:

- In alignment with and contributing to the innovation strategy
- Consistent between individual initiatives within the overall portfolio
- Synergistic using existing structures and efforts and supporting those
- Balanced between risk and returns
- Communicated

SUMMARY

An excellent plan in the file cabinet is no plan at all.

H. James Harrington

Planning for the implementation of an IMS must include adequate planning that considers not only the opportunities but also the risks involved. In addition, innovation objectives should be developed along with supporting plans to achieve those objectives. These plans need to be

- In alignment with the strategy of the organization,
- Defined with specific deliverables and expected results,

- Properly resourced,
- Adequately monitored and adjusted over time to assure completion, and
- Fit within either existing supportive organizational structures or within new structures that are specifically designated for the purpose of supporting the IMS.

Another concept that is critical to the success of an IMS is the creation and management of innovation portfolios. Similar to the planning these need to be:

- In alignment with and contributing to the innovation strategy
- Be consistent between individual initiatives within the overall portfolio
- Synergistic using existing structures and efforts and supporting those
- Balanced between risk and returns
- Communicated
- Improved as time goes on

Remember that ISO 56002:2019 title is "Innovation Management System – Guidance" standard. This Standard states that it is "an innovation management system guide to recommend best innovative practices to an organization like its innovation vision, strategy, policy, and objectives and to establish the support and processes needed to achieve the intended outcomes." The Standard is not intended to define the sub-process, activity, or task involved in managing a comprehensive innovation. It does not provide guidance on specific tools and/or methodologies related to innovation because they could be considered self-serving and would be difficult to keep up-to-date with the rapidly changing innovation technology.

ISO Standard 56000:2020 defined innovation as a new or changed entity realizing or redistributing value. Introduction of something new includes the development and implementation of a new idea, design, method, product or service. We are concerned that the standard definition for innovation does not require that innovation results in add value. We feel that any activity that doesn't add positive value may be creative, but it is not innovative. We are also concerned that the ISO definition does not require the impact of the project to be evaluated from all the stakeholders' point of view. Frequently, the positive value added to one stakeholder is more than offset by the negative value added to another stakeholder.

The purpose of this book is to provide the reader with a better understanding of ISO 56002:2019 and help them in using the Standard to guide their project to design, install, perform and sustain the objective that has been established for the IMS. It also provides some additional tools, methods, and technologies that will assist your organization in developing an IMS that is uniquely designed to support your specific organizations products, customers, services, and culture. Those organizations, where the ISO 56002:2019 IMS provides guidance along with the added interpretations in this book, will have the capabilities to develop an innovative management culture and performance that you will be proud of. If the guidance in Clause 6.0 is followed, the organization will have a road map that will lead to an effective and efficient IMS. But it is like an automobile race; you can never win the race if you don't start your car.

5

Clause 7: Support

PURPOSE

This clause provides guidance on how to put together the resources needed to establish, implement, maintain, and improve a support system for your IMS. In this chapter, you will learn how to use resources and capabilities, understand the importance of managing and engaging people and teams, and how to secure funding to your innovation activities and programs.

OVERVIEW

This chapter discusses some of best practices on how to establish a support system for innovation programs and activities. It discusses the role of people, rewards, knowledge, and infrastructure such as innovation labs in enhancing the performance if an IMS. It also describes how organizations should address collaboration and change management, as well as IP issues. Finally, the chapter discusses some known tools and methods used in the industry to engage teams in creativity and innovative thinking. The chapter consist of the following subclauses:

- Resources (people, time, knowledge, finance, infrastructure)
- Competence
- Awareness
- Communication
- Documented information

- Tools and methods
- Strategic intelligence management
- Intellectual property management

BENEFITS

This chapter shows you how to assemble different components to support your IMS taking into consideration the specifics of your organization. It provides a wide range of examples and practices from which you can take what applies to your size, your industry, and your level of maturity.

CLASSIFICATION OF ACTIONS

This chapter is written as a *Should do* type of activity, giving you the choice of implementing practices that works better for your circumstances.

SUBCLAUSE 7.1: INNOVATION RESOURCES

The organization should determine and provide in a timely manner the resources needed for the establishment, implementation, maintenance, and continual improvement of the innovation management system.[*]

Clause 7 of ISO 56002:2019 addresses support and all the things you need to do to put in place your IMS and support your innovation activities and programs. Because Clause 7 of ISO 56002:2019 addresses all the support issues, it is actually the longest clause in ISO 56002:2019, so we will not dwell too much on the obvious support actions like time,

---

[*]©ISO. This material is excerpted from ISO 56002:2019, with permission of the American National Standards Institute (ANSI) on behalf of the International Organization for Standardization. All rights reserved.

documentation, infrastructure, and awareness. These are general recommendations that most organizations with a mature management system should have already in place. For instance, a healthy organizational culture that wants to invest in innovation should dedicate time to support innovation activities and programs. Usually, that time investment is in the form of building capacity, such as training, teaching, collaboration, mentoring, certification, internship, and so forth. Your HR department, and perhaps the training and development department as well, have a dedicated time effort for that.

A mature management system should also have a good documentation system that allows the organization to record, track, and follow up with different procedures and processes. We will not address awareness and communication, because we have already addressed them in the leadership clause (Clause 5). We will focus, however, on the support actions that directly impact the success of your IMS. These support actions are:

1. Resources and capabilities (Subclause 7.1.1)
2. People and teams' development (Subclause 7.1.2)
3. Knowledge management (Subclause 7.1.4)
4. Funding and financial issues (Subclause 7.1.5)
5. Infrastructure (Subclause 7.1.6)
6. Innovation competency framework (Subclause 7.2)
7. Tools and methods (Subclause 7.6)
8. Strategic intelligence management (Subclause 7.7)
9. Intellectual property management (Subclause 7.8)*

To achieve a competitive advantage that helps you improve your performance and achieve your strategic goals, you will need to be able to acquire, develop, and bundle your resources in a way that supports your innovation capability and enhance your IMS. In the strategic management literature, authors such as Wernerfelt, Prahalad, and Hamel, who led the development of the Resources Based View (RVB) approach to strategic management, argue that for companies to compete and successfully outperform their rivals they have to invest in their resources.

According to this approach, rather than looking outside of the organization, managers need to look inside the organization and frequently analyze their internal environment to develop, manage, acquire, and improve their resources. While resources by themselves do not lead to success, it is the bundling of resources and capabilities that allow a company to succeed.

Having a state-of-the-art facility, for instance, and a strong financial position does not create by itself a capability. What creates a capability is your ability to manage the state-of-the-art facility and bundle it with your financial position to lure talents and incentivize innovators to succeed.

The resource-based view makes a distinction between two types of resources: Tangible and Intangible.

- Tangible resources often refer to physical resources, such as infrastructure, technology, borrowing capacity, structure, and reporting lines.
- Intangible resources refer to talent, management capabilities, trust, knowledge, brand-name, and customer service.

You can use any of these resources to develop or harness your innovation capability. For instance, you may combine your borrowing capacity with your reputation and brand name to attract and retain innovators, independent thinkers, and entrepreneurs seeking to develop new products. ISO 56002:2019 suggests that you need to manage these resources in a proactive way, transparent and flexible manner to enhance your innovation capabilities.

For these resources to realize the value and help you develop innovation capabilities, they must have the following attributes:

- Resources must be valuable, meaning they help you create a differentiation that sets your organization apart from the competition.
- They must be rare, owned by a few, or difficult to acquire.
- They must be costly to imitate. If your competitor wants to acquire them, then they will have to pay a higher price. For instance, if your competitor wants to acquire a data scientist to develop or train neural networks, they will have to pay them more, which could be a constraint on their budget.

- And finally, resources have to be bundled, organized, and structured in a way that makes your organization unique. For instance, if you have a tech lab and great talents, but your talents are not allowed to use the facility then your resources are not creating a capability.

As a general approach to managing resources, ISO 56002:2019 suggests that you take the following action:

- Decide what resources you can develop internally and what resources you can acquire so you can manage the make-buy decision in a flexible and adaptable approach.
- Segregate the resources that are directly linked to your innovation capability from other resources so you can focus your efforts on managing and developing what matters to innovation.
- Adopt a long-term approach to developing your innovation capabilities by investing in resources that have a long-term impact. For instance, rather than buying an AI technology, focus on developing an internal Machine Learning Team that helps your company learn how to build the new technology internally.
- Proactively manage and acquire resources so they support or enhance your innovation capability.

Generally speaking, a capability, used as a noun, is an ability of an organization to do certain things. Capabilities are defined by opposition to other business concepts such as process and activity.

Managers and employees struggle to define what a capability means. You will be surprised how your team may not have the same understanding of the same capability, and what is considered as a capability and what is not. To help your team develop a good understanding of the concept of capability and have a common language around the same concept, take the following steps.

- Assemble a small team of three to five managers with enough experience and knowledge about the company and the business.
- Have the team develop an initial list of what they think your organizational capabilities are.

- Run the initial list by your senior managers, directors, different processes owners, and managers to check the list. Ask them to enrich it or amend it.
- In the second draft of this iteration process, ask your managers, the following questions "What ability do we have that supports our innovation?"
- In the third and final iteration, compare the suggestions made by your senior managers and process owners with ISO Innovation documentation: ISO 56000:2020 Terminology, ISO 56002:2019 Innovation Management System Guidance, ISO 56003 Innovation Partnership, ISO/TR56004 Innovation Management Assessment, ISO 56006 Strategic Intelligence Management, and ISO 56007 Idea Management.
- Make a final and approved list of all your innovation capabilities and share it with all your decision makers, as well as your teams and innovators to allow for people to tap into different organizational capabilities.
- Finally, capabilities are like living organisms; they grow and die so make sure you update your capability by running this process every three years.

Subclause 7.1.2: Managing People

In the management literature, we often ask the question, "Who is more important to innovation – the people or the process?" While companies may take different ways of answering these questions, in practice research shows that for innovation to work effectively, you need to have both. That is, you need creative people willing to contribute with new ideas, and an organizational environment that incentivizes employees to engage, and protects their rights to their intellectual contribution. ISO 56002:2019 provides a clear direction on what you need to do to manage people, so they are driving innovation. In this clause, we will address five action items:

- Managing people's pipeline from recruiting to retention
- Manage innovation teams
- Create enough incentives that lure creative people to innovation
- Provide a risk-free environment for people to innovate
- Develop a process that clarifies ownership

There are two additional actions you need to take to foster innovation: attracting creative people and innovators, and provide incentives so you can retain innovators. Your HR recruiting system must have a selection tool that helps your company target and recruit innovators whether you are recruiting from colleges or directly from the labor market. Use tools that help you predict the innovativeness skills of the recruit and learn about their creativity skills. Focus on discovery skills that differentiate innovators and creative people. In their book, *The Innovator's DNA*, authors Dyer, Gregerson and Christensen, argue that innovator people, unlike average people, have five discovery skills. These skills are crucial to innovation. Association skills, questioning skills, observation skills, experimenting skills, and networking skills differentiate innovators from average employees.

- **Association Skills**

    According to the authors, the association ability is a mental skill that allows people to link things that are seemingly not connected. While ordinary people may look at three different things and see no connection between them, those who are gifted with association skill may see a link. A common example used to illustrate this skill is the example of Google's co-founder Larry Page when he developed the algorithm that runs Google. When Larry Page was a graduate student at Stanford University working on his Ph.D., the search engine of that time was quite limited in its capability. When you enter a keyword, you get tons of documents and webpages that have no relevance to what you are looking for. Larry's ability to associate the amount of data with its relevance, a skill that he developed in graduate school as a researcher, led him to come up with a better system that organizes data.

- **Questioning Skills**

    The second skill you need to target in recruits, or help your current employees harness it, is questioning. Questioning is a skill of not being satisfied with the current state and an ambition for a better tomorrow. While we are all born with a certain level of curiosity, innovators' questioning mindset makes them challenge the status quo continuously. Those with a questioning mindset tend to ask questions such as "why and why not," "what if," "how should we do things differently," "in what way we might…" "How might we do things?" In these lines of questions, the innovator may stumble on the right question that challenges some fundamental assumptions.

- **Observation Skills**

    Innovators have a particular passion for observing processes and behaviors to spot a problem, a difference, a frustration, or an improvement. These observation skills, when combined with the ability to question things, becomes a crucial skill that leads to innovative ideas.

- **Experimenting Skills**

    The fourth skill that you need to target in your selection and recruiting process is experimentation. Innovators play with experimentation to test out unusual ideas. This experimentation does not have to be an elaborate one or in a high-tech lab. It can be a simple one and in common places. The experimentation skills are associated with another common skill found in entrepreneurs and innovators called playfulness. Innovators like to try things out and play with things to experiment and test things out.

- **Networking Skills**

    The last skill discussed by the authors of *The Innovator's DNA* is networking. Networking is different from the previous skills outlined here in the sense that you can acquire it and encourage your employee to develop it. You can incentivize your would-be innovators to develop a networking skill by creating events for people to meet and network, while also encouraging and supporting them to participate outside of the company's networking opportunities. Networking helps employees learn about other challenges and how people are dealing with them, which could spark a creative moment.

Managing Innovation Teams

Teams' management is the third support action suggested by ISO 56002:2019 to help you establish and manage your Innovation Management teams. When forming innovation teams, you need to look at two important issues: size and diversity.

- **Size**

    The size of the team is critical. What we refer to in the management literature as the overstaffing bias in teams, is a situation in which the team is so big that it affects its ability to make decisions and engage people. Most researchers tend to agree that the ideal size of innovation teams is about ten people. Larger teams also increase conformity pressure, which is a factor in silencing independent thinkers. People in larger teams tend to lose the connection and the chemistry that fuels the team's identity. Jeff Bezos, CEO, and founder of Amazon created a rule in making teams at Amazon, "Every team should be small enough that it can be fed by two pizzas."

- **Diversity**

  The second issue in teams' formation is to make sure that your teams are highly diverse. While diversity may seem to be a barrier to fast decision making, it is a good practice to have in innovation teams. ISO 56002:2019 suggests that, when putting together your innovation teams, you need to mix people from different disciplines, different professional backgrounds and expertise, and different cultural and geographic backgrounds. Cognitive diversity is another crucial component of creative thinking. Cognitive diversity impacts divergent thinking and helps members develop questioning skills, an essential step to ideation. Diversity also helps cross-pollinate ideas, taking one idea from one specific context and applying it to a different context, which could spark *Eureka* moments for team members.

  Diversity is also important as it helps teams avoid group-think, a pitfall in which people adopt a similar pattern of thinking; and the Abilene paradox, another pitfall in which group members attempt to conform to the more dominant voice in the team.

  Furthermore, diversity has been proven in research as well as in practice, to help team members learn from each other, and be challenged or questioned about some of their basic taken for granted professional assumptions. When a trained financial analyst works with an engineer, both people learn how to recognize thinking patterns and reasoning from a different perspective, which can help the team improve its creative and integrative thinking. Your role as an innovation leader is to engineer highly diverse teams, otherwise, people default to homogeneity as most of us tend to gravitate with people we know and people we are comfortable with.

Finally, and as we leave the clause on teams, it is important to mention the Google study called Project Aristotle. Project Aristotle is a famous two-year study conducted by Google to understand how teams perform. In this study, which gathered 180 Google teams, researchers analyzed more than 250 different team attributes and conducted more than 200 interviews. They found that the single most predictor of team success is psychological safety. Psychological safety means that team members feel that they are safe in making mistakes, sharing thoughts, and failing without being penalized. This is particularly true for innovation. When team members feel that there is a lack of psychological safety, they revert to group-think and compliance with norms, a behavior that is in-compatible with creative and innovative thinking.

Rewards and Recognition

ISO 56002:2019 recommends that you establish an appropriate incentive program to motivate and engage employees in innovation. When es-tablishing your reward and recognition programs, it is crucial that you make a distinction between factors that have a direct impact on moti-vation and factors that indirectly support motivation. This distinction is crucial because it helps your reward program become more efficient.

In the motivation literature, we make the distinction between two important concepts: hygiene factors and motivation factors. Hygiene factors impact people's satisfaction with the job. They reduce job dis-satisfaction but have little impact on engagement. Motivation factors, on the other hand, help increase job satisfaction and impact directly per-formance. Hygiene factors are found in every organization and, by themselves, they do not directly motivate and incentivize people. Salary, job security, status, and good management are all factors that help avoid dissatisfaction, but they do not impact motivation. Once employees get confirmed in their position, the salary or the status does not become a source of motivation; rather, it is considered almost as an entitlement that employees lose them only in extreme cases such as termination. We also call these factors extrinsic motivation factors.

Motivation factors, also called intrinsic factors of motivation, on the other hand, have a direct impact on motivation. Factors such as achievement, the nature of work, autonomy, and growth are considered to have a more direct impact on engaging innovators. Because these factors individualize people and performance, employees tend to respond to them positively. These factors take into consideration the individuality of the person and speak directly to their desire and ambition. They help employees perceive themselves as different. The distinction between hygiene factors and motivation factors is a well-known motivation theory in the United States and has been critical in designing programs that drive innovation in big consulting firms as well as in startups.

In designing your reward and incentive program to support innovation and establishing your IMS, focus on the following three motivation pillars: purpose, autonomy, and mastery. These are the new trends in motivation that have been championed by author Daniel Pink in his well-known book *Drive: The Surprising Truth of What Motivates Us.*

Autonomy

Autonomy is the ability to direct your behavior. Empirical evidence shows that employees, and especially millennials, are willing to give up to 20% of their raise if they get in exchange a better control over their work, according to a study published in 2016 by Price Waterhouse and Coopers. For most people, once they achieve a certain level of wage, autonomy becomes more relevant. It is important to mention that, autonomy does not mean independence from work; it simply means the ability to manage your own time. The famous 20% Google's rule, in which employees are given time off up to 20% of their overall work time, to work on projects that have some personal interest to them, is also a good example of how a company can design an incentive program around the concept of autonomy.

Mastery

The second concept in the new motivation theory is mastery. According to Daniel Pink, people achieve better results when they care about something; and when they care about something, they invest more time and effort to master it. Similar to people who do programming, not for cash but just to get good at it, or people who spend hours playing guitar to master it; mastery is a key driver that engages people in what they do. Your role as an innovation champion is to figure out the things your innovator wants to get good at and provide them with time and a framework to master it while aligning them with your innovation goals.

Purpose

The third factor in motivating people is the notion of purpose. The purpose is an important concept that drives engagement because it provides meaning and allows people to define what work means for them. Purpose allows people to constantly re-engineer their role inside the organization to make it fit the overall nature of work. People driven by purpose tend to think about a higher goal of seeing their work as a means to it. If you can help your employees find a meaning and a purpose, then you can achieve your goal in making them engaged in your innovation programs.

Subclause 7.1.4: Knowledge Management

If you look at the contribution of the United States economy to the global GDP, you will find that the United States' share of the global economy in the 1970s was about 70%. Most of the United States contributions were in the form of manufacturing outputs, service exports, merchandise exports, and so forth. But if you take a look at the share of the United States of the global economy now, you will see a fundamental change in the type of product and services the US economy put on the global market. According to a study conducted by the Business Intelligence Unit of the *Economist* in 2015, about 70% of products put on the global market by the United States economy are technology-oriented products, such as software, cloud computing, social media platforms, financial-oriented products such as venture capital investment, foreign exchange reserve, and investment banking products, and finally, intellectual properties products in the form of R&D and patents. This fundamental shift in the product and services the United States economy puts on the global market denotes an underline fundamental shift that took place in the United States economy since the late 1970s.

The United States economy has shifted towards a knowledge-based economy. With the acceleration of technical production and scientific discovery the United States economy now relies more on intellectual capital, such as IP, R&D, design, management, and consulting, then physical output or natural resources. The proliferation of the personal computer in the late 1980s and the upsurge of social networks, cloud computing, big data, Artificial Intelligence, and Blockchain are making the United States a knowledge and innovation-based economy. The year 2016 marked a rupture between the old and the new economy when Apple, Microsoft, Alphabet (Google), Amazon, and Facebook emerged as the leading global companies by market capitalization, thus surpassing traditional companies that have dominated the global economies for decades from sectors such as finance, gas, and oil. In 2020 for instance, Microsoft had a market cap of $1.3 Trillion, while Apple and Amazon had a market cap of $1.2 Trillion each.

Why this is important to mention for an IMS? Well, the shift that took place in the United States now places more emphasis on innovation. United States companies are getting better at managing knowledge and innovation, which puts more pressure on companies to creates a better ecosystem to manage knowledge and innovation. ISO 56002:2019 suggests three important actions: capturing knowledge, facilitating access to knowledge, and maintaining access and improving knowledge. Let's look at these three recommendations one by one. But before that, let's see how knowledge management is defined.

Definition of Knowledge Management

Gartner defines knowledge management as a "discipline that promotes an integrated approach to identifying, capturing, evaluating, retrieving all of enterprise information assets." These assets may include databases, documents, policies, procedures, captured expertise, and the experience of individual employees. In the knowledge hierarchy, we make a distinction between data, information, and knowledge.

- **Data**

  Data refers to nonprocessed information or raw data. This could be nonprocessed information that you may have about your customers, such as age and location. It will not help you unless you have processed it, organized it, and structured it to use it during your decision-making process. For instance, a random number of 1,000 customers, or a single fact about your customer or your competitor, means nothing until you can convert it into information.

- **Information**

  Information is the conversion of raw data into a structure that helps you decide. When data is contextualized, it becomes information and then it becomes relevant to your decision-making process. For instance, when you connect the number of traffic accidents to a specific behavior or a specific road intersection, then the raw data becomes valuable information that can help you make informed business decisions.

- **Knowledge**

    With knowledge comes power and wisdom. When you process, organize, and structure data and information, you get knowledge. Knowledge helps you decide not only about current situations but more importantly, decide about future situations. Knowledge, when well exploited, helps recognize patterns, predict the future, and make sound business decisions. There are two types of knowledge: tacit and explicit.

    1. **Tacit knowledge**

        Tacit knowledge is the type of knowledge that one has and develops over time as a result of a long process of learning and training. Tacit knowledge is very difficult to share or teach because it is intimately linked to the person's experience, skills, ability, career path, and educational background. Examples of tacit knowledge could be the way a musician plays an instrument or a pilot lands an aircraft. Tacit knowledge cannot be captured by traditional formal ways of teaching. Rather, you capture tacit knowledge in a context similar to the context that links a master with a student, through observation and mentoring. When a company does not capture tacit knowledge, it can be easily lost when the individual leaves the company.

    2. **Explicit knowledge**

        By opposition to tacit knowledge, explicit knowledge, or expressive knowledge, can be easily captured, codified, transcribed, and transferred to others. Your ability to manage knowledge shows in the way you organize and diffuse explicit knowledge. Business intelligence platforms, your company's own internal network, or sharing platform are a good example of where you can store explicit knowledge, like policies, manuals, how-to, and other data that is important.

Now that we have defined knowledge, data, and information, let's look at what ISO 56002:2019 recommends to manage knowledge to support your IMS. ISO 56002:2019 suggests two important actions: capture knowledge, and facilitate access to it. Let's review these two actions.

Capture Knowledge

You may have a lot of data and information in your company's network, but unless you turn that into knowledge that informs your decision-making process, and your innovation activities and programs, the data and information you have is worthless. Some of the actions you can take are:

- Capture and store information about your customers, employees, competitors, and the world you interact with.
- Create, manage, and organize your external sources of knowledge such as customers, users, partners, providers, competitors, consultants, database experts, network researchers.
- Create context for some of the most important information and data you have, such as failed projects and products, returned products, good customers, bad customers incidents, issues, and challenges you have faced.
- Review failures and lessons learned from previous projects as well as from other initiatives launched.

Facilitate Access to Knowledge

There is no meaning to investing time and effort in capturing, organizing, and structuring knowledge if employees do not have access to it or are not incentivized to use it. Your role is to incentivize collaboration and break silos so employees can access information and store knowledge. Use the well-known model called SECI developed by Nonaka and Takeuchi to help your employees access knowledge, disseminate, and transfer knowledge.

- Socialization: Transfer tacit knowledge by observation and mentorship (tacit to tacit).
- Externalization: Transfer knowledge by teaching, codifying it, and training people on it (tacit to explicit).
- Combination: Disseminate knowledge through a combination of tacit and explicit knowledge.
- Internalization: Transfer knowledge through teaching, coaching, and mentor (explicit to tacit).

Finally, and as we leave this clause, it is very important to develop a knowledge management lifecycle to formalize and codify the process that helps employees and helps you manage knowledge. There are a lot of models out there that you can choose from. One of them is ISO Standard 30401:2018 Knowledge management systems—Requirements. In this standard you will learn how to establish an effective management system to manage knowledge.

Finance

> "Innovation has nothing to do with how many R&D dollars you have. When Apple came up with the Mac, IBM was spending at least 100 times more on R&D. It's not about the money. It's about the people you have, how you're led, and how much you get it."

> *Steve Jobs, 1998*

When planning your innovation strategy, your IMS must address the question of the funding of innovation. While big and multinational organizations might find it easy to address the question of budget, because innovation tends to be more mature in these organizations, in Small and Medium Enterprises SME the funding of innovation is an issue. CEOs and CFOs tend to be reluctant to fund projects that have a lot of unknowns in organizations that are asked to do more with less.

It is important to mention that, in practice as well as in management literature, there is a consensus around the idea that big spending does not always correlate with innovation output. A PWC study conducted in 2018 found that

> "The relationship between a company's level of innovation expanding and economic success is, however, tenuous at best. Over the past dozen years, our annual Global Innovation 1000 study has found no statistical relationship between dollars spent on research and development and financial performance, suggesting that the way you spend your innovation dollars is more important than how many of those dollars you spent."

> *PricewaterhouseCoopers. Strategy, not size, matters in innovation spend*
> *https://www.pwc.com/us/en/services/consulting/library/investing-in-innovation.html*

Agile Funding Process: A Lean Budgeting Approach

Those who worked with or are in finance and accounting know quite well that the budgeting process by design is rigid. It is made that way for legal and compliance reasons. However, this approach does not work for funding innovation. Innovation outputs and innovation products are not the results of mega-budget spending on big projects that turn into innovation overnight. The true and real innovation is the result of an agile management process, nimble planning, leaps and starts, and small baby steps of learning from many failures. This is why ISO 56002:2019 recommends a flexible approach to managing the innovation budget. In the following, I will discuss important actions recommended by ISO 56002:2019 to manage innovation finance.

- Rather than using ad hoc allocations, err on the side of an annual budget with a flexible planning process that allows for the unknowns. Because innovation is inherently unpredictable, managing your innovation budget with a traditional process may stifle innovative thinking and demotivate talents willing to experiment.
- Make sure that in your planning process you split your budget between everyday operational expenses, learning, and development, testing, and experimentation to gain better flexibility in how you manage your expenses.
- When planning your innovation product don't pack the product with a lot of features that the consumer may or may not need. This could be also very expensive for the development process. Often, those who work on innovation tends to see the customers throughout their prism falling into the trap of perfecting the product, in the hope that this would impress more customers. Start always with a lean product and if customers want more features, you will know that during the prototyping. An MVP (Minimum Viable Product) approach, in which you develop the minimum that you believe your customer will be happy with, will allow you to manage your budget prudently while making progress towards perfecting the product.

Innovation Is Not About the Next Big Thing

Innovation is not always about the next big idea. Being an innovative company means also that you can save time and labor by improving efficiencies and reducing the cost to enhance your productivity and profitability and manage better the funding constraints. Ellis Booker, an expert on innovation and writer for *CIO* magazine, suggests three creative ways that help you overcome financial challenges:

- *Small bets with a clear definition of success and failure gates*
  According to Booker, in a lot of companies, the CFO tends to resist the idea of allocating a big budget for a big project. Leadership understands a good investment, and the idea of giving a single bet a big check could be a scary one. So, your strategy is to define small innovative initiatives that can show some results in the short term. This can help you leverage the resources you have but more importantly help your finance manager overcome the fear of unknowns. This is especially true for the IT department that tends to innovate incrementally.
- *Invest in people's time*
  The second idea Booker suggests is to use the budget allocated for training programs to turn them into an experiential learning opportunity. In experiential learning, innovators can build products, test them, and prototype them. According to Booker, this strategy is being implemented at PayPal and it has led to a change in the culture of innovation where most of PayPal employees who go through the experiential learning program find themselves innovating.
- *Separate legacy system expenses from your true innovation expenses*
  Particularly true for old and big organizations, the legacy system is a major inhibitor of innovation. Organizations that have not kept up with technological progress, find themselves spending a lot of dollars to maintain, fix, and update old applications. If you are an IT manager wanting to innovate in this environment, you need to address with your senior leadership the issue of legacy system cost and make sure it is separated from the cost of innovation. A recent survey of government senior IT managers found that, federal agencies spend half of their annual IT budgets on maintaining and supporting archaic applications.

Infrastructure

In Subclause 7.1.6, ISO 56002:2019 suggests that for an IMS to work effectively, organizations need to have an appropriate infrastructure that supports and facilitates different innovation activities and programs. This infrastructure, according to ISO 56002:2019, could be a physical one like building, laboratory, incubator, accelerator, and other physical spaces that would allow innovators to connect with the outside world and engage in design thinking activities as well as testing out different ideas and innovations. This infrastructure could be also virtual. Platforms, sharing apps, software programs, and other online innovation labs are also, according to the standard, considered as infrastructure and should provide your IMS with the means to achieve its objectives.

But in recent years, a new infrastructure concept emerged and start to gain attraction. Inspired by the success of older versions of innovation labs, such as the Y Incubator in the United States, which gave birth to successful startups, like Airbnb and Dropbox, or more recently innovation lab successes stories, such as the IMotion Venture, the Innovation lab created by Jaguar Land Rover, or the Wayra Innovation Lab created by Telefonica. Business leaders are now rushing to create corporate innovation labs in order to provide innovators and creative employees with the innovation space they need to engage in innovative activities.

In the following, we will discuss the idea of the innovation lab by providing some trends and share some industry-proven best practices on how to manage them.

What is an Innovation Lab? A Conceptual Framework

An innovation lab is a physical environment that can be located in a separate building or adjacent to the parent company. They are similar to the idea of industrial parks of the 1970s and the idea of incubators of the 1990s in the sense that, they are meant to help managers and business leaders incubate new ideas, test out new products and services, and accelerate the development of mature products to scale MVPs minimum viable products. Conceived as a co-creation space, they serve primarily as a focal point for innovation activities. Successful innovation labs are more than space. They are an approach and a method that helps the parent company understand the challenge and transform customer's need into a product. Whether they are called "centers," "labs," "studio," "incubator," or "accelerator," innovation labs perform the same function.

Depending on the level of sophistication of the industry in which you operate, the attention and the resources you provide, the innovation lab plays an important role in connecting the company with the world of innovation and research. They are the ideal space for connecting the company with the outside ecosystem and help the organization stay alert about innovations that might threaten their established products. Steve Blanks, a Silicon Valley entrepreneur and a thought leader on innovation, calls innovation lab "innovation outpost." According to him, they perform two important functions.

First, they serve as "the ears and eyes" of the parent corporation. A corporate innovation lab, according to Steve Blank, helps decision-makers predict future breakthroughs by sensing the change taking place in the economy and the industry. By connecting the organization with outside entrepreneurs, the lab engages the organization in the economic cluster in which it operates, and helps management understand the change and the disruption taking place in the market.

Second, a corporate innovation lab helps also the parent company understand change and assess threats and possible disruptions that can take over their innovation. When an innovation lab works with the outside ecosystem, it becomes, as well described by Steve Blank, "an innovation identification vehicle" that provides early warning on a new threat, change, and disruption.

Setting Up a Corporate Innovation Lab

While ISO 56002:2019 does not suggest any specific way to organize your innovation lab, there are some industry-proven best practices that you can take advantage of when setting up an innovation lab. In the following, we will summarize some important steps that you need to take.

- *Innovation lab location: Decide where to locate the innovation lab*
  While some companies choose to build it closer to the parent company or the business unit, other companies choose to build it away from the parent corporation. Scott Krisner is CEO and Co-founder of Innovation Leaders, a company that provides innovative consulting services, argues that if you want your lab to focus on breakthrough innovation, then setting it up away from the core business is much better. Being away from the parent company,

allows the lab to connect better with the outside ecosystem and gain some autonomy from the everyday focus on narrow operational issues. On the contrary, if you want your innovation lab to work on incremental innovation, then being closer to the core makes more sense. Being closer to the business unit, helps decision makers interact better with the lab.

- *Connecting the lab to the business unit (BU)*

  Often when innovation labs are created, they tend to gain progressively certain autonomy that disengages them from the core business. Innovators working on new products quickly get disconnected from the real work happening at the business unit and start working on things that have no relevance or impact on the bottom line. To avoid this issue, and to help your lab stay connected to the bottom line, build support bridges between innovators working in the lab and business units. Appoint a trusted manager that has some credibility with different entrepreneurs and business unit managers to manage the lab. Use the lab as a facility for the BU to meet and mingle with innovators. As well argued by Anthony Furrier, the CEO of Culturevate, a company that helps organizations create an innovation culture, innovation labs tend to fail when there is not enough trust between the innovation lab management and business unit management. When this relationship is characterized by toxic politics, ideas that are sent to the lab never come back and ideas that come out of the lab never see the light.

- *Create a sense of idea ownership*

  Before sending ideas from the BU to the innovation lab, make sure that the idea has a champion in the BU. The champion's role is to push for resources, attention, follow up, and provide customers' feedback to those working on the solution so innovators know that the business unit is behind the idea. When there is a lack of ownership from the BU, there is less accountability and innovators get easily disengaged.

- *Open your innovation lab to the outside world*

  The secret sauce of innovation in the 21st century is collaborations and openness. The 20th century's mentality of "everything has to be invented here" is a *passé*. While it is important to protect your trade secrets and your innovations, it is equally important that you open your mindset to collaboration by inviting startups, re-searchers, academia, and customers to collaborate on the challenges you are trying to solve. A good example of this is VISA's Innovation Center in San Francisco where VISA brings customers to collabo-rate on new solutions being developed to tackle the future of payment.

- *De-risk innovation*

    Innovation is an inherently risky activity. Use the lab as a space to test out big transformation initiatives that you can't implement in the core. For instance, if you are trying to figure how to implement a new change initiative, such as a digital transformation or an AI strategy, use the lab as a miniature environment to test the effects of the transformation. By running scenarios in the lab and proto-typing the transformation process you want to implement, you develop a better idea about the issues and the problems as well as the best ways to tackle them.

- *Rotate your key business leaders and functional managers to lead and manage the innovation lab.*

    This practice, developed by Johnson & Johnsons, helps strengthen the ties between the innovation lab and the business unit and create a better alignment between the daily operations of the center and the corporate strategy.

- *Embrace customer centricity*

    For your innovation lab to succeed, it has to be intimately linked to the strategic imperative of the organization, but more importantly, it has to develop a customer-centric mindset. You won't be able to solve your customer challenge and understand customer needs if you are not thinking like a customer and looking at the thing from the customer's perspective. A good example of a customer-centric approach is Lowe's Innovation Lab (LiL LABS) located in the United States. The mission and the focus of the innovation labs are to understand how technology, visualization, and robotics impact customers and employees. Created to "accelerate the future of retail," the lab embraces a customer-centric approach to understand how technology will impact customers in the future.

Competency

A competency model is a framework that helps an organization define the knowledge, skills, and attitudes (KSA) that are specific to the context of the organization and the context of the industry in which you operate. It is an inventory of skills and behavior that are required for the organization to succeed. It answers a very basic question: "What type of knowledge, skills, and abilities my IMS needs to have in order to support innovation programs and activities in my organization?"

You need to work with your HR department to develop the innovation competency model. A typical competency model, as well described by a PWC study, has to have "4C's": clarity of what is required to succeed, consistency in how you measure the skills needed, connecting skills and competencies to the organizational strategy, and continuity in the approach and the message being taught.

While ISO 56002:2019 does not prescribe any set of competencies, it suggests a few actions that may help you build the model. The standard recommends that you:

- Define the competencies needed to support the IMS.
- Create an inventory of existing competencies and identify gaps.
- Collaborate with the outside world to create the competencies needed.

Generally speaking, innovation requires four types of competencies:

- Ability to lead and manage change
- Ability to conduct research and manage uncertainties
- Ability to use insights to identify market opportunities
- Ability to create ideas and validate concepts

Central Michigan University, through a collaboration of authors, developed a good innovation competency model. To the best of my knowledge, this is the only innovation competency that integrates different skills and competencies. This framework has four components:

- **Creativity**
  The ability of people to generate ideas, think critically and solve problems using new and recycled ideas. This competency is a core

competency for innovation. Your IMS will not be able to succeed if you have not included creativity as competency in your organization.

- **Entrepreneurial mindset**

   The ability for people to take initiatives, suggest ideas, and being self-directed and engaged without the need for them to be managed. Team members who are independent thinkers, take initiatives, seek solutions, and constantly work to improve the system, should be your priority. You should also train people to develop these skills by challenging them to become entrepreneurial, or entrepreneurs inside your organization.

- **Integrating perspective**

   This cluster of competencies is very important in linking your IMS output to the industry and the economic sector in which you operate. The integration ability helps your employees answer basic questions in innovation: For what purpose is this product going to be made? Those who have developed an integrative perspective can easily connect and link things that are happening outside the company with the internal functioning of the IMS. You can identify people and teams with this behavior by tracking those who participate in outside activities such as peer-review networking events, industry conferences, research symposia, and collaborate with the outside world.

- **Managing and leading change**

   This cluster of competencies is the most important innovation. Innovation is about change so let's dive into it.

Innovation and Change Management (ICM)

Innovation is about change. No organization in the world claims to be an innovative organization without being open to change and transformation. Change and disruption have become synonymous with success in today's global economy and if you don't lead your disruption, most likely you will be disrupted by forces over which you have no control. ISO 56002:2019 links the ability of an organization to innovate to its ability to manage change. Change is mentioned more than 20 times in different clauses of ISO 56002:2019, and it is discussed as a core principle of the Innovation Management Principles.

All the clauses between Subclause 7.2.2 and Subclause 7.4 are about the ability of the organization to manage change and disruption, whether in the way you set your processes, build competencies, or communicate. So, let's take a look at how you manage and lead change to support your IMS.

One of the most known frameworks of change management is the framework suggested by Harvard professor John Kotter. In his book *Leading Change*, Kotter (2012) suggests a framework that helps organizations design, implement, and lead change. This framework is taught in many business schools and has been implemented in a variety of organizations. Below we will describe this model and link it to ISO 56002:2019 and the establishment of the IMS.

- **Creating a Sense of Urgency**

    The first step in Kotter's framework is to create a sense of urgency. The sense of urgency is part of your effort to get the organization ready to accept change. The reason you innovate is that there is a threatening event forcing you to change the way you conduct your business. This threatening event could be an innovation coming from your competitor that may displace your core product; poor performance of your stock; or simply a new vision and a new strategic direction coming from your CEO.

    The sense of urgency is an important step that motivates people, rallies skeptics, and drives new behavior in the organization. The sense of urgency helps employees adopt a mentality of an emergency crisis happening now and that needs to be dealt with immediately and not later. It is a step that you need to take to help your team understand that, unless innovation is taken as an urgent matter, things will not work. The sense of urgency is a powerful marketing tool that helps you deal with complacency and make your team seize on the change opportunity. Without a sense of urgency innovation defaults to a backseat position on people's busy schedule. So, make your IMS change strategy a now-priority task versus a tomorrow-plan wish. In a survey conducted by Deloitte, it was found that 41% of top managers find that a major barrier to digital transformation is other "competing priorities" that they deal with. If you don't inject that sense of urgency in your change and innovation strategy, it would be difficult for people to give your IMS the attention it needs.

- **Build the Guiding Team**

    The second step you need to take to implement your change strategy is to build the team that will lead the change and establish the IMS IMS. ISO 56002:2019. When choosing people who lead the implementation of the IMS, use the following suggestions:
    - Identify employees available to meet every two weeks and are likely to stay in the company.
    - Identify people who have an innovation management background and have skills that foster innovative thinking, such as creativity, design thinking, collaborative work, and are comfortable with change.
    - Identify one senior leader willing to commit to this team and who understand the behavior that drives change.
    - Identify people who can give at least 10% to 15% of their working time to build the IMS.

- **Get the Right Vision**

    Getting the right vision simply means that, in Kotter's model, you explain the goal and the purpose of the IMS and why the company needs to change. ISO 56002:2019 provides enough information on how you can develop an innovation vision, but following are a few steps you can take to help your team understand change.
    - Engage the team in charge of establishing IMS to discuss the vision of your innovation strategy. This discussion should be directly linked to the overall strategy of the company. The discussion also should show how IMS can support the strategic goals of the organization.
    - Using ISO 56002:2019 as a reference, identify the most important goals that your organization strives to achieve and come up with a vision that captures your organization's aspirations. Show your team how your organization attempts to differentiate itself from the crowd through innovative thinking.
    - Connect those aspirations to how your IMS functions and outline for the team how the different parts of the IMS should be integrated to support change and innovation.

- **Communicate for Buy-In**

    In the fourth step of Kotter's model, you need to communicate how the new IMS and the change you are seeking will affect the entire organization. In this step, what you are doing is overcoming the "cognitive hurdle" of the organization, your first step to change execution. Your communication strategy should be as direct as possible to make your employees and your team in charge of the implementation of the IMS see and experience the change. Put them face-to-face with your worst operational crisis like an angry customer describing his or her experience on a viral post, or a distractor on your Net Promoter Score bashing your product. These tactics of making people feel, see, and live the experience are very powerful in driving change and help employees overcome their internal resistance.

- **Empower Action**

  The fifth step on Kotter's framework describes actions you need to take to empower employees and the organization to sustain your IMS. The following are a few suggestions for empowering employees:

  - Turn your salaried employees into entrepreneurs hungry for a new and creative idea by providing more incentives to innovators. Empowered employees–entrepreneurs can be a powerful engine for your IMS. Teach your employees to take a risk and help them take initiative without worrying too much about the consequences. Turn your culture into a permissive culture rather than a prohibitive culture and inspire your employees to "ask for forgiveness not for permission" to help them take risks. When employees feel that they are free to try out options and that they are backed by management, they become more engaged.

  - Take advantage of the implementation of ISO 56002:2019 to review your HR policies and provide your employees with time off, using the Google 20% rule, to support your employees working on projects they are passionate about.

  - Teach your employees collaboration skills and encourage them to meet and network with other employees from other functions and departments. One of the most powerful tools that can spark a moment of innovation and creativity, is cross-departmental and cross-functional collaboration. In this space, people develop new skills, learn about other functions' challenges, and complement each other's skills.

In change management creating short-term wins is a must. At a certain point in the implementation of the IMS, people need to take a break from change to see what they have achieved. These moments are important to build the camaraderie needed for teamwork and reflect on the achievement and the progress of the new IMS. Short term wins are also an opportunity for you to help people visualize their achievements. Short-term wins are usually between six to eighteen months and must be about achievement that is tangible such as an innovation lab, an incubator, a new process, or a new partnership.

- **Perseverance**

The last step in Kotter's model is perseverance. Kotter calls this step the "don't let up and make it stick" step. In today's new business environment, characterized by disruptions and adversity, the new normal that is, perseverance has become one of the most powerful characteristics in leadership. It goes beyond traditional leadership traits, such as intelligence and talents. It is your determination and your perseverance that will allow you to put the new IMS in place. It is perseverance that will help you put your innovation strategy in place. You will face tremendous resistance and many people will question the changes you suggest, even among those who welcome innovation. It is your determination and your stamina that will make IMS a reality.

Awareness and Communication

Communication is a critical dimension of every work managers job, but when it comes to innovation, it is a must. Often managers engage in activities that are meant to support their innovation capabilities, but when they ignore the communication dimension of the initiative, failure becomes unavoidable. Particularly true for activities and procedures that are meant to strengthen your IMS, if you ignore the communication, the marketing, and the public awareness campaigns, you will not get the engagement you need from your employees. Lack of communication kills the creativity that is the fuel of innovation.

Let everyone know about how your IMS functions, and what incentives people have access to when they engage with the system. Hold innovation campaigns to keep people interested in innovation and keep the process transparent so people can open up and volunteer their time and effort to support activities and programs that make your innovation ecosystem fluid. Share information and charts, like the innovation strategy, the innovation policy, the innovation journey, the incentives, and the achievements, on walls and public places where employees can see them. Design campaigns that target innovators every three months, so people know that the organization is behind them when they engage with the system.

Below are a few suggestions on how you should communicate about your IMS.

- Know your audience. It may be important for you to define several audiences and design a campaign for each audience according to the size of your company. You may have a campaign for your employees and one for your managers and senior executives. In the ones that addresses management, you need to explain the added value of the innovation policy, how the different parts of the IMS relate to each other, and more importantly, what is expected from them to make the IMS a successful one.
- Design an elevator speech around the "why" of an IMS and aggressively push it down to all levels and ranks so people can use it to explain the shift happening in the organization.
- Build a persona and choose a relevant name and a position for it. Create an issue around the difficulty of managing innovation and provide the new solution through the voice of the persona. Show the expected added value of the IMS.
- Create marketing content to explain the policy and the intent of the IMS and distribute the material using all channels available to you: Email, intranet, posters, social media, meetings events, etc.
- Use the company's events and gathering platforms to explain the IMS and show how the new policy is meant to help boost the Innovation capability of the organization.

SUBCLAUSE 7.5: DOCUMENTED INFORMATION

The clause on documentation is a familiar requirement. It is similar to the requirements of ISO 9001:2015 as well as ISO 14001:2015 (Environmental Management System) and ISO 45001:2018 (Occupational Health and Safety). There are two types of documents that you need to think about when addressing this clause. The documents suggested by ISO 56002:2019 and the documents you deem necessary for a good functioning of the IMS.

This is the documentation suggested by ISO 56002:2019:

- The scope of the IMS (Subclause 4.3)
- Innovation vision (Subclause 5.1.3)
- Innovation strategy (Subclause 5.1.4.1)
- The communication policy (Subclause 5.2.2)
- Innovation objectives (Subclause 6.2.1)
- Innovation initiatives and processes (Subclause 8.1)
- Results of the analysis and evaluation (Subclause 9.1.2.1)
- The audit program (Subclause 9.2.2)
- The management review (Subclause 9.3.3)
- The nature of deviation and nonconformity as well as subsequent actions taken (Subclause 10.2).*

In addition to these documents, you can also retain and control documents that you believe are necessary to a good functioning of the IMS, taking into consideration the complexity level of different operations and processes, the size of the organization, and the nature of the industry in which you operate.

Furthermore, the Standard also suggests that, when creating or updating any documentation, you need to describe and identify documents in an appropriate way and similar to ISO 9001:2015 requirements (title, date, author, reference). You need also to identify the format such as the language, the software version, the graphics, and the type of media electronics and/or paper.

---

*©ISO. This material is excerpted from ISO 56002:2019, with permission of the American National Standards Institute (ANSI) on behalf of the International Organization for Standardization. All rights reserved

Finally, a control procedure should also be defined to ensure that the content is protected against loss or improper use, and the access level, as well as the distribution procedures, are well identified.

SUBCLAUSE 7.6: TOOLS AND METHODS

In Subclause 7.6, ISO 56002:2019 suggests that you develop a mix of tools and methods to help you manage innovation and creativity. Depending on the sector and the industry in which you operate, tools can be a powerful technique to engage people in innovation activities and support their work to achieve their goals. Innovation tools and methods are also helpful techniques in exploring insights, learning more about the customers, and engage the workforce in solving problems. ISO 56002:2019 provides a few examples of tools, such as ethnographic research, backcasting, brainstorming, and inclusive design, but there are more tools and techniques that you can use depending on the nature of the problems and the industry in which you operate.

The International Association of Innovation Professionals (IAOIP) conducted a detailed two-year study to determine what tools/methodologies are most frequently used and/or were the most effective. The study included inputs from innovative businesses, innovative consultants, and other methods and tools taught at universities. The original study revealed that there were over 250 tools/methodologies presently being used, proposed for use, or being taught. Faced with this staggering number of tools and methodologies, the study group decided that they had to narrow this list down to a reasonable size. As a result, they went back out to a sample of the population and asked them to look at each of the 250+ tools/methodologies and indicate which of the following statements best reflected their experience in the way a tool or a methodology was being used to create innovation:

1. This tool or methodology is used on almost all the innovation projects.
2. This tool or methodology is used on a minimum of two out of five innovative projects.

3. This tool or methodology is seldom, if ever, used on innovative projects.
4. Not familiar with the tool or methodology.
5. Never used or recommended this tool or methodology in doing any innovation projects.

The group objective was to narrow the 250+ tools/methodologies down to 75. They were able to reduce it down to 76. A list of these tools can be found in Appendix B. The result of this study was documented into three books published by CRC press. The book titles are:

- *The Innovation Tools Handbook, Volume 1: Organizational and Operational Tools, Methods, and Techniques that Every Innovator Must Know* (2016).
- *The Innovation Tools Handbook, Volume 2: Evolutionary and Improvement Tools that Every Innovator Must Know* (2016).
- *The Innovation Tools Handbook, Volume 3: Creative Tools, Methods, and Techniques that Every Innovator Must Know* (2016).

There are more tools and techniques that you can use depending on the nature of the problems and the industry in which you operate. In the following, I will discuss the top ten tools used in the industry based on some best practices from leading companies such as Google, IDEO, and Frog Design.

- **Collective Action Tool (CAT)**

    CAT is an ensemble of methods and techniques designed to help companies manage the creative thinking process. It provides a nice framework to manage innovation and channel employee's creative thinking ability. Designed by a company called Frog Design, the toolkit is used by a variety of industry leaders in the profit, nonprofit, and government sectors. It is made of six steps that help your team clarify the problem, seek new ideas, imagine new solutions, and plan for actions. Each stage is made of sub-steps that guide the team during their innovative thinking. You can download it for free from the company's website at frogdesign.com.

- **The Seven Rules of Brainstorming**

  This approach to innovation and creativity was developed by the design firm IDEO to help organizations develop a richer and more structured approach to brainstorming. While brainstorming has been used for some time in a variety of ways, this tool helps organization structure better the process of brainstorming to enrich it and help participants focus on the goal without judging ideas. The seven rules, according to IDEO are: defer judgment, encourage wild ideas, build on others' ideas, stay on topic, one conversation at a time, be visual, and go for quantity. These rules are a good framework that helps you take the chaos out of brainstorming and create a safe environment for team members to come up with ideas without feeling intimidated or compelled to comply with the consensus.

- **The Mohamed Bin Rashid Center for Government Innovation**

  Mohammed Bin Rashid Center for Government Innovation is a great source in the United Arab Emirates that provides a variety of tools and frameworks to manage innovation and creative thinking. The MBRCGI's framework is made of seven steps with each step having its technique. Some of these techniques are future vision, board intelligence game, one + one = one, and the building block/the hanger. The framework is a free kit that you can download from mbrcgi.gov.ae.

- **Innovation Flow Chart**

  Developed by the Development Impact and YOU (DIY) and Nesta, this tool provides a highly structured and very detailed process for generating ideas. The chart lists all the stages and the steps that you need to go through to solve a specific problem. What is important about this chart, is that in each stage it provides suggestions on the budget needed as well as the skills and the type of people suited for the specific stage. The flowchart is a free download that you can get from DIYtoolkit.org.

- **Attribute Listening**

  This is a method that helps your innovation team understand complex problems with multiple dimensions and multiple facets. The goal of this method is to breakdown the challenge into smaller pieces to list the attributes of each small piece. Once the problem has been broken into smaller pieces, and all the attributes have been identified, it becomes easier for the team to visualize the connections and cause-effect relationship. This should help participants identify solutions based on the nature of the connection between different pieces and the nature of the cause-effect relationship.

- **Innovation Hackathon**

    In recent years, hackathons have become a popular way to solve big challenges. Conceived originally in the computer and IT industry, hackathons are now used in a variety of sectors. The goal of the hackathon is to define a problem, or challenge, and invite people to compete to solve it. It is a form of crowdsourcing used in open in-novation. Hackathon is open to internal employees as well as to external people to the organization. When it is open to the outside world, it can also be a good source for talent scouting. Kaggle Days is a Polish startup that is gaining some traction in organizing and managing hackathons in Europe and the Middle East.

- **Force Field Analysis (FFA)**

    FFA is a tool used in management to identify the strengths and weaknesses of an idea. This technique is not suited for generating ideas but rather for testing the selected ideas. The goal is to understand how an idea measures up in the real world, and what resistance it will face during the implementation. The outcome of this method is a decision matrix that helps you either choose the idea, ignore it, or amend it.

- **Design Sprint**

    Designed by Google Venture, this approach to innovation is a five-day discussion process to solve a problem. For five days that start on Monday and end on Friday, participants use a variety of techniques to come up with a final solution to the challenge. The five days are planned as follow:

    - Monday: Map
    - Tuesday: Sketch
    - Wednesday: Decide
    - Thursday: Prototype
    - Friday: Test

    According to Google Ventures, Design Sprint helps companies compress the time it takes to produce a Minimum Viable Product (MVP) In five days, you can generate tremendous data that can help you decide about the features of the products. According to the Google Ventures website, Design Sprint was used with a variety of startups such as Medium to help them explore market opportunities and develop innovative market entry strategies. There is a detailed description of the Google Ventures website (gv.com) that helps you plan and use the tool.

- **Trend Mapping**

    This tool helps you map out the most important current and future trends affecting your company, your industry, and the economic cluster in which you operate. It is also a method that helps you think about future foresight to identify changes that the average person in the industry may not be able to identify. The important aspect of this tool is that it provides you with a cognitive organizer to inspire participants and help them focus on the trends that are more relevant to the issue being discussed.

- **Fast Prototyping**

    This is an innovative technique that helps your team working on innovative products to get quick feedback from users on the product or the experiment being developed. By inviting users to discuss your prototype, you get a quick idea of the weaknesses and strengths as well as the shortcomings of the prototype which you can feedback into the design of the product.

Finally, it is important to mention that ISO 56002:2019 does not recommend any specific tool. As long as you can adapt the tool to your specific context, you can use any tool you want. Conducted well, these tools have the potential to engage everyone in the organization and infuse an innovative culture into the work processes of the organization. ISO 56002:2019 also recommends that once you choose your tools you create an awareness campaign to share and inform different teams about these tools so they can integrate them into their work. You can also add them to your yearly training and development plan to help employees acquire new skills in managing innovation. This will provide a solid foundation for your IMS.

SUBCLAUSE 7.7: STRATEGIC INTELLIGENCE MANAGEMENT

Strategic Intelligence Management refers to the ability of the organization to acquire, collect, analyze, and evaluate data and information in order to forecast future events that may impact the performance of its innovation activities. The term intelligence, in an organizational context, refers to the effort of scanning, monitoring, assessing, and integrating data and information into the decision-making process. ISO 56002:2019 recommends that, for the IMS to be effective, managers need to develop a process that helps them anchor an intelligence culture that would allow top leadership to manage uncertainties, predict future events, and anticipate competitor's behavior while preempting actions that may be a source of future threat to the company's innovation pipeline.

ISO has another standard that is part of the innovation management family of standards that addresses specifically the needs of organizations seeking to understand and implement a strategic intelligence management practice. Called Innovation Management Tools and Methods for Strategic Intelligence, ISO 56006 provides a useful framework that helps organizations set up a strategic intelligence management practice and provides managers with the tools and methods on how to link the strategic intelligence management effort to the IMS. It also provides suggestions on how to integrate intelligence management into other organizational management systems in order to support the innovation culture of the organization.

While the Innovation Management System Standard ISO 56002:2019, does not provide a model for setting up the strategic intelligence management practice and only calls for an approach to strategic intelligence, it might be appropriate and more helpful to adopt the model developed by ISO/DIS 56006 Innovation Management — Tools and methods for strategic intelligence management — Guidance. This standard provides a comprehensive approach that is simple to follow and intuitive for most employees to integrate into their work. The model is made of five steps. In the following, I will discuss each step and provide examples and explanations.

ISO/DIS 56006 Model: Identify the Strategic Intelligence Needs

The first step of the Strategic Intelligence Model (SIM) is to identify the data and the information needed that support different innovation activities and innovation programs. The data may be related to the future of technological breakthroughs, such as AI, Blockchain, quantum computing, nanotechnologies, and other transforming and exponential technologies, or it could be related to the specifics of the industry in which you operate. When collecting data about your industry, it is important that you look at trends affecting the power of suppliers, the power of buyers, the dynamic of product substitutes, and the intensity of the competitive environment. These are the five forces in Porter's model that define the level of industry competitiveness.

In addition to the technological trends and industry analysis, you need also to understand trends affecting the economy and the socio-cultural environment. The inflation rate, interest rates changes, and how shifts in demographics shape consumer taste and behavior, are also an important component of the data identification you need in this step.

Framing

Once you gather the data and the information needed for your Strategic Intelligence Management, you need to identify and select the issues that you think will impact your innovation activities. This is what we mean by framing. Framing allows you to link the change and the issues you identified to the innovation vision and the innovation strategy of the organization. Framing helps you contextualize the data you identified in order to explain how the change you foresee will impact your IMS. For instance, if in the first step you identified regional changes as an important opportunity or a serious threat, then in this step you need to frame this change in the context of your organization by looking, for instance, at emerging markets that either can provide you with an opportunity to leverage your innovation capabilities or can take innovation products away from you.

Gathering and Analyzing

Once you frame the issue that will impact your innovation strategy, you need to dive deeper into the data and the issue to create a model that helps you shape the decisions. In this step, your challenge is to be able to develop a reliable process for analyzing data. Some of the tools you can use are popular cloud-based platforms such as Tableau, the RapidMind, KNIME analytics, and DataMell. These applications, and others, are a great tool that help you extract valuable insights from your raw data.

You can also use other machine learning-based applications to analyze data and train models at making predictions. When using AI-based applications to train your models at predictions, it is critically important that you pay attention to common errors that could lead to an erroneous interpretation of the data. Common data errors to avoid are:

- Overfitting: The error of forcing an explanation into a dataset.
- Sampling bias: The error in which your selection of the sample did not account for the entire population you are supposed to include.
- False causality: The error in which you mistakenly link a cause and an effect.
- Confirmation bias: The error in which you seek information and data that confirm your initial belief about a trend or an event.
- Unconscious or implicit bias: The error in which you unfairly choose a course of action like choosing to invest in technology XY simply because you happen to like this technology.
- Anchoring bias: The error of overly focusing on one piece of information or data, with no evidence that this piece of data has any relevance to the decision being made.

These biases are serious data errors that can seep into your decision-making process and affect the outcome of the innovation program or the innovation activities you intend to pursue. They are also serious errors that may affect the reliability and validity of the Strategic Intelligence Management practice you intend to put in place.

Interpretation

This is the most important step of the entire process. In the interpretation step, you are making a sense of the data as it relates to your internal organizational environment, such as capabilities and resources (things you can do), and as it relates to the external environment to describe the opportunities that you may seize on. The interpretation requires a cognitive skill, such as the ability to integrate data and information and to present it in a visually simple way so management and leadership can understand it and see the connections. The interpretation is the actual output of the Strategic Intelligence Management model. And it is this interpretation that will help you make the recommendations.

Recommendations

This is the last step in the Strategic Intelligence Management process. In the recommendations stage you are providing top management with options to act and scenarios to follow. Examples of recommendation can be a go or no-go decision, risk reduction, responding to opportunities, collaborate, or build a strategic alliance.

The PESTEL Model

Another model known in the industry and that can help you develop a Strategic Intelligence Management practice is a called PESTEL. This model looks at six important factors.

- Political factors, in which you look at the role of the government and how public policy shapes and affect innovation.
- Economic factors, in which you look at the macro and micro-economic trends, such as interest rates, supply and demand forces, spending income, and the role of incentives in building a national innovation ecosystem.
- Social factors, which focus on how changes in age, gender, culture, ethnicity, and more generally how changes in demographics impact shifts in consumer behavior.
- Technological factors which look at the trends in technology and how tech breakthrough affects the speed of innovation.
- Environmental factors, which look at the scarcity of raw materials and the sustainability of the economic activity, as well as the ethics of the decision-making process in managing breakthroughs.
- Legal factors, in which we look at the impact of law and regulations on the performance of different innovation programs, in terms of health and safety as well as the advertising, consumer rights, and privacy laws.

BOX 5.1 THE FORESIGHT COMPETENCY MODEL

Future Foresight is an academic discipline that has gained some popularity in recent years as it has been intimately linked to the ability of the organization to manage its innovation activities and programs. The ability of an organization to predict the future can be tremendously helpful in its ability to manage change and innovation. Future Foresight is also a competency that you can help your employees to acquire and develop. The Association of Professional Futurist provides a Foresight Competency Model made of five competencies.

- Effectiveness
- Academic
- Workplace
- Foresight Technical
- Foresight Sector

Tier Four of this model, called Foresight Technical Competencies, defines the skills and competencies an employee needs to have in order to be able to practice as a futurist. These competencies are:

1. Framing: Scoping the project and defining the focal issues.
2. Scanning: Understanding and explore signals of the future.
3. Futurists: Identified a baseline and alternative future.
4. Visioning: Developing and committing to a profound future.
5. Designing: Developing a prototype, offering, or artifacts to achieve the vision and the goal.
6. Adapting: Enabling organizations to generate options to an alternative future.

Teaching and training your innovators on acquiring these competencies could be very helpful in managing your innovation. These competencies help innovators understand the change happening in the market and the emerging needs that they can translate into an innovative product.

(Source: The Association of Professional Futurist www.apf.org)

SUBCLAUSE 7.8: INTELLECTUAL PROPERTY MANAGEMENT

There is no innovation without a strong Intellectual Property Management (IPM) framework. Strong evidence from leading innovative organizations, as well as from research conducted on the subject, shows that the only way for an organization to keep its innovation momentum and boost its IMS is by providing strong protection to its innovators and creative thinkers willing to invest time and effort in creating new things. There are two benefits to a strong IP framework. First, it provides entrepreneurs and innovators inside the organization with a strong reward to engage with innovation. When employees feel that their intellectual work is protected and patented through the organization and that the organization stands behind their creative work and intellectual property, they are more willing to engage. The IP framework in this case acts as a motivator for employees and helps the organization lure more entrepreneurs and innovators into the innovation process.

The second benefit of a strong IP framework is that it provides an assurance to investors willing to invest in the company. When the organization holds many patents, it suggests to the external world that there is a strong IP framework, which in turn acts as an incentive for investors willing to take risks. The IP framework, in this case, becomes an indicator of a good management system that sends a positive message. The Silicon Valley model, which has dominated the global economy during the last 30 years is a good example of how good ideas when combined with an IP management system, lead to great success.

Types of Intellectual Property Protection

According to the World Organization for Intellectual Property (WIPO) there are four types of intellectual property: patents, trademarks, trade secrets, and copyrights.

- **Patent**
    A patent is legal protection provided by the law. In legal terms, a patent provides exclusive protection to the inventor. It helps the owner prevent others from commercially exploiting their invention. Patents are valid for 20 years and in principle valid only in the country in which the application has been submitted.
- **Trademark**
    A trademark is a symbol, or a sign, a phrase, or a sentence that differentiates a company from another one. A trademark is valid for ten years and is protected by the law once the application process is

completed. A good example of trademark is the Nike symbol or the colors identifying a Coca-Cola drink.

- **Trade Secret**

    A trade secret is a formula, a process, a recipe, or information such as a customer list. It could be also an algorithm or a method on how to compute or execute a business model. It is also valid for 20 years and gives the bearer an exclusive right to exploit commercially the trade secret to which it is entitled.

- **Copyrights**

    Copyright is the right of an author that protects the work of authorship like in the work of music, literacy, or artwork. In the United States, and for work created after January 11, 1978, a copyright lasts for the entire life of the author plus an additional 70 years.

Intellectual Property Management Framework

Subclause 7.8 of ISO 56002:2019 recommends that for a company to be able to take advantage of its IMS, it has to develop an IP framework. ISO 56002:2019 recommends four critical actions that need to take place.

1. **Define IP Assets**

    Management needs to define the innovation output that needs protection. Work with your legal counsel and your top leadership to identify the critical IP assets that need protection. Generally speaking, and depending on the sector in which you operate, examples of IP assets could be software, data, technologies, know-how, inventions, literary, scientific, or artistic work, symbols, designs, methodologies, names or images, or any output of your IMS, These are all work that can be identified as an IP asset.

2. **Provide a Rationale for Your IP Framework**

    Once you identify your IP assets, you need to provide a rationale explaining why the company needs to provide IP protection. The reason you need to provide a rationale explaining the why of your IP framework is to help investors, regulators, and other stakeholders link your IP framework to the company's mission, vision, and strategy. For instance, a company may be using patents to realize value, protect authorship from infringement, or simply obtaining the freedom to operate. A rationale helps stakeholders understand your IMS and the actions you take to protect your intellectual property.

3. **Clarify Copyrights Ownership**

The third action recommended by ISO 56002:2019 is to clarify the ownership of the IP assets. It is critical that the IP framework clarifies who owns the rights to innovation, especially when a third party is involved through a joint venture or other forms of the collaborative framework. Defining the ownership, or at least defining the conditions and the circumstances under which an innovation right may be claimed, helps you address litigation risks and preempt other legal and business issues.

4. **Protecting the Innovation**

Restricting access to areas inside the premise where the new products or a process is being developed, and work with the legal advisor to monitor national legislation and other legislations where your product is being sold or being developed, helps you protect your innovation.

Developing an IP Framework

A new standard has been approved and published recently that specifically addresses the issue of IP. ISO 56005:2020 Innovation Management—Tools and Methods for Intellectual Property Management—Guidance, is a new standard that was published in 2020 and aims at helping organizations create a framework to protect their IP. This new standard defines three actions that can strengthen your IP framework.

1. Integrate the IP management into the IMS by linking the two systems.

Understand the connection between IP management and the innovation activities and how these two dimensions support the overall strategy of the organization. Questions that you may want to ask at this stage are:

- Why do we want to create an IP strategy?
- What are the innovations that we need to protect, and what are the ones that we need to leverage with a third party through licensing?
- What are our objectives in setting up an IP strategy?

- What is the link between IP vision and the overall mission and strategy of the organization?
- What are the barriers that we may run into by protecting our IP? Barriers may relate to the type of process we use, the kind of people we hire, or the type of recording methodologies we adopt.
- Should we develop or acquired an IP asset?
- How do we compare with others in the industry in terms of IP maturity, IP culture, IP capability, and IP experience?

2. Define the ways you want to exploit your innovation.

   There are many ways for companies to exploit their IP, but generally speaking, ISO defines six ways to exploit any IP:

   - **Direct exploitation:** Commercially using your own patent, trade secret, copyright, or intellectual work.
   - **Licensing:** Exploiting your IP by granting a third party the right to exploit the intellectual property against a fee.
   - **Collaboration**: Exploiting your IP using any form of collaborative agreement, such as M&A, strategic alliance, or joint venture so you are able to explore the new IP.
   - **Spin-off:** Exploiting your IP by creating a new entity to utilize the new innovation. Companies use a spin-off to venture out with a new product, or a new service, to avoid distractions, or to disturb the core.
   - **Sale:** Exploiting your IP through a sale of the IP, or an auction of it, or simply re-assign its ownership to a new purchaser. This usually takes place when the business ceases to exist or changes the direction.
   - **Investment:** Exploiting your IP to attract investors in order to increase the valuation of the company.

3. Risk mitigation

   The third action recommended by ISO 56002:2019 is to establish a risk management process in order to protect your IP framework. In establishing the risk management process, you need first to identify the origin of the risk. The risk may be at the beginning or at the end of the innovation project and can be internal or external. An internal risk example could be the risk that relates to employees' management like in the case of conducting an IP background on employees to find out where they signed a confidentiality agreement. An external risk could be the risk related to the partnership you intend to create.

It is also recommended that you map out the risk. A typical mapping out exercise would be made of a chart of high-mediumlow risk with an explanation of the actions needed to take a place.

SUMMARY

Sometimes we get so excited and involved in "fighting the dragons or swimming hard not to drown" that we lose sight of how dependent our personal performance is based upon the support we get from the rest of the organization. This clause was designed to remind us that when involved in problem-solving, we find ourselves spending too much of our time and energy ignoring the rest of our responsibilities. All of a sudden, we find ourselves all alone in command without the support that we need to get our job accomplished on time and at a level that we are proud of.

In this chapter, we discussed how the organization should be formed in order to provide us with the resources we need to perform at a level that is in keeping with the organization's principles and vision. Every part of the organization is responsible for providing new creative ideas, maintaining our current assignments, and providing support to other parts of the organization that depends upon us.

The support activities that we often take for granted are absolutely essential. People, time, knowledge, funding, infrastructure, communication, intellectual capital protection, tools, and methods, for too many of us, are taken for granted unless we don't have them. It's only human nature to complain. We get up in the morning and arthritis in our knees bothers us for 30 minutes or there's a spot on that white shirt we planned to wear. It seems the world is treating us badly. Why is it that we don't think about how lucky we are to be able to get out of bed or that we own a shirt? Or about how lucky we are to be living here in the United States? Most of us are lucky to be working in an established organization that has all of the services billed into the organizational structure. But even then, we spend far too much of our time complaining about already established systems that are struggling to meet the changing demands of today. It is a very different story for small and startup organizations that start out fresh without any imminent infrastructure. My father can remember the time when IBM didn't have the finances to meet pay the bills and for months every employee had their pay cut by 50% and to take that worthless IBM stock in place of their full salary. If my father had saved "that worthless piece of paper" instead of trading it in for $150 to buy a home, I wouldn't have had to work a day in my life. Often, some of the best things in our lives are created from some of the worst things in our life. Be thankful for what you have, rather than being unhappy about the things you don't have.

6

Clause 8: Operations

PURPOSE

To provide guidance on how to manage the innovation process and how to orchestrate different operations that are needed to support the innovation process. The chapter describes the control mechanisms of collaboration, criteria by which you define innovation, and the agile governance framework that needs to be put in place to ensure a more fluid innovation process.

OVERVIEW

This chapter focuses on how to manage innovation initiatives and how to prepare the innovation process: create a concept, identify opportunities validate concept developed solution, and deploy solutions. It also provides tools and best practices on how to evaluate the idea at the end of each step, and provides a risk assessment matrix at the end of each step benefits. The chapter helps you understand what activities are needed to operate your innovation process cycle while identifying some best practices for using the ideation process. At the end of each chapter, you will be able to implement the innovation process. The chapter consist of the following subclauses:

- Operational planning and control
- Innovation initiatives
- Innovation processes

BENEFITS

This chapter shows you how to assemble different components to support your Innovation Management System (IMS), taking into consideration the specifics of your organization. It provides a wide range of examples and practices from which you can take by what applies to your size, your industry, and your level of maturity.

CLASSIFICATION OF ACTIONS

This chapter is written as a *Should do* type of activity, giving you the choice of implementing practices that works better for your circumstances.

CLAUSE 8.1: GENERAL FRAMEWORK TO OPERATIONAL CONTROL

The organization should plan, implement, and control innovation initiatives, processes, structures and support needed to address innovation opportunities, meet requirements, and to implement the actions determined in 6.2.[*]

Operational control is about the way you apply and administer different systems, processes, and metrics to manage efficiently the innovation system and align different organizational resources to create the harmony and the coherence needed. Clause 8 of the ISO 56002:2019 provides three key ideas that, from an operational point of view, if well implemented, will allow your IMS to function effectively and efficiently. These key ideas are agility and partnerships (Clause 8.1), innovation initiatives (Clause 8.2), and the innovation process (Clause 8.3). Let's go over these key ideas.

---

[*]©ISO. This material is excerpted from ISO 56002:2019, with permission of the American National Standards Institute (ANSI) on behalf of the International Organization for Standardization. All rights reserved.

Organization Agility

Agility, as a conceptual framework, refers to the ability of the organization to respond quickly to market changes, while still focusing on your innovation projects and operations. The concept of agility has been defined by different authors. Aaron Smith (2015), a principal at McKinsey and expert at organizational design, defines agility as "the ability of the organization to be dynamic, nimble, flexible, and moving fast to address change, while still focusing on core operations and key planning process." According to the author, agility can manifest itself in three key areas: Structure where resources are allocated; governance, where decisions are made; and processes where operations are done.

Let us use this framework to show you how you can embed the concept of agility during the implementation of ISO 56002:2019.

Structure: Create a Cross-Functional and Self-Directed Team to Manage Innovation

Organizational structure is an important tool that helps companies deploy strategies and allocate resources but for innovation, structures such as the functional approach and the matrix approach, are not appropriate. Cross-functional teams and self-managed teams are recommended more for managing innovation processes and operations because they provide better flexibility to change and they are nimbler in addressing issues that may affect innovation. When choosing your teams, focus on diversity. The diversity of professional backgrounds, as well as cultural background, helps team members become more creative and avoid group thinking and other pitfalls to teams we discussed in the previous chapter (Support Clause 7).

Governance: Review Your Decision-Making Process

Innovation activities and procedures need a decision-making process that is fast and flexible. You cannot make decisions about creativity and innovation in the same way you make decisions about budget planning. A start-up mindset is what is needed for innovation management. Empower your team leaders and members to make decisions by allowing them room for failure. Agility requires team members to act fast, and if team leaders have to wait for decisions or have to go through different lines of bureaucracy to make decisions, then your innovation operation will suffer.

Process: Standardize Your Key Processes

Companies struggling with implementing processes struggle because either the process is too complex, i.e., not intuitive, or it has not been well taught to employees. A process that is ill-designed, or not well explained, creates bottlenecks for the workflow and adds more waste. People spend endless time in meetings asking basic questions about steps that are sometimes obvious. We hear often people saying that the process is getting in the way of innovation. This can be true only if the process is complex for people to digest and understand. World-class organizations invest tremendous time to create intuitive processes that are standardized so people can implement them seamlessly. The study conducted by Aaron Smith of McKinsey shows that signature processes, such as Amazon's synchronized supply chain, or P&G product development and external communication processes, are critical elements of the companies' strategy. These companies invest tremendously in designing their processes in an intuitive way and spend much time training employees on how to implement them, so people know who does what at different touchpoints of the workflow.

Generally speaking, there are three problems that hinder the performance of a process:

- Lack of governance. In this situation, the process is not well mapped out or the person in charge is not identified correctly on the process map. People spend a lot of time figuring out where to go to execute simple tasks. We suggest that you spend time mapping out different workflow procedures that relate to the management of innovation initiatives, programs, and activities, and create an innovator's journey that clarifies the process of employees willing to be part of the innovation process.
- Lack of employees' skills. The second obstacle that tends to hinder the performance of a process is the lack of skills and information. A sub-process can hinder the main process if employees lack the competency they need during the execution of the process. Here

you need to spend time teaching people how to use the process, provide them with information, knowledge, and training to become nimble. Create a common language around that process so you can easily standardize it.

- Lack of employees' engagement. This situation can affect tremendously different innovation operations. In this situation, people are not "interested" in doing what they are supposed to do, even when the process is simple and intuitive. People lacking engagement, start creating shortcuts, performing at the minimum threshold not going the extra mile to fix and improve things. Your role as the innovation leader is to empower employees by creating incentives that engage them. Motivate people and make them become the center of the process so they know that if they do not do their parts innovation operations get affected.

Collaboration and Partnership

In innovation, collaboration and partnership are a must. There is no way for a company today to innovate without being engaged in a network of collaboration where participants share information, data, and research. So when you engage in a collaborative arrangement, it is critical that you take control of that arrangement and you get involved in different operations. ISO 56002:2019 suggests that when you outsource your collaboration initiatives, you need to make sure that you are in charge of managing the agreement and that you are fully involved in that partnership by creating control tools and gating mechanisms that help you to manage different operations.

A good framework to use to implement collaboration and partnerships is the ISO 56003:2019 Innovation Management – Tools and Methods for Innovation Partnership, Guidance. This standard is part of the ISO innovation series and can be helpful in creating and managing collaboration and partnerships.

Generally speaking, to implement an innovation collaborative initiative you need three important steps: Decide whether to enter into an innovation collaborative initiative, identify and select partners, and align the perception of the value. Let us look at these steps one by one.

Decide Whether to Enter into an Innovation Collaboration Initiative

There are many reasons for a company seeking to develop its innovation capabilities to enter into a collaborative agreement. The reason you would want to enter into a collaborative agreement is to get easy and free access to resources and capabilities that may add value to your current resources and capabilities. Complementarity is an important reason for collaboration. You may have a strong borrowing capacity, but you lack customer insights. You may have an important stock of technology, but you do not have a scientific research capability. And finally, you may have an attractive physical location, but you do not have access to talents. These are situations in which complementarity may help overcome resource constraints in developing an innovation ecosystem.

So, before you decide to enter into a collaborative agreement, ask yourself the following gating questions:

- Gating question 1: Will the partnership add value to my innovation capabilities and in what ways? If the alliance does not add any value to my innovation ecosystem, then the partnership does not make sense.
- Gating question 2: What type of synergy will I develop by creating the partnership, and how will the synergy boost my innovation capabilities?
- Gating question 3: Will there be a cultural fit between the two organizations that will boost collaboration, creativity, and cohesion between the teams?

Select and Identify the Right Partner

The second step in managing collaboration is to identify and select the right partner. ISO 56002:2019 provides a long list of potential organizations that can be a good target, but generally speaking, partners can be identified from four different main categories: R&D laboratories, business clusters, competitors, and customers. In this step, you need also to ask three gating questions:

- Gating question 1: Is there enough trust between the two organizations so teams can work openly and share information and knowledge in a way that boosts my innovation ecosystem internally?

- Gating question 2: Have we addressed the issues that relate to intellectual property rights in order to manage innovation input?
- Gating question 3: Is there a cultural alignment between the two organizations that would allow us to align our perception of value in the collaboration?

Align the Perception of Value

A successful partnership is one that relies on good management practices. You need to put in place mechanisms that allow the partnership to run smoothly and solve practical issues that may arise. You need also to establish control systems, whether these control systems are financial, strategic, or structural in order to be able to reap the benefit of the partnership.

Finally, and as we have been arguing throughout this chapter, innovation is an inherently human activity. It relies on trust and openness to flourish. If trust is not there, the collaborative agreement runs into issues that manifest themselves later in the form of cultural clashes. If you have not conducted cultural due diligence in order to test the culture, the perception, and the values of your partner, it may be difficult to create a smooth partnership that helps you boost your innovation operations.

CLAUSE 8.2: INNOVATION INITIATIVES

The second clause of Clause 8 of ISO 56002:2019 addresses innovation initiatives. By innovation initiatives, ISO 56002:2019 refers to any actions that you may take to innovate. This can be a project, a program, an initiative, or any suggestions that focus on innovation. As long as the initiative has a novelty dimension, a starting and ending point, is coordinated and adds value to the organization's stakeholders, while addressing a new or an emerging issue, the action can be considered as an innovation initiative according to ISO 56002:2019.

To manage the innovation initiative, ISO 56002:2019 suggests 12 actions (Clause 8.2.1 a to l). Of all these actions, there are some that are a must-have and you need to put them in place as a requirement of your IMS. Without them, you cannot run an IMS.

Other actions, in our view, are nice to have and while important, they are not critical for a beginner. Depending on the specifics of your situation, and the level of innovation maturity of your organization, we suggest that you start with the critical recommendation, and delay the other ones for a later time.

Below, we will first outline the must-have recommendations (Clause 8.2.1 Clauses: a to e, plus Clause h). Then we will address the rest of the recommendations, which are important but not critical; these are the nice-to-have recommendations.

Review the Scope of the Innovation Initiative

A *sine qua none* condition to a successful IMS is the ability of a manager to establish a process by which he or she continuously monitors and reviews the scope of the initiative, its goal, objectives, and its expected outcomes.

By asking the following questions and periodically revising them, you will be able to manage well your innovation initiative.

- What goal or goals, objective or objectives, the initiative intends to achieve?
- What exactly are the long-term, midterm, and short-term goals of the initiative?
- How is the initiative going to help you solve the problems and address the unmet needs of your customers?
- What metrics and milestones we have to set for this initiative?
- What are the triggers that we need to set to call off the initiative?

Establish Innovation Metrics and Risk Trigger

Nothing is achieved without measurement or metrics that tell you whether the innovation initiative is delivering or not. The importance of an evaluation system for an innovation initiative is that it helps you learn about the shortcoming, the issues, the overall performance of the initiative, and how you can fix it. Keep in mind that the first set of metrics you choose may change as the contour of the initiative changes. In other words, you may find yourself changing the metrics themselves to allow for the initiative to grow and breathe and that is totally fine. Often, people set metrics at the start of the initiative and then they get attached to them, even when the situation changes. Do not be afraid to question the evaluation process and the measurement that you have set initially if this is what needs to be done.

Decide About Structure

The third recommendation of ISO 56002:2019, that we believe is a must-have action, is the need to establish a management structure to manage the initiative. Regardless of the type of structure you choose, a cross-functional team, a steering committee, or even a new temporary unit, the structure has to be flexible and agile enough to adapt to a changing environment.

Define who will be in charge: the leadership of the initiative.

Nothing is achieved without a clear and well-defined leadership role. Make sure that the initiative has a leader that is able to secure the resources, tangible and intangible, to lead the initiative. Make sure also that the leader you choose has the leadership profile and the attributes the initiative requires in terms of knowledge of the business, expertise, and other characters such as trust and the ability to inspire and empower team members.

People and Competencies

The last must-have action in managing your innovation initiative is the choice of people. If the initiative is an interesting one, then everyone wants to get on the team. And if the initiative is deemed not of interest, then no one volunteers to be on the team. Your job is to establish a set of selection criteria that would allow you to choose the right people. We suggest that you choose members based on their technical skills, what they can bring to the initiative, knowledge of the organization, and their ability to perform in the new team. Examples of skills you can look for are entrepreneurial skills, negotiation skills, time management, collaboration, creativity, and the set of technical skills required by the nature of the initiative. You need also to include a set of selection criteria that identify people's intrinsic and extrinsic motivation, as well as their drive to success.

The second set of recommendations ISO 56002:2019 suggests are not a must. If you are a beginner and you believe the innovation maturity is still low, then you do not have to worry about them. However, as the innovation initiative takes off and gets more steam, you need to think of putting the following clauses in place.

Roles and Responsibilities

Once the initiative takes off, and after the first few meetings of the innovation initiative, you need to start documenting the roles and responsibilities of different people involved in the initiative. Identifying who does what is particularly important for the long term and midterm initiatives. The clarity in roles and responsibilities alleviates confusion and motivates people to be more engaged in what they do. When the lines of authorities are clearly defined, and people know the expectations, they will perform better. They will also be more open to improvements and open to coaching from initiative leaders.

Collaboration

In the hyper-connected world in which we live, nothing is achieved without collaboration with internal and external parties. A good IMS should have a well-defined collaboration framework that provides clarity of the role and responsibilities of different parties. Below are a few suggestions on how to establish this framework:

- First, you need to identify those with whom you will be collaborating: These can be organizations in your ecosystem, competitors, vendors, research centers, consulting firms, or otherwise. Clearly state what you mean by the collaboration and mechanisms you need to have.
- Second, establish metrics, or milestones that will help you measure the progress of collaboration, and whether it is adding value to the initiative, or not.
- Finally, establish the contribution weight of the partner. In other words, how much value is this partner adding to the initiative? And how is this partner helping me achieve the goals of the innovation

initiative? Is it 10%, 20%, 30%, or less? The importance of quantifying the contribution of your partner is helpful but may not be critical. It may help you, for instance, assess the quality of the collaboration, and whether you would want to continue the collaboration in the future or not.

IP and Continuous Learning

Every innovation initiative is a learning opportunity so you should establish a process by which you capture the failure and the learning, and how you intend to disseminate that learning to the innovation team. Important also is to address upfront the IP issues, especially if the initiative involves a collaboration with an external partner in which there might be a technology development process. I would even argue that if this is the case, then you need to consider Subclause 8.2 of ISO 56002:2019 as a must action that needs to be taken care of at the beginning of the process.

CLAUSE 8.3 INNOVATION PROCESS

The organization should configure the innovation processes to suit the innovation initiative.[*]

This subclause defines a process where an innovative opportunity can be transformed into a deployable solution. It is important to point out that this basic innovation management process will not totally incorporate all of the activities defined. Each initiative should modify the basic process to meet the unique needs of the individual entity. Your final design process should be flexible and adaptable taking on unique configurations depending upon the type of innovation the organization is involved in.

---

[*]©ISO. This material is excerpted from ISO 56002:2019, with permission of the American National Standards Institute (ANSI) on behalf of the International Organization for Standardization. All rights reserved.

- Definition of system: a system is a set of interrelated or interacting acting elements.
- Definition of process: a process is a set of interrelated or interacting activities that used input to deliver an intended result.

This planning activity includes defining opportunities, developing strategies, defining organizational structures, preparing value propositions, and conducting a business case analysis, and defining maintenance processes. These can neatly be defined by three distinct phases (see Figure 6.1).

To prepare an IMS, all the processes related to the organization's appropriate process groupings should be defined and documented. You will note that we called the 12 clauses Process Groupings, because each of them is made up of a number of different processes that need to work in harmony. For some, innovation specific processes may not be relevant. In these cases, the design process can be excluded from the project.

Due to the extremely high failure rate of innovative projects, we feel that five tollgates need to be added to the process.

- A very brief one is at the end of Process Group 1 – Opportunity Identification.
- The second one is at the end of Process Group 3 – Value Proposition.

Phase I. Creation

- Process Grouping 1. Opportunity Identification
- Process Grouping 2. Opportunity Development
- Process Grouping 3. Value Proposition
- Process Grouping 4. Concept Validation

Phase II. Preparation and Production

- Process Grouping 5. Business Case Analysis
- Process Grouping 6. Resource Management
- Process Grouping 7. Documentation
- Process Grouping 8. Production

Phase III. Delivery

- Process Grouping 9. Marketing, Sales, and Delivery
- Process Grouping 10. After-Sales Services
- Process Grouping 11. Performance Analysis
- Process Grouping 12. Transformation

FIGURE 6.1
Three Phases of the Innovative Process.

- The third one is at the end of Process Group 5 – Business Case Analysis.
- The fourth one is at the Process Group 8 – Production.
- The fifth one is at Process Group 11 – Performance Analysis.

The ISO 56002:2019 standard divides up the IMS implementation process into five process groupings (phases). The process doesn't include tollgates. The ISO 56002:2019 standard has five implementation cycle phases. They are:

- Phase I. Opportunity Identification
- Phase II. Concept Creation
- Phase III. Concept Validation
- Phase IV. Solution Development
- Phase V. Solution Deployment

ISO 56002:2019 was written to help an organization develop its IMS. In reality, it is designed to help guide, design, and implement a project whose scope is to develop operating procedures and processes that other projects/programs will use/consider to successfully meet their objectives. This project, like all projects, is formed with a set of objectives, a beginning and end date with the output from when the project is turned over to the normal management staff to maintain, update, and improve.

The success of the IMS project is not the procedures and processes that they develop, document, and install. The success of the IMS project can only be measured by how efficiently and effectively the individual innovative initiatives flow through the process and the adaptability of the process to meet unexpected or unique requirements. The IMS project team should continuously ask the question, "Are we developing innovative processes and procedures that set our organization apart from the competition?" When we talk about managing the innovative system, we are addressing how we can control and improve the processes and procedures that are used in the innovative cycle.

There are many different ways that the innovation process is divided into phases based on different focus points of interest and challenge. Most of them put their primary focus on the design/creation activities even though that is a small portion of the cost and cycle time related to the innovative product cycle. Other organizations focus on sales and marketing activities because they can have a bigger impact on customer perception of the product than the uniqueness the design has. You can take a very innovative product design and tie it to poor marketing and selling activity and you have a failed product. On the other hand, you can take an average design product and tie it in with superb marketing and sales activities and you can have a successful product. For innovation to make an organization successful, it has to do an innovative job throughout the total innovative cycle. Just one weak link in the chain will cause the project to fail. Marketing studies indicate that if you tell an individual something three times, they will start to believe it.

ISO 56002:2019 provides enough flexibility to implement the five phases. Particularly, these phases can:

- Follow a linear or nonlinear approach
- Enjoy a certain level of iteration between different units
- Be implemented independently or in connection with other processes and sub-process from other units
- Should interact with other processes such as R&D, marketing, sales, and partnership processes

In other words, ISO 56002:2019 provides a blueprint that you can use and reconfigure in any way you want to. As long as you are using the five steps, you are free to design the process in the way that better fits your size, your industry, and the market in which you operate. Let us look at the five-step framework suggested by ISO 56002:2019.

Phase I. Opportunity Identification

The first step suggested by ISO 56002:2019 to manage the innovation process is to start with the opportunities that are open to you. A major input that helps you do a good job in identifying opportunities is your understanding of the organization's context, as well as the intent of the innovation.

There are three major tasks related to opportunity identification. They are:

- Identifying the potential opportunity.
  Most people will easily identify many improvement opportunities in a very short period of time.

- Quantify the potential opportunities.

  Most of the potential opportunities will be rejected immediately due to some lack of skill, interest, or resources. For the others, a very quick analysis needs to be done to determine the advantages, disadvantages, and resources expended narrowing your search down to one or two that you would like to be authorized to pursue.
- Opportunity selection.

  The individual who can legitimize the pursuit of the opportunity needs to approve a scope statement for the effort.

The major output from the opportunity identification step is an approved scope statement by an individual who can legitimize the expenditure of the required resources and the resources required to complete the activities necessary to have a value proposition prepared and presented.

Scope of IMS

Scope boxes in a specific program, project, or product. It's a lot like the organization's mission statement as it defines what activities are assigned to the specific program, project, or product. It has a defined start and end date; plus, the items that enter the activity and those items that leave the activity before the end item is delivered.

The scope defines the following:

- what is included in the project,
- what is not included in the project,
- what the outputs are from the project,
- what the inputs to the project, and
- what parts of the organization are involved in the project.

Project scope is the statement that defines the full extent of the project assignment. It includes things like scope description, criteria for acceptance, projected deliverables, assigned personnel, and duration of the project. It provides the trigger that sets up a new project and provides resources to support it. They should be released under an executive signature that has the authority to authorize the project.

Strict adherence to the scope specification will help reduce the overruns and expansions to the program. The context and the strengths, weaknesses, opportunities, and threats (SWOT) analysis you conducted, as we have seen earlier, should provide you with insights on the trends that could inspire your team to come up with a new concept. The intent of the innovation should help you define the scope of the innovation, the category of innovation (product/process, business model, market, or technology), and the type of innovation you want to be in (incremental, disruptive, breakthrough, or architectural). In addition, it should include any other previous learning experiences that you may have had from failed or successful initiatives.

- Definition of charter: A charter is an expansion of the scope statement, which documents the reason that the activity was brought into existence, a description of the entity, who is sponsoring it, and why.

A charter can also include things like project objectives, description of the purpose, the justification for initiating the project, how success will be measured, and often budgeted amount. Often this leads directly to the work breakdown structure in the project plan and it must agree with the approved scope statement. We recommend that it is prepared by the opportunity team that is accountable for the successful completion of the activities.

Of special consideration in previous experiences is the issue of failure and how it should not handicap your team's thinking. Help your team develop a fail-fast mindset to overcome psychological barriers and turn failed experience into teaching and learning moments.

Next are a few suggestions that will help you identify opportunities.

- Start with customer insight and what the customer is telling you in terms of their unmet needs. What were the limitations of previous products, and how should you improve them? How did the customer react to your previous improvement? And what did you learn? How was the journey of your customer with the product, and what can you do to improve it?
- Use big data analytics and artificial intelligence tools to identify trends and changes in your customer's attitudes and behavior. What can you learn from your channels about your customer? What AI applications you can adopt that help you understand

better your customer? How do your customers connect to your product? And what experience they have?

- Understand how the competition is reacting to market changes: Where do your products stand in the market and how do they measure with respect to the competition? What other things are happening in the market and in your economic cluster that is changing and that can open an opportunity for you, i.e., things like regulations, demographics, interest rates, and global expansion?

There are many tools for you to identify these opportunities. The most well-known are market research, ethnographic studies, focus groups, benchmarking, and crowdsourcing. But new tools that relate to big data, predictive analytics, and use of AI are of critical importance, especially if you have been engaged enough with your customer and you own the data. This could be a golden opportunity for ideas.

Phase II. Concept Creation

Once you identify the opportunities and your customer's unmet needs, you need to move to the next step: Concept Creation. Below are few suggestions on how you can run the concept creation phase.

- The ideation process
  In this step, you are primarily brainstorming about what to do with the opportunity you identified previously. The more expertise and knowledge in the team you have and the more diversity you can get in terms of the professional and cultural background of team members, the deeper you get into the ideation process. Here are a few suggestions on how to manage the ideation process.
  - Conceptual fluency
    Encourage people with conceptual fluency and open-mindedness to attend the ideation process. Conceptual fluency is the ability of people to use, understand, and interact with abstract concepts. People with conceptual fluency are better at coming up with new ideas because they can think in abstract terms and can imagine solutions that do not exist yet. They do not need to anchor their thinking into tangible things to speak

their imagination. In other words, they can see abstract things that normal people do not see.

- Originality and playfulness

  Playfulness is the ability to create a nonthreatening environment that sends a positive message to the team. It helps the ideation team think of challenges and innovation research questions in a lighthearted way which should engage and stimulate the team's imagination. Playfulness humanizes the rigid process of testing by injecting kindness, humor, and positivity while helping people relate to experimentation, especially when it involves hard science.

- Decrease authority and increase ownership

  The less authority you assert in the ideation process, the richer the ideation process becomes. When people fear authority, they become less visible in the discussion. Encourage them by refraining from commenting on their discussion. In some cases, it is even better to ideate without the manager around the team.

- Encourage people with both convergent and divergent thinking.

  Create an inclusive process in which convergent and divergent thinkers work together on the same challenges so you have better chances of "stumbling" on solutions that you would have never thought about had you used only one type of thinking.

Tollgate 1 – Opportunity Analysis

- Definition of tollgate: For an IMS, a tollgate defines a point in a new project cycle where the status of an individual project is evaluated to determine if it should continue or be terminated.

Between each phase or step, many companies employ a "tollgate" to control the process. The tollgate defines a number of conditions that need to be met for the process to move into the next phase. We like to insert a tollgate at the end of the opportunity identification process to be sure that the project is in line with the organization's mission goals and objectives, which should also be capable of providing real value-added to the organization's stakeholders if it is successfully taken advantage of. Successful completion of this tollgate will result in the initial scope statement being approved by management who can authorize the expenditure of funds required to prepare a value proposition. Tollgates may also be placed at the end of preparing the value proposition, business case analysis, and just before the first customer ship.

The Idea Evaluation Process

After you have completed the first step of the concept creation phase, the ideation process, you move to the second step which is the evaluation of the ideas the ideation process produced. You will realize that not all the ideas you generated in the ideation process will be good and applicable. So an important step you need to do is to evaluate the ideas. ISO 56002:2019 suggests that at the end of the ideation process, you investigate and assess potential ideas that may present a solution to your problem. ISO 56002:2019 suggests the following rubrics:

- Novelty: To what extent the idea is novel and has the potential to be patented?
- Risk: What risk (strategic risk, business risk, operational risk, legal risk, or social risk) the idea may have for the organization or the project?
- Feasibility: Is the idea feasible? Can it be implemented? And in what way it can be operationalized?
- Desirability: Will the idea be desirable by your customer and your stakeholders? Would they accept it? Would they embrace and interact with it?
- Sustainability: How sustainable is the idea? For how long you can use the solution? And would the solution be consistent over time?
- Intellectual Property Right: Is the idea patentable? Can we claim it is an IP? And if so, what implication could this have on our business?

A great way to evaluate and assess the idea is to design an assessment rubric that helps your team come up with a decision to rate and grade ideas.

We like to target five different solutions based upon slightly different objectives. For example:

1. Does the solution have time and/or cost limitation?
2. What solution can you come up with that can be implemented within one month?

3. What solution can you come up with if you only have $500,000 to spend on implementation?
4. What solution can you come up with if your competition is selling an equivalent product for less than the cost to produce it?
5. How can I make it simpler to use?

Often, when we come up with three potential alternatives, a fourth potential alternative pops out that is better than any one of the three based upon combining the three thoughts together. In Table 6.1 you will find a simple individual innovative evaluation form. (Legend – 1 is minimum or none and 5 is high or outstanding.)

Once you evaluate your ideas, you need to link them to the solution. In this stage, you are creating a business concept. And when you get to the business concept creation, make sure that you:

TABLE 6.1

Simple Individual Innovative Evaluation Form

Idea		1 2 3 4 5
1 Novelty	To what extent is the idea novel and has the potential to be patented?	1 2 3 4 5
2 Risk	What risk (strategic risk, business risk, operational risk, legal risk, or social risk) the idea may have for organization or the project?	1 2 3 4 5
3 Feasibility	Is the idea feasible? Can it be implemented? And in what way can it operationalize?	1 2 3 4
4 Desirability	Will the idea be desirable by your customer and your stakeholders? Would they accept it? Would they embrace and interact with it?	1 2 3 4 5
5 Sustainability	How sustainable is the idea? For how long can you use the solution? And would the solution be consistent over time?	1 2 3 4 5
6 Intellectual property right	Is the idea patentable? Can we claim it is an IP? And if so, what implication could this have on our business?	1 2 3 4 5

- Define the proposition: What is the benefit of the concept and how does it help your customers, your market, and your position?
- Develop a granular business model that defines the different components you need such as marketing, sales, operational, and finance.
- Define the assumptions under each model. Assumptions are important to spell out for each scenario, as they allow for people to understand the rationale behind your choice. Assumptions provide clues to your thinking, which should help your stakeholders understand the decision-making process.

Prepare the Value Proposition

- Definition of value proposition: A value proposition is a document that defines the benefits that will result from the implementation of a change or the use of output as viewed by one or more of the organization's stakeholders. A value proposition can apply to an entire organization, part thereof, or consumer account, product, service, or internal process.

The following is a typical example of what a value proposition document's Table of Contents might look like.

- Title and the names of the originators of the proposed change
- Table of contents
- Executive overview
  - Description of the proposed change
  - Description of the AS/IS state
  - Value-added content that the proposed change would bring about
  - Overall cost and time frame to implement the change
  - Other solutions that were considered and why they were not chosen
  - Risk and obstacles related to the change
  - Recommendations
- List of the key people associated with the value proposition (executive sponsor, individuals recommending the change, individuals that created the value proposition)
- Financial calculations

- Details related to other value-added results. (Examples: cycle time reduction, stock reduction, improved customer satisfaction, reduced defect levels, increase market share, etc.)
- List of risks and exposures
- List of assumptions
- Other solutions that were considered and why they were not chosen.
- Implementation plan
- Three-year projection of the situation if the proposed change is not approved
- The net value added when the cost (money and other resources) related to installation of the change is subtracted from the value added content
- Detailed recommendations
- References

Tollgate 2 – Value Proposition Approval

This is a meeting with the appropriate management team to review the innovation project team's charter and evaluate if the projected value-added result from the project/program is sufficient to justify the resources that will be applied. As a result of this meeting, qualified project managers may be assigned to assist the individual responsible for the project.

Phase III. Concept Validation

Concept validation, called also Proof of Concept (POC), is a critical step in innovation. It allows you to test your product in the real world and collect information, data, reactions, and level of acceptability about your product. In the validation stage, you are producing a minimum viable product to get feedback and market reaction. In this stage, you are testing and piloting the minimum version that your customers will accept. This version of your final product needs to be attractive enough to get your customer hooked on the concept. The more you are engaged with the customer, the better knowledge you develop about the concept.

The validation stage helps you in two ways. First, it reduces the initial amount of uncertainty by allowing you to stress test your assumptions. This is a critical dimension of the proof of concept. When we develop a new product, we tend to make certain assumptions about the customer, the product, the market, the timing, the competition and so forth. The goal of the validation process is primarily to understand whether the set of assumptions you made are correct or not. For instance, if one of your assumptions was that your product would be attractive to a specific segment of the customer, say for instance high school students, then in the validation, you are trying to figure out whether high school students will engage with your product.

Second, in this stage you are producing a minimum version of the product, and you want to understand what improvements you would want to add. The minimum viable product (MVP) approach is a limited version of the final product that is used primarily to engage with the customer. In the MVP version, you set many checkpoints that would allow you to rethink your product as evidence becomes clearer about the level of acceptability of the product.

The Innovator Board, an educational site dedicated to innovation, suggests three ideas in the validation process:

- First define your focus: What is it that you need to validate and what type of information and data you are seeking? Define your customer personae and how you want to reach them.
- Second, map out your assumptions: During the concept creation, you must have operated under certain assumptions such as timing, age group, design, economic condition, and so forth. In this stage what assumptions are you trying to test out?
- Third, decide on the method of validation: Is it experimentation? User interview? Lab testing? Or research questions? Of course, this will depend greatly on the nature of the product.

ISO 56002:2019 provides three examples of possible validation approaches: Tests, experiments, pilots, and studies. ISO 56002:2019 provides these methods as a suggestion, but, in fact, it all depends on the type of product you are validating. For instance, a validation of a pharmaceutical product will be subject to more requirements by the Food and Drug Administration (FDA) than a validation of a new business idea or a software product, and therefore the method and the approach may differ.

Once you validate the technical part of the product, i.e., whether technically it works or not, you need to validate the product with the

202 • *The ISO 56002 Innovation Management System*

customer. In customer validation, user research, and market research are of paramount importance. Customer validation is necessary for almost any product. In this stage, you are collecting evidence on whether your product will find a customer. But for most of the product, a customer interview is necessary. Jim Semick (2020), the founder and chief strategist at ProductPlan, argues that customer validation interviews help in providing a clear answer to the problem, the solution, and the pain points. He provides the following suggestions on how to conduct customer validation interviews:

- Make your interview long enough to develop a better insight into how the customer connects with the product. Longer interviews are said to provide a more accurate picture of how the interviewee identifies himself or herself with the product.
- Conduct enough interviews to develop a better sense of market potential. Talk to as many people as you can to understand the market breadth and the range of issues that your product can or cannot solve.
- Face-to-face interviews are the best medium for collecting information for validation purposes. Face-to-face interviews allow you to read people's body language and develop an accurate reading of their true feeling vis-a-vis your product.
- It is critical that you talk to users but also you need to include decision makers. If you are targeting a business that will hopefully use your product, then talking to the finance manager, as well argued by Jim Semick, will allow you to gauge buying willingness as well.
- Ask "why" and let the customer do the talking. Do not overwhelm the customer or lead them with your questions. Let your questions and your body language be as neutral as possible.
- Document customer reaction. The best way to keep track of people's interviews is to stick to a template in which you write down all the questions. The template will help to conduct a structural interview with a higher degree of reliability of the customer feel.
- Ask open-ended questions and focus on the relationship between the problems and the solution your product is offering. When you focus on the relationship and you let the customer do the talking you will get better insights.

Tollgate 3 – Business Case Analysis

- Definition of business case analysis: Business case analysis is an evaluation of the potential impact of a problem or opportunity and on the organization to determine if it is worthwhile investing the resources of the opportunity. The individual case competes against all other present and proposed activities/projects to determine which existing activities will continue to be active on the organization's portfolio of activities/projects and what new ones will be added.

This is a very critical tollgate as new initiatives are announced once they are added to the organization's portfolio of activities/projects. It also triggers the start for industrial engineering and manufacturing engineering to procure the space and equipment required to handle the estimated output demands.

Phase IV. Solution Development

After the entity successfully completes Tollgate #3, you validate the product and do the tweaking needed for your innovation based on customer interviews; then you need to work on developing the solution. In this stage, ISO 56002:2019 suggests three *Must do* activities and we have added a fourth *Must do* activity. These are:

- The first *Must do* activity is to define the new value realization: In this step, you need to move from concept discussion to the solution discussion. In other words, your innovation becomes more tangible and therefore you should be able to articulate well what the customer value in your product. Your customer will measure this value through the different touchpoints that the product journey offers them. So it is critical that you also work on mapping out the customer journey the product is offering.
- The second important action you need to address in the solution development step is to decide whether you want to develop the solution by yourself or with others. All options are open, and you should choose based on what you believe, will help your innovation succeed. If you decide to go it alone, then your responsibility in the

deployment phase will become more complex than if you decide to partner. If you decide to sell the solution or let yourself be acquired, then you lose control of the innovation.

- The third *Must do* action ISO 56002:2019 suggests is the need to engage early on with your legal department to spell out and map out the risk associated with the innovation. More importantly, you need to make sure that your IP legal experts are fully engaged to make sure that you are not infringing on other's intellectual properties and that your innovation is well protected. These are the two most critical risks you need to address at this point. It is also at this stage that you need to start addressing the patentability issue. In other words, do you need to patent the innovation? And if so how and when?

- The fourth *Must do* activity is to prepare the paperwork, facility, equipment, people, and other required resources that will allow the entity to be activated. Typical paperwork that could be required:
  - From Product Engineering: assembly drawings, blueprints, product specifications, performance specifications, maintenance manuals, and patent applications.
  - From Manufacturing Engineering: production routings, setup instructions, job instructions, automation requirements, inspection instructions, tooling drawings, fixture drawings, and performance specifications.
  - From Industrial Engineering: equipment layout requirements, storage requirements, shipping containers, electrical layout drawings, and maintenance procedures for fire in safety approvals.

The list can go on and on, as everyone has their set of papers that need to be customized to meet their needs including production control, procurement, quality, personnel, and separate unique reporting for each member of the executive team. The paperwork requirements keep pouring in until we are buried up to the neck in reams of paper. What happened to the paperless organization? It seems like the only organization that is using less paper is the daily newspaper.

The paperwork is not the only commodity that we need to take advantage of as an innovative opportunity. Personnel needs to provide people who are properly trained to turn the wheels of this mighty new "dragon," not the system that we are creating. They need someone to

TABLE 6.2

A Risk Management Matrix

Develop the Solution Alone	Develop the Solution with a Partner
• Achieve better control over the innovation development • Better flexibility in managing the innovation product • Enjoy better return	• Quick entry into an industry or country • Sharing the risk of failure • Developing learning opportunities • Avoids cost development and deployment

install all the desks and the equipment that they will need, someone who's going to certify suppliers based upon the first article of inspection and reliability test. Production Control prepares a schedule usage list in order that the required parts are purchased and provides a warehouse to store the compliments and finished goods inventory. Marketing is pressured to prepare flyers, pamphlets, advertising for newspapers and magazines, sales campaigns, salesperson training, radio, and television slots. Let's face it – this is only the tip of the iceberg. There are literally thousands of opportunities to follow-up during the development solution phase that can make an innovative design unattractive to the general public.

At the end of this stage, you should be able to have three outputs:

- A road map that defines the value realization of the innovation along with a customer journey road map that also spells different touchpoints.
- A clear strategy on how you will develop the solution and whether you want to partner or go it alone.
- A risk management matrix that identifies possible issues with the innovation (see Table 6.2).

Phase V. Solution Deployment

Once you develop the solution, you need to deploy it. In this stage, you are pushing the new innovation into the market to make it a fully accepted product. Your first step is to organize yourself to create an aggressive campaign for the launch of the product. Your engagement with the users, customers, and partners should be part of the campaign and fully documented in order to build a database about customers' reactions and customer feedback.

To accomplish this, you must first turn on your production process to eliminate any incompatible links. It is not unusual for many problems to be identified as the many individual processes mold together into a production system for the first time. Early samples of the hard tool production facilities should first be evaluated in extreme detail to be sure that they match the engineering specifications. In the beginning, this often leads to many problems related to the engineering design and manufacturing capabilities, requiring changes in both the engineering design and the manufacturing equipment. Pre-customer delivery process outputs should be set aside to be evaluated from a performance and reliability standpoint. We recommend to use some of the early pre-customer ship outputs to run a beta test at organizations that agreed to a set pre-customer ship sample to evaluate in the customer environment. I personally have seen this used very effectively in restaurants, where a chef brings out a free new dessert and asks us to try it and tell him what we think of it.

In parallel with setting up and activating your customize facility, the marketing group should create an aggressive campaign for launching the production process outputs. Your engagement with the users, customers, and partners should be part of the campaign and fully documented in order to build a database about customers' reaction and customer feedback.

ISO 56002:2019 suggests three actions. These actions are:

- Develop a launch campaign that allows you to promote the new innovation through well-crafted communication and marketing strategies. The goal of this communication strategy is to create awareness about the new innovation while engaging with your customers
- Create a process by which you measure the adoption rate. Generally speaking, the adaption rate is the total of the new user divided by the number of existing users. But because your product is new, you need to start building metrics so over time you are able to track and measure the progress of adoption.

- Finally, it is critical to creating a mechanism by which you collect the customer feedback in order to improve the product, but more importantly, capture new knowledge that would allow you to develop new opportunities.

The IMS Cycle

There are three major types of plans used in most organizations. They are:

- Total organizational planning

  These are the four types of plans that make up the Organizational Master Plan. These are made up of many individual plans that fall into the specific planning group. They are the combined plan of all the individual projects, individual programs, individual needs, individual ongoing sources requirements, etc. plans related to the total organization.
- Specific objective plans

  These are plans that are related to a specific need or objective that has a start and end date and a specific measurement of success. Typically there are individual projects, research studies, potential customer studies, acquisitions, etc. Upgrading your IMS would be classified as a project and would operate using the project management guidelines and the present IMS cycle guidelines.
- Ongoing operations planning

  These are plans for maintaining the presently approved and implemented projects, systems, and products. These are directed at sustaining present operations and products based upon future projections. Frequently, continuous improvement objectives of 55% to 10% are included in this category. The maintenance of the IMS after the upgraded system has been installed is an example of ongoing operations planning.

Based upon these definitions, implementing a portfolio of projects that follow these guidelines results in an organization having an IMS that is capable of establishment, implementation, maintenance, and continuous improvement and breakthrough improvement in its operating systems; all that adds value to its stakeholders.

SUMMARY

We believe that the creativity phase of an innovative product cycle is the most fun and exciting and receives the most recognition in all the phases in the IMS cycle. However, it requires far less skill and ability than is needed to set up a complete self-sufficient facility to produce and sell that innovative output.

7

Clause 9: Performance Evaluation

PURPOSE

This chapter describes the process by which you evaluate the performance of the IMS. It provides the general framework to help you create and implement a monitoring system that allows you to measure, analyze, and evaluate the performance of innovation activities and programs. It describes the steps needed to establish the monitoring system and discusses the tools and methods needed to evaluate the IMS. It also provides a discussion of the difference between qualitative and quantitative methods to help you decide about the types of metrics you need to create and install the evaluation system.

OVERVIEW

This focuses on the general framework that allows you to put together a coherent evaluation system, and how to link it to your internal audit, and annual management review process. The chapter shows you how to align these three actions to create coherence in the functioning of the IMS evaluation.

- Monitoring, measurement, analysis, and evaluation of the IMS
- Internal audit
- Management review

BENEFITS

At the end of this chapter, you will learn how to structure the overall IMS evaluation system, and how to design metrics that provide you with an indication of how well the system is functioning. There are examples of metrics, with a discussion of each different type of measurement indicator.

CLASSIFICATION OF ACTIONS

This chapter provides recommendations needed to support the monitoring and evaluation system of your IMS and provides some examples and best practices on how to implement metrics, and from which you can choose based on the specific circumstances of your organization.

Subclause 9.1.1.1 Monitoring, Measurement, Analysis, and Evaluation

The organization should determine what needs to be monitored and measured, including which innovation performance indicators are to be used.

*(Subclause 9.1.1.1. a)**

The success of any management system depends a great deal on its evaluation. No system in the world can function without proper mechanisms that provide accurate data and information on how well the system is or is not working, and how well is or not achieving its goals. IMS is no different.

ISO 56002:2019 makes the evaluation of the performance of the IMS a critical step that helps decision makers understand the contribution of innovation programs and activities to achieving organizational strategy and how well IMS is aligning different innovation activities inside the organization.

---

*©ISO. This material is excerpted from ISO 56002:2019, with permission of the American National Standards Institute (ANSI) on behalf of the International Organization for Standardization. All rights reserved.

In this clause, we will address three *Must do* activities:

- The evaluation of the IMS
- The auditing process of the IMS
- The review frequency of the IMS

Planning the Evaluation

The purpose of the evaluation system is to generate evidence about how effective and how efficient the IMS is working. The goal of an evaluation is to be able to make evidence-based decisions about changes and improvement to the system. Before you start the evaluation, you need to decide about three actions: the scope of the evaluation (what do I evaluate), the tools and method (how do I evaluate), and who will perform the evaluation (people engaged in the evaluation).

The Scope of the Evaluation: What Do You Evaluate?

Depending on the specific situation of your organization, you can choose the scope of the evaluation based on the nature, the size, the specific industry, the goals and the objectives you assigned to your IMS. If you are a government agency and you want to understand the contribution of innovation at the macro-level to the country's GDP performance, you can look at the economic competitiveness, how innovation is contributing to the job market, or how it is helping nascent industries thrive. At the micro-level, and for organizations in general, the evaluation helps you assess whether innovation has helped you achieve your strategic goals, as you defined them.

ISO 56002:2019 provides enough flexibility for organizations to evaluate what is deemed necessary based on the geography, the size, the nature, and the industry in which you operate. You can choose to evaluate:

- The entire integration IMS;
- Only part of the system, such as outcomes or results;
- The interaction of different parts of the system;
- Focus on innovation portfolio; or
- You can focus on the maturity level of innovation, as an indicator of your capabilities.

Another approach to deciding about the scope would be simply to focus on the dimension of ISO 56002:2019 itself. Here you can evaluate the following components:

- How well the leadership is engaged in innovation programs and activities
- How well the planning process, including the strategy, the structure, and innovation portfolio, is helping the organization achieve its strategic goals
- How well the support system provides to innovation, such as structure, people, time, knowledge, and finance is helping with the fluidity of the IMS
- How well operation activities and innovation processes, are aligned to help the ideation process as well as validation and deployment of new innovative initiatives
- The assessment of the evaluation process itself. In other words, how accurate and valid is data and the methods we use to measure the effectiveness of innovation programs and activities
- The improvement process and how corrective actions and learning is injected back into the system is helping the organization improve its capabilities

Tools and Methods: How to Evaluate?

In this step, you are deciding about the tools and the methods to use to conduct the evaluation. There are a plethora of tools and methods, so it is important that you choose the right ones. More importantly, it is critical to define the rationale behind the choice of a specific method. Depending on the circumstances of your organization, a mix of methods and approaches is always helpful in generating better and valid data.

We make a distinction between qualitative methods and quantitative methods. In qualitative methods, we use a variety of unstructured or semi-structured tools such as interviews, case studies, and focus groups to generate ideas, insights, and opinions. You use these types of methods to dive deeper into what motivates people to behave the way they do, how they make choices, and what prompts them to make certain decisions.

In quantitative methods, the goal is to quantify a problem or an issue by generating hard data, such as statistics that help you make inferences about

TABLE 7.1

The Nature of Indicators: What Indicators to Use?

	Quantitative	Qualitative
Goal	Discover facts, explore the phenomenon, and explain causation	Focus on the true meaning of what people are doing and why
Research question	What, when, and who	Why and how
Sample	Large population	Small groups
Data	Gathered through a survey or other statistical methods	Focus on participant, observation, and behavior
Analysis	Statistical methods	Analysis is done by classification and information is categorized by themes

certain behaviors. Quantitative methods include statistical data analysis, model methodologies, cost–benefits analysis, online surveys, expert interviews, and peer reviews. For instance, the number of ideas generated over a quarter can help you make an inference about how employees are innovative in your team, while the number of employees trained on the innovation framework can help you make an inference about how leadership is committed to innovation. But remember, these are just inferences that may or may not lead to the actual outcome you need.

Here is a summary of the difference between quantitative and qualitative methods provided by author Stacey McDonald, from the knowledge center in Ontario, Canada (2018) (see Table 7.1).

The next subclause of ISO 56002:2019 deals with the type of indicators to use to monitor and evaluate the IMS. ISO 56002:2019 suggests the adoption of a combination of indicators, both qualitative and quantitative, to capture the true meaning of your measurement system. Thus, you can measure your IMS using three types of indicators:

- **Input-related indicators**

    The importance of input-related indicators is that it gives you an idea about the level of richness of the material you use to produce innovative products. In other words, if your ideas come from a variety of sources, such as employees, customers, partners, and so forth, then your innovation product will be more affluent and will cater to a variety of segments of your stakeholder map. Examples of input-related indicators could be ideas and initiatives coming from employees, ideas, and initiatives coming from vendors, new sources of knowledge, etc.

- **Throughput-related indicators**

    In the throughput-related indicators, the notion of speed, learning, and how ideas are processed is of extreme value to the efficiency of your IMS. You can choose indicators that capture the ability of employees to collaborate, process new information and new knowledge, collaborate, and how quickly they develop new capabilities. You should also choose indicators that capture the speed to get your product to the customer.

- **Output-related indicators**

    The importance of output-related indicators is that it gives you information on the impact of your innovation on your market activities. This could be captured by market share indicators, user satisfaction, cost savings, new user adoption, or any indicators that show the effect of your innovation on your customer.

Who and When to Conduct an Evaluation?

The last two questions you need to address in the performance evaluation process is when and by whom the performance evaluation should be conducted. With respect to the first question, a good practice is to conduct the evaluation every quarter or at least once a year, or when the results are available.

As to who should conduct the assessment, ISO 56002:2019 provides enough flexibility. You can have the evaluation done internally by your audit department, or externally by an outside provider. The internal assessment can be as frequent as you want without overwhelming the system and the people in charge of the system with too much unnecessary evaluation. We believe the yearly assessment should be conducted by a third-party provider to ensure objectivity, impartiality, and fairness.

Subclause 9.1.2 Conducting the Analysis and the Evaluation

After you decide about the measurement system, the type of data you need, how to collect it, and who conducts the assessment, you need to get to the next step, which is the actual analysis and evaluation. The most critical dimension of the analysis phase has to do with the effectiveness and efficiency of your IMS. Effectiveness is defined as "the extent to which planned activities are realized and planned results are achieved." (ISO 9001:2015). In other words, whether you have conducted the activities you planned in an effective way and whether you achieved the results you hoped for. In other words, did you achieve the goals that you set for the system at the beginning of the year? Here are two examples:

- If one of my goals was to achieve X number of innovations at each stage in an innovation cycle (the experiment cycle time) and I received below that X number, then the effectiveness of my IMS is below expectation.
- If one of my goals was to reduce the time to market of new product by an X number and I have not achieved that number, then my effectiveness is below expectation.

The second criterion in the analysis of the IMS is efficiency. Efficiency refers to the number of resources used to manage the IMS. The less waste you have in the system while being effective in achieving your goals, the better your system is. However, when it comes to measuring innovation activities, the ISO definition of efficiency has to be taken in relative terms. Return on innovation investment tends to require more time. Spending on R&D, training, and experimentation have less of an immediate return, and therefore subjecting innovation activities to the same stringent requirements of a manufacturing assembly line could harm your IMS. While the ideal solution is to achieve the right goal with the right amount of resources or achieve a higher ROI while being cost-effective, in innovation you need to be aware of the fact that efficiency pushed to its extreme may kill innovation activities.

What to Measure

Once you gather data and measurement tools, and you define your approach to measurement, you are ready to evaluate the performance of your innovation system. Subclause 9.1.2.2 provides few areas to which you can apply your analysis. You can use the following questions:

- How well you understood the context
- How well is your leadership engaged in supporting your IMS
- How effective you were in taking risks to seize opportunities
- How effective your innovation strategy was in achieving results
- How efficient and how effective the process and the support provided by your IMS to innovation activities
- How well you learned from success and failure
- How important is it to the organization to recognize opportunities and make improvements to your IMS to make it better

Of course, all this process of evaluation has to be fully documented.

Internal Audit

The third step recommended by ISO 56002:2019 for the performance evaluation is to conduct an internal audit of your IMS. The goal of an internal audit is to make sure that the IMS is working according to the requirements you have identified, and that the IMS is functioning effectively and efficiently. It is important to understand however that, while some people in the organization may be apprehensive about the audit function and tend to view it in a negative way, when conducted in a professional and appropriate manner, auditing helps organizations gather data about the weaknesses and strengths of the IMS. It also signals to different teams the interest and engagement of leadership and that ought to keep them focused on their innovation activities.

The Audit Program

ISO 56002:2019 recommends that you establish an audit program that has the following components:

- The definition of audit methods, responsibilities requirements, as well as how frequently the audit should be conducted.
- The objectives and the scope of each audit.
- Objectivity and impartiality are important to any audit process, and therefore, it is critical that you choose your internal auditor carefully. You can also enlist an external auditor who should be subject-matter experts in innovation.

- The purpose of the audit is to identify the weaknesses in the systems. When you write a report, in addition to outlining the weaknesses, it is important that you provide the solution as well by pointing out the corrective actions needed.
- Auditing reports need to be looked at as an opportunity for improvement and learning. When you conduct an audit, it is helpful to follow up with other supporting activities, such as workshops, training, meeting, or any activities that help teams understand, accept, and implement the recommendations of the report.

Management Review

The review of your IMS by management is a needed action to ensure that the system is working effectively and efficiently. It is also the time for management to review the results of internal audits, conducted by internal teams or external audit during the previous cycle.

When to review and how deep you get into the review of the system is a decision left to the organization. Typically, a quarterly review is recommended. If not, at least once every six months. You also do not have to review the entire system. You can choose what is relevant to the system.

- You may focus on the depth of the idea like whether the ideas are coming from a variety of stakeholders (employees, partners, customers, vendors … etc.).
- Or you may focus on improvements that are meant to reduce the cost of doing business (cost improvement rate).
- Or any other dimension of the system.

Management Review Input (What data to use to conduct the review)

The data and the input to the review process can come from a variety of sources. ISO 56002:2019 suggests eight action sources to consider (Subclauses a through h in Subclause 9.3.1).

- The first input to the review is previous reports. A status check on what has been achieved since the last review and whether all the previous recommendations and comments have been taken care of is the first step. It is actually a requirement of quality management and it applies here as well.

- Change in the external or internal environment that may affect the process of innovation. An example of external change is an acquisition or a merger that has affected the internal organizational chart. Another example of external change is a change in regulation or a government mandate for an organization that is involved with social innovation.
- Other information on how the IMS has been performing, including a check on whether the IMS has achieved its value realization (Subclause 5.1.2).
- Whether the goals and the objectives of the innovation have been met (Subclause 6.2).
- How well the process, the initiative, and the innovation portfolio have been performing (Subclause 8.2).
- How well the organization and the team are sharing knowledge about success and failure (Subclause 7.1).
- In what way the organization deals with deviations nonconformity, and corrective actions suggested (Subclause 10.2).
- And finally, the results of the audit, what, and how should management address them.

Furthermore, you need also to address the following:

- Discrepancy or consistency between the strategy and policy of the organization, as well as the strategic direction, especially if there has been a change in the structure of the organization (Subclause 5).
- The issue of support, and the availability of resources, financially or otherwise, as well as the availability of competencies needed for the system to perform the function effectively (Clause 9). This is an important discussion to have especially in difficult times, or during economic downturn.
- The need to update or change indicators to make them more relevant to the current situation and capture what is effectively being measured (Subclause 9.1).
- And finally, how effective is the action taken to seize on a new opportunity, including the opportunity to learn and to continuously improve.

Management Review Output

ISO 56002:2019 recommends that the management review should be documented. This is a crucial recommendation because it helps management keep track of their recommendations so they can use them in the next review cycle. A typical documentation example could include action to improve the IMS, a change in the measurement system, or a change to the strategy and policy of innovation.

8

Clause 10: Improvement

PURPOSE

The purpose of the chapter is to provide guidance on how to implement an improvement system and manage the different steps that link it to the shortcomings and the weaknesses identified by the IMS evaluation process. It helps you understand how you can install corrective actions to immediately stop the deviation, and establish a preventive action plan to avoid future problems.

OVERVIEW

The focus of this chapter is on steps you need to take to install a leading system that helps you identify the weaknesses and how to prevent them from happening in the future. At the end of the chapter, you will have learned how to conduct an improvement strategy based on output from your evaluation system. You will also have learned how to communicate with different parties and stakeholders internally to improve the IMS classification. There are two components to this clause:

- Deviation, non-conformity, and corrective actions
- Continual improvement

BENEFITS

At the end of this chapter, you will learn how to conduct an improvement strategy based on output from your evaluation system. You will also learn how to communicate with different parties and stakeholders internally to improve the Innovation Management System (IMS) classification.

CLASSIFICATION OF ACTIONS

The chapter is written as a *Should do* type of activity. It provides a list of best practices that can be implemented to enhance your IMS based on the specific circumstances of your organization.

SUBCLAUSE 10.1

> *The organization should determine and select opportunities for improvement and implement any necessary actions and changes to the innovation management system, considering performance evaluation results.*[*]

Clause 10 of ISO 56002:2019:2019 deals with improvement, deviation, nonconformity, and continual improvement. At the end of the performance evaluation, and as a result of the management review, you should have a relatively good idea of where the weaknesses and the strengths are of IMS. There are three actions that you need to keep in mind:

- Changes you need to introduce to improve and enhance the strength of the system.
- How you address the shortcoming of the IMS performance and how you solve the issues identified earlier during the evaluation phase.
- What actions you need to take to correct deviations from what has been set as the performance target and how your address nonconformity.

Before we get into the details, let us go over a few terminologies used by the standard.

- The deviation is an undesirable result or a gap between the actual performance and the initial target performance of the system. Examples of a deviation could be a lack of engagement of employees in the process of ideation or a final product that does not meet market expectations.
- Nonconformity, on the other hand, is simply the nonfulfillment of a required condition, like not being able to define an innovation goal or an innovation policy for your IMS.

There are three types of action you need to take when there is a deviation or a nonconformity.

- Deal with the consequences of the deviation, which simply means that you accept the consequences and try to learn from it fast, while at the same time take actions to correct it.
- Understand why the deviation happened in the first place by studying and analyzing the station.
- Update or make changes to the IMS based on your understanding of the shortcoming.

Of these three suggestions, the second one is the most important recommendation as it helps you conduct a root-cause analysis to understand the source of the deviation, where it comes from, and how and why the organization missed it in the first place. It also helps you to identify what can be done differently to avoid the same problem in the future.

Corrective Actions and Preventive Actions

Corrective Actions and Preventive Actions (CAPA) is a framework that helps managers structure efforts to conduct a root-cause analysis of the deviation and take actions to predict what could trigger the deviation or nonconformity in the future. Professor Nathan Conover, president of the consulting firm, Pathways, defines CAPA as the "immune system of the organization." It helps you identify the risk before it happens and disseminate a culture of prevention among team members.

Corrective Actions

Corrective actions help you identify deviation and nonconformity in the IMS in the following ways.

- When there is a deviation, CAPA allows you to initiate corrective actions, which should allow you to take immediate actions to eliminate the problem. For instance, if the quality of ideas coming into the funnel from your employees does not meet your target and has been identified as a deviation, then you need to enlist more employees into the system, or design an aggressive marketing campaign that targets specifically the idea suggestion system of the organization. This would be an immediate action you can take to address the deviation.
- Corrective action helps you eliminate the cause of the deviation or the cause of the nonconformity permanently. In the root-cause analysis, you should have gathered data on what happened, how it happened, why it happened, and what should be done to avoid it in the future. Generally speaking, the root-cause analysis addresses three types of problems: human error (an employee not following the protocol), a technical glitch (like in the case of a suggestions system not recording the number of ideas submitted into the system), or a process error (like in the case of sending feedback to the wrong department).

Preventive Actions

Once you corrected immediately the deviation in the preventive actions, you are putting in place a system that helps you predict when a problem is going to happen and how you could prevent it. It is like putting in place a trigger and an alarm system that sends signals when a problem is about to occur.

Of critical importance to CAPA methodology and the improvement system in general is the documentation. Documenting the source of the problem, how it was identified, and how it was solved is critical to preventing the same problem from occurring in the future.

Continual Improvement

The purpose of the root-cause analysis and the CAPA technique is to be able to standardize a process of analyzing a deviation and a nonconformity.

Once this is done, a decision about how to improve the system will have to be made.

The Standard suggests focusing on four elements of the improvement: suitability, adequacy, effectiveness, and efficiency. We have already discussed effectiveness and efficiency in performance evaluation. Let us take a look at suitability and adequacy.

Suitability simply refers to whether the functions provided by the system are suited for the goals and objectives of the IMS. Functional suitability helps you understand whether the IMS as designed, has accomplished the task assigned to it. For instance, if you assigned to the system the function to improve your innovation competitiveness, the question you need to ask is whether or not this has been achieved.

The Subclause that relates continual improvement to the IMS is the last clause in ISO 56002:2019.

> The ability to be creative and recognize innovation opportunities is the human characteristic that has set us apart from the rest of the animals and fish.
>
> *H. James Harrington*

Bibliography

Abrahamson, E. (2000). Change Without Pain. Harvard Business Review. July-August 2000.

Aghina, L., De Smet, A. and Weerda, K. (2015). Agility: It Rhymes with Stability. McKinsey Quarterly. Retrieved from https://www.mckinsey.com/business-functions/organization/our-insights/agility-it-rhymes-with-stability

Blank, S. (2015). How to Build a Corporate Innovation Lab that Works. Retrieved from https://venturebeat.com/2015/12/26/how-to-build-a-corporate-innovation-lab-that-works/

Board of Innovation. (2020). Innovation A to Z. Retrieved from https://www.boardofinnovation.com/

Bodell, L. (2014). Four Simple Steps For Defining Your Company's Innovation Vision. https://www.forbes.com/sites/groupthink/2014/11/07/four-simple-steps-for-defining-your-companys-innovation-vision/#44a2ec577357

Booker, E. (2018). 5 Ways To Fund Innovation On A Budget. Retrieved from https://www.cio.com/article/3282445/5-ways-to-fund-innovation-on-a-budget.html

Catalfamo, J. (2017). Why You Want Value Realization, Not Value Creation. Retrieved from https://www.salesforce.com/blog/2017/09/value-realization-not-value-creation.html

Central Michigan University (2011). Innovation Competency Model. Retrieved from https://drewboyd.com/innovation-competency-model/

Christensen, C., McDonald, R., Altman, E. and Palmer, J. (2018). Disruptive Innovation: An Intellectual History and Directions for Future Research. Retrieved from https://www.researchgate.net/publication/325803847_Disruptive_Innovation_An_Intellectual_History_and_Directions_for_Future_Research [accessed Apr14 2020].

Conover, C. (2020). What Is Corrective and Preventive Action? Retrieved from https://www.smartsheet.com/corrective-and-preventive-action

Trice, D., Peteraf, M. and Leih, S. (2016). Dynamic Capability and Organizational Agility: Risk, Uncertainty, and Strategy in the Innovation Economy. California Management Review. Vol 58. No 4. Summer 2016.

DeNisco Rayome, A. (2017). 91% of Top Companies use AI to Boost Customer Service, Improve Branding. Retrieved from https://www.techrepublic.com/article/91-of-top-companies-use-ai-to-boost-customer-service-improve-branding/

DeSmith, A. (2015). The Keys to Organizational Agility. Retrieved from https://www.mckinsey.com/business-functions/organization/our-insights/the-keys-to-organizational-agility

Dyer, J., Gregerson, H. and Christensen, C. (2011). Harvard Business Review. The Innovator's DNA: Mastering the Five Skills of Disruptive Innovators. Harvard Business Review Press.

Ferrier, A. (2015). Building an Effective Innovation Incubator/Accelerator: A New Approach. Retrieved from https://blog.hypeinnovation.com/building-an-effective-innovation-incubator

https://www.forbes.com/sites/robertbtucker/2017/11/20/starting-an-innovation-lab-avoid-these-pitfalls/?sh=113c08e97a2b

Harrington, H. J. and James S. (1994). Total Improvement Management: The Next Generation in Performance Improvement. McGraw Hill.

Harrington, H. J., Comner, D. and Horney, N. (1991). Project Change Management. McGraw Hill.

Harrington, H. J. and Trusko, B. (2014). Maximizing Value Propositions to Increase Project Success Rate. Productivity Press.

Innovator Board. (2020). Validation Guide: 24 Ways to Test Your Business Idea. Retrieved from https://www.boardofinnovation.com/tools/assumption-mapper/

Kotter, J. P. (2012). Leading Change. Boston, Mass.: Harvard Business Review Press.

Krisner, S. (2017). Starting An Innovation Lab? Avoid These Pitfalls.

Lengrand & Associates. (2006). SMART INNOVATION: A Practical Guide to Evaluating Innovation Programmes. Retrived from https://www.academia.edu/16037979/Smart_Innovation_A_Practical_Guide_to_Evaluating_Innovation_Programmes_Supporting_the_Monitoring_and_Evaluation_of_Innovation_Programmes

McDonald, S. (2018). Some Differences Between Quantitative and Qualitative Data. Retrieved from https://share.otf.ca/t/some-differences-between-quantitative-and-qualitative-data/639

Nonaka, I. and Takeuchi, H. (1995). The Knowledge-Creating Company: How Japanese Companies Create the Dynamics of Innovation. New York: Oxford University Press.

Pink, D. H. (2009). Drive: The Surprising Truth About What Motivates Us. Riverhead Books.

Porter, M. E. (1980). Competitive Strategy: Techniques for Analyzing Industries and Competitors. New York: Free Press.

Miller, W. L. and Morris, L. (1999). Fourth Generation R&D: Managing Knowledge, Technology, and Innovation.

Semick, J. (2020). 9 Tips for Better Customer Validation Interviews. Retrieved from https://www.productplan.com/customer-validation-interviews/

Stigler, G. (1934). Production and Distribution in the Short Run. Journal of Political Economy. 47/3.

Swabey, S. (2017). Culture clash – the challenge of innovation through acquisition. Retrieved from https://eiuperspectives.economist.com/technology-innovation/innovating-scale/article/culture-clash-challenge-innovation-through-acquisition

Thompson, A., Peteraf, M., Gamble, J. and Strickland, A. (2020). Crafting & Executing Strategy: Concepts and Cases. (22nd edition). Boston: McGraw-Hill/Irwin.

Voehl, C., Harrington H. J. and Ruggles W. (2017). Effective Portfolio Management Systems. CRC Press.

Zenger, J. (2015). Nine Behaviors That Drive Innovation. Retrieved from https://www.forbes.com/sites/jackzenger/2015/05/14/9-behaviors-that-drive-innovation/#5404a4f67593

Appendix A

Glossary

Acronyms Connation

AI	Artificial Intelligence
AIDS	Acquired Immunodeficiency Syndrome
ANSI	American National Standards Institute
ASQC	American Society for Quality Control
ASTM	American Society for Testing Materials
BU	Business Unit
CAPA	Corrective Actions and Preventive Actions
CAT	Collective Action Tool
CCM	Culture Change Management
CINO	Chief Innovation Officer
COVID-19	Coronavirus Disease 19
CRM	Customer Relations Management
4Cs	Clarity, Consistency, Communication and Competencies
CX	Customer Experience
DIY	Development, Impact, and YOU
DFD	Data-Flow Diagram
FDA	US Food and Drug Administration
FFA	Force Field Analysis
GDP	Gross Domestic Product
HIV	Human Immunodeficiency Virus
IAOIP	International Association of Innovation Professionals
IMP	Innovation Management Principles
IMS	Innovation Management Systems
IP	Innovation Policy
IPM	Intellectual Property Management
ISC	Innovation Systems Cycle
ISO	International Organization for Standardization
IST	Innovative Systems Team
KSA	Knowledge, Skills and Attitude
LiL LABS	Lowe's Innovation Lab
ML	Machine Learning
MBRCGI	Mohamed Bin Rashid Center for Government Innovation
NSD	New Service Development
NSF Intl	National Sanitation Foundation International
OCM	Organizational Change Management

OECD	Organization for Economic Co-operation and Development
OMP	Organizational Master Plan
PESTEL	Political, Economic, Social, Technological, Environmental, and Legal
PCM	Pulse Code Modulation
PDCA	Plan-Do-Check-Act
POC	Proof of Concept
PWC	Price Waterhouse and Coopers
OPM	Organizational Portfolios Management
R & D	Research and Development
ROI	Return On Investment
SECI	Socialization, Externalization, Combination, and Internalization
SIM	Strategic Intelligence Model
SIPOC	Supplier, Input, Process, Output, and Customer model
SME	Small Medium Enterprise
SSADM	Structured-Systems Analysis and Design Method
STEM	Science, Technology, Engineering, and Mathematics
SWOT	Strengths, Weaknesses, Opportunities, and Threats
TIME	Total Innovative Management Excellence
WBS	Work Breakdown Structure
WIPO	World Organization for Intellectual Property

INNOVATION DEFINITIONS

The following definitions are from a variety of sources.

- We have noted under each definition those that were taken directly from ISO 56000:2000.
- Some of the definitions are direct quotes from the IAOIP "Study Guide to the Basic Certification Exam." The study guide is used to prepare individuals for the basic exam to be certified as a professional innovator by IAOIP. These were taken from what the IAOIP is using as the Body of Knowledge for the innovation professional.

Note: In some cases there is more than one definition for the same tool/ methodology. In most of these cases all the definitions are acceptable and often the additional definitions just help to clarify what the methodology/ tool is. In some cases the preferred definition is identified.

- **5 Whys:** A simple but effective method of asking five times why a problem occurred. After each answer, ask why again using the previous response. It is surprising how this may lead to a root cause of the problem, but it does not solve the problem.
- **76 Standard Solutions:** A collection of problem solving concepts intended to help innovators develop solutions. A list was developed from referenced works and published in a comparison with the 40 principles to show that, those who are familiar with the 40 principles will be able to expand their problem solving capability. They are grouped into five categories as follows:

  1. Improving the system with no or little change; 13 standard solutions
  2. Improving the system by changing the system; 23 standard solutions
  3. System transitions; 6 standard solutions
  4. Detection and measurement; 17 standard solutions
  5. Strategies for simplification and improvement; 17 standard solutions

- **7-14-28 Processes:** This is a task-analysis assessment that involves breaking a process down into 7 tasks, then breaking it further into 14 tasks, and then another level further into 28 tasks.
- **40 Inventive Principles:** The 40 Inventive Principles that form a core part of the TRIZ methodology invented by G.S. Altshuller. These are 40 tools used to overcome technical contradictions. Each is a generic suggestion for performing an action to, and within, a technical system. For example, principle #1 (Segmentation) suggests finding a way to separate two elements of a technical system into many small interconnected elements.
- **Advocate:** The individual or group that wants to achieve a change but lacks the power to sanction it.
- **AEIOU Frameworks:** It stands for activities, environments, interactions, objects, and users. It serves as a series of prompts to remind the observer to record the multiple dimensions of a situation with textured focus on the user and their interactions with their environment.
- **ARIZ (Algorithm for Creative Problem Solving):** A procedure to guide the TRIZ student from the statement of the ideal final result (IFR) to a redefinition of the problem to be solved and then to the solutions to the problem.

- **Absence Thinking:** Absence thinking involves training the mind to think creatively about what it is thinking and not thinking. When you are thinking about a specific something, you often notice what is not there, you watch what people are not doing, and you make lists of things that you normally forget.
- **Abstract rules** are those unarticulated, yet essential, guidelines, norms, and traditions that people within a social setting tend to follow.
- **Abundance and Redundancy:** Abundance and redundancy is based on belief (not necessarily factual) that if you want a good invention that solves a problem, you need lots of ideas.
- **Administrative process** specifies what tasks need to be done and the order in which they should be accomplished, but does not give any, or at least very little, insight as to how those tasks should be realized.
- **Affinity Diagram:** Affinity diagram is a technique for organizing a variety of subjective data into categories based on the intuitive relationships among individual pieces of information. It is often used to find commonalties among concerns and ideas. It lets new patterns and relationships between ideas be discovered.
- **Affordable loss [principle]** stipulates that entrepreneurs risk no more than they are willing to lose.
- **Agile innovation** is a procedure used to create a streamlined innovation process that involves everyone. If an innovation process already exists, then the procedure can be used to improve the process resulting in a reduction of development time, resources required, costs, delays and faults.
- **Analogical Thinking and Mental Simulations:** Method of using past successes applied to similar problems by mental simulations and testing.
- **Application of Technology:** These people are intrigued by the inner workings of things. They may be engineers, but even if not, they like to analyze processes, get under the hood, and they like to use technology to solve problems (business or technical).
- **Architect:** Designs (or authorizes others to design) an end-to-end, integrated innovation process, and also promotes organization design for innovation, where each function contributes to innovation capability.

- **Attribute Listing, Morphological Analysis, and Matrix Analysis:** Attribute listing, morphological analysis, and matrix analysis techniques are good for finding new combinations of products or services. We use attribute listing and morphological analysis to generate new products and services. Matrix analysis focuses on businesses. It is used to generate new approaches, using attributes such as market sectors, customer needs, products, promotional methods, etc.
- **Attributes Based Questions:** Questions based on attributes are ones in which you look for a specific attribute of an object or idea.
- **Balanced breakthrough mode** suggests that successful new products and services are desirable for users, viable from a business perspective, and technologically feasible.
- **Barrier buster** helps navigate political landmines and removes organizational obstacles.
- **Benchmark (BMK):** A standard by which an item can be measured or judged.
- **Benchmarking (BMKG):** A systematic way to identify, understand and creatively evolve superior products, services, designs, equipment, processes, and practices to improve your organization's real performance.
- **Benchmarking Innovation:** A form of contradiction. Doing something completely new – applying an invention in a new way – it means that others are not doing the same thing. Thus, there is nothing to benchmarking.
- **Beliefs:** Beliefs is an acceptance of something to be true. They, in fact, may or may not be true.
- **Biomimicry:** Biomimetic or biomimicry is the imitation of the models, systems, and elements of nature for the purpose of solving complex human problems (Wikipedia). The transfer of ideas from biology to technology, it is the design and production of materials, structures, and systems that are modeled on biological entities and processes. The process involves understanding a problem and observational capability together with the capacity to synthesize different observations into a vision for solving a problem.
- **Bottom-Up Planning for innovation:** A process where innovations are described in portfolio requirements to meet business objectives.

- **Brainstorming:** A technique used by a group to quickly generate large lists of ideas, problems, or issues. The emphasis is on quantity of ideas, not quality.
- **Brainstorming or Operational Creativity:** Brainstorming combines a relaxed, informal approach to problem solving with lateral thinking. In most cases, brainstorming provides a free and open environment that encourages everyone to participate. While brainstorming can be effective, it's important to approach it with an open mind and a spirit of nonjudgment.
- **Brain-Writing 6-3-5:** An organized brainstorming with writing technique to come up with ideas in the aid of innovation process stimulating creativity.
- **Breakthrough, Disruptive, New–to-the-World Innovation:** Paradigm shifts that reframe existing categories. Disruptive innovation drives significant, sustainable growth by creating new consumption occasions and transforming or obsolescing markets.
- **Business Case:** A business case captures the reasoning for initiating a project or task. It is most often presented in a well-structured written document, but in some cases may come in the form of a short verbal agreement or presentation
- **Business Case Analysis:** Business case analysis is an evaluation of the potential impact a problem or opportunity and on the organization to determine if it is worthwhile investing the resources to of the opportunity.
- **Business Innovation Maturity Model (BIMM)** offers a road map to innovation management maturity.
- **Business Model Generation Canvas:** This is a tool that maps what exists. The business model canvas is a strategic management and entrepreneurial tool comprising the building blocks of a business model. The business is expressed visually on a canvas with the articulation of the nine interlocking building blocks in four cluster areas: (1) offering: value proposition, (2) customer: customer segments, customer relationships, (3) infrastructure: distribution channels, key resources, key partnerships, key activities, and (4) value: cost structure and revenue model.
- **Business model innovation** changes the method by which an organization creates and delivers value to its customers and how, in turn, it will generate revenue (capture value).

- **Business Plan:** A business plan is a formal statement of a set of business goals, the reason they are believed to be obtainable, the plan for reaching these goals. It also contains background information about the organization or team attempting to reach these goals.
- **Capital Investment:** This is the cost of manufacturing equipment, packaging equipment, and change parts.
- **Cause-and-Effect Diagram:** A visual representation of possible causes of a specific problem or condition. The effect is listed on the right hand side and the causes take the shape of fish bones. This is the reason it is sometimes called a Fishbone Diagram or an Ishikawa Diagram.
- **Change Agent:** The individual or group responsible for facilitating the implementation of the change.
- **Charter:** A charter is an expansion of the scope statement, which documents the reason that the activity was brought into existence, a description of the entity, who is sponsoring it, and why.
- **Clause:** A clause is a unit of grammatical organization next below the sentence in rank and in traditional grammar said to consist of a subject and predicate.
- **Co-Creation Innovation:** A way to introduce external catalysts, unfamiliar partners, and disruptive thinking into an organization in order to ignite innovation. The term co-creation innovation can be used in two ways: co-development and the delivery of products and services by two or more enterprises; and co-creation of products and services with customers.
- **Collaboration** is a working practice whereby individuals work together to a common purpose to achieve business benefit. Collaboration enables individuals to work together to achieve a defined and common business purpose.
- **Collective Effectiveness**: In a complex and highly competitive business environment, it is hard to sustain support R&D and innovation expenses. Networking allows firms access to different external resources like expertise, equipment, and overall know-how that has already been proven with less cost and in a shorter period.
- **Collective Learning:** Networking not only helps firms gain access to expensive resources like machinery, laboratory equipment, and technology, but it also facilitates shared learning via experience and

good practice sharing events. This brings new insight and ideas for a firms' current and future innovation projects.

- **Combination Methods:** A by-product of already applied process, system, product, service wise solutions integrated into a one solution system to produce one end-result that is unique.
- **Communication of Innovation Information:** Employees vary greatly in their ability to evaluate potentially significant market information and convey qualified information to pertinent receivers in the product development stream.
- **Comparative Analysis:** A detailed study/comparison of an organization's product and/or service to the competitors' comparable product and or service.
- **Competitive Analysis:** It consists of a detailed study of an organization's competitor products, services, and methods to identify their strengths and weaknesses.
- **Competitive shopping** (sometimes called mystery shopper) is the use of an individual or a group of individuals that goes to a competitor's facilities or directly interacts with the competitor's facilities to collect information related to how the competitor's processes, services and or products are interfacing with the external customer. Data is collected related to key external customer impact areas and compared to the way the organization is operating in those areas.
- **Conceptual Clustering:** The inherent structure of the data (concepts) that drives cluster formation. Since this technique is dependent on language, it is open to interpretation and consensus is required.
- **Concept Tree (See Conceptual Clustering)**
- **Confirmation Bias:** The tendency of people to include or exclude data that does not fit a preconceived position.
- **Consumer co-creation** means fostering individualized interactions and experience outcomes between a consumer and the producer of the producers organization output. This can be done throughout the whole product lifecycle. Customers may share their needs and comments and even help to spread the word or create communities in the commercialization phase.
- **Context:** ISO 56000 defines context as the combination of internal and external issues they can have an effect on the organization's

approach to developing and achieving is objectives. It is also sometimes called organizational environment.*

- **Context of the Organization:** The combination of internal and external factors and conditions that can have an effect on an organization's approach to its products, services, and investments.
- **Contingency Planning:** A process that primarily delivers a risk management strategy for a business to deal with the unexpected events effectively and the strategy for the business recovery to the normal position. The output of this process is called "contingency plan" or "business continuity and recovery plan."
- **Contradiction Analysis:** The process of identifying and modeling contradictory requirements within a system, which, if unresolved, will limit the performance of the system in some manner.
- **Contradictions:** TRIZ defines two kinds of contradictions, physical and technical.
- **Convergent Thinking:** Vetting the various ideas to identify the best workable solutions.
- **Copyrights:** Legal protection of original works of artistic authorship.
- **Core or line extensions, renovation, sustaining close-in innovation** extends and adds value to an existing line or platform of products via size, flavor, or format. It is incremental improvement to existing products.
- **Cost–Benefit Analysis (CBA):** A financial analysis where the cost of providing (producing) a benefit is compared the expected value of the benefit to the customer, stakeholder, etc.
- **Counseling and Mentoring:** These people love teaching, coaching, and mentoring. They like to guide employees, peers, and even their clients to better performance
- **Crazy quilt principle** is based on the expert entrepreneur's strategy to continuously seek out people who may become valuable contributors to his or her venture.
- **Create:** Make something: to bring something into existence. The difference between creativity and innovation is the output from the

---

*©ISO. This material is excerpted from ISO 56000:2020, with permission of the American National Standards Institute (ANSI) on behalf of the International Organization for Standardization. All rights reserved.

innovation has to be a value added output while the output from creativity does not have to be value added.

- **Creative (Preferred Definition):** Using the ability to make or think of new things involving the process by which new ideas, stories, products, etc., are created.
- **Creative Problem Solving (CPS):** A methodology developed in the 1950s by Osborn and Parnes. The method calls for solving problems in sequential stages with the systematic alternation of divergent and convergent thinking. It can be enhanced by the use of various creative tools and techniques during different stages of the process.
- **Creative Production:** These people love beginning projects, making something original, and making something out of nothing. This can include processes or services as well as tangible objects. They are most engaged when inventing unconventional solutions. In an innovation process, these people may thrive on the ideation phase, creating multiple solutions to the identified problems.
- **Creative Thinking:** Creative thinking is all about finding fresh and innovative solutions to problems, and identifying opportunities to improve the way that we do things, along with finding and developing new and different ideas. It can be described as a way of looking at problems or situations from a fresh perspective that suggests unorthodox solutions, which may look unsettling at first.
- **Creativity:** Creativity is using the ability to make or think of new things involving the process by which new ideas, stories, products, etc., are created.

  (**Note:** You can have creativity which is not innovative, but you cannot have innovative activities that are not creative.)
- **Cross-Industry Innovation:** refers to innovations stemming from cross-industry affinities and approaches involving transfers from one industry to another.
- **Crowdfunding:** The collective effort of individuals who network and pool their money, usually via the Internet, to support efforts initiated by other people or organizations.
- **Crowdsourcing:** A term for a varied group of methods that share the attribute that they all depend on some contribution from the crowd.
- **Culture** is all about how people behave, treat each other, and treat customers. It is created based upon a person's background, history, heritage, religion, and beliefs.

- **Culture creator e**nsures the spirit of innovation is understood, celebrated, and aligned with the strategy of the organization.
- **Customer advocate** keeps the voice of the customer alive in the hearts, minds, and actions of innovators and teams.
- **Customer profile:** Empathy Map is a technique for creating a profile of your customer beyond the simple demographics of age, gender, and income that has been in use for some time
- **Decision:** A decision is a specific result that a person or system aims to achieve within a time frame and with available resources.
- **DVF model (desirable, viable, feasible):** Another name for the balanced breakthrough model.
- **Design innovation** focuses on the functional dimension of the job-to-be-done, as well as the social and emotional dimensions, which are sometimes more important than functional aspects.
- **Design for X (DFX):** Both a philosophy and methodology that can help organizations change the way that they manage product development and become more competitive. DFX is defined as a knowledge-based approach for designing products to have as many desirable characteristics as possible. The desirable characteristics include: quality, reliability, serviceability, safety, user friendliness, etc. This approach goes beyond the traditional quality aspects of function, features, and appearance of the item.
- **Design of Experiments:** This method is a statistically based method that can reduce the number of experiments needed to establish a mathematical relationship between a dependent variable and independent variables in a system.
- **Directed Innovation:** Directed innovation is a systematic approach that helps cross-functional teams apply problem-solving methods like brainstorming, TRIZ, creative problem solving, assumption storming, inventing, and provocation to a specifically defined problem in order to create novel and patentable solutions
- **Direction setter** creates and communicates vision and business strategy in a compelling manner, and ensures innovation priorities are clear.
- **Disruptive innovation** is a process where a product or service takes root initially in simple applications at the bottom of a market and then relentlessly moves upmarket, eventually displacing established competitors.
- **Divergent Thinking:** Coming up with many ideas or solutions to a problem.

- **Diversity Trumps Ability Theorem** states that a randomly selected collection of problem solvers outperforms a collection of the best individual problem solvers.
- **Drive to Acquire:** The drive to acquire tangible goods such as food, clothing, housing, and money, but also intangible goods such as experiences, or events that improve social status.
- **Drive to Bond:** The need for common kinship bonding to larger collectives such as organizations, associations, and nations.
- **Drive to Comprehend:** People want to be challenged by their jobs, to grow and learn.
- **Drive to defend** includes defending your role and accomplishments. Fulfilling the drive to defend leads to feelings of security and confidence.
- **Edison method** consists of five strategies that cover the full spectrum of innovation necessary for success.
- **Effectuation** is taking action toward unpredictable future states using currently controlled resources and with imperfect knowledge about current circumstances.
- **Ekvall:** Ekvall's model of the creative climate identifies ten factors that need to be present: idea time; challenge; freedom; idea support; conflicts; debates; playfulness, humor; trust, openness; dynamism; liveliness.
- **Elevator Speech:** An elevator speech is a clear, brief message or "commercial" about the innovative idea you are in the process of implementing. It communicates what it is, what you're looking for and how it can benefit a company or organization. It's typically no more than two minutes, or the time it takes people to ride from the top to the bottom of a building in an elevator.
- **Emergent collaboration** is a social network activity where a shared perspective emerges from a group through spontaneous (unplanned) interactions.
- **Emotional Rollercoaster:** It is a notion, similar to journey mapping, that identifies areas of high anxiety in a process and, as such, exposes opportunities for new solutions
- **Enterprise Control:** These people love to run projects or teams and control the assets. They enjoy owning a transaction or sale, and tend to ask for as much responsibility as possible in work situations.

- **Entity:** ISO 56000:2020 defines entity as anything perceivable or conceivable. For example, a product, service, process, model, method, or a combination thereof.[*]
- **Entrepreneur:** Someone who exercises initiative by organizing a venture to take benefit of an opportunity and, as the decision maker, decides what, how, and how much of a good or service will be produced. An entrepreneur supplies risk capital as a risk taker, and monitors and controls the business activities.
- **Era-based questions** require that you put yourself in the position of thinking about a question in a different time or place from the one you are currently in. For example, instead of asking yourself the general question,
- **Experiments** in this context represent a mixture of surveys and observations in an artificial setting and can be summarized as test procedures.
- **FAST:** An innovative technique to develop a graphical representation showing the logical relationships between the functions of a project, product, process or service based on the questions "How" and "Why."
- **Fast Action Solution Team (FAST):** This is a methodology that sets aside a group of individuals for two consecutive days to solve a specific problem, game management concurrence with a solution, and get agreement on how the problem was dissolved and who will take the action.
- **Failure Mode Effects Analysis:** A matrix-based method used to investigate potential serious problems in a proposed system prior to final design. It creates a risk priority number that can be used to create a ranking of the biggest risks and then ranks the proposed solution.
- **Financial management** activities and manages financial programs and operations, including acquiring funding for the project, accounting liaison and pay services; budget preparation and execution; program, cost, and economic analysis; and non-appropriated fund oversight. It is held responsible and accountable for the ethical and intelligent use of investors' resources.

- **Financial reporting** includes the main financial statements (income statement, balance sheet, statement of cash flows, statement of retained earnings, and statement of stockholders' equity) plus other financial information such as annual reports, press releases, etc.
- **Fishbone Diagrams, aka Ishikawa Diagrams:** A mnemonic diagram that looks like the skeleton of a fish and has words for the major spurs that prompt causes for the problem.
- **Five Dimensions of a Service Innovation Model:**

  1. Organizational
  2. Product
  3. Market
  4. Process
  5. Input

- **Flowcharting:** A method of graphically describing an existing or proposed process by using simple symbols, lines and words to pictorially display the sequence of activities. Flowcharts are used to understand, analyze, and communicate the activities that make up major processes throughout an organization. It can be used to graphically display movement of product, communications, and knowledge related to anything takes an input and value to it and produces an output.
- **Focus group** is made up of a group of individuals that are knowledgeable of and or would make use of the subject being discussed. The facilitator is used to lead the discussions and record key information related to the discussions. The group is brought together so that the organizer and gain information and insight into a specific subject or the reaction to a proposed product.
- **Force Field Analysis:** A visual aid for pinpointing and analyzing elements which resist change (restraining forces) or push for change (driving forces). This technique helps drive improvement by developing plans to overcome the restrainers and make maximum use of the driving forces.
- **Forecasting** is predicting what the future will look like.
- **Four Dimensions of Innovation:**

  1. Technology: technical uncertainty of innovation projects
  2. Market: targeting of innovations on new or not previously satisfied customer needs

3. Organization: the extent of organizational change
4. Innovation environment: impact of innovations on the innovation environment

- **Four Square Model:** The four-square model is a design process that is composed of two sets of polar extremes: understand-make and abstract-concrete. It consists of five steps:

  1. Problem framing: identify what problem we intend to solve and outline a general approach for how we will solve it.
  2. Research: gather qualitative and quantitative data related to the problem frame.
  3. Analysis: unpack and interpret the data, building conceptual models that help explain what we found.
  4. Synthesis: generate ideas and recommendations using the conceptual model as a guide.
  5. Decision making: conduct evaluative research to determine which concepts or recommendations best fit the desirable, viable, and feasible criteria.

- **Functional Analysis:** A standard method of systems engineering that has been adapted into TRIZ. The subject-action-object method is most frequently used now. It is a graphical and primarily qualitative methodology used to focus the problem solver on the functional relationships (good or bad) between system components.
- **Functional Model:** A structured representation of the functions (activities, actions, processes, operations) within the modeled system or subject area.
- **Functional innovation** involves identifying the functional components of a problem or challenge and then addressing the processes underlying those functions which are in need of improvement. Through this process, overlaps, gaps, discontinuities, and other inefficiencies can be identified.
- **Futurist:** Looks toward the future, scouts new opportunities, helps everyone see their potential. Enables people throughout the organization to discover the emerging trends that most impact their work.
- **Generic creativity tools** are a set of commonly used tools that are designed to assist individuals and groups to originate new and different thought patterns. They have many common characteristics

like thinking positive, not criticizing ideas, thinking out of the box, right brain thinking, etc. Some of the typical tools are benchmarking, brainstorming, six thinking hats, storyboarding, and TRIZ.

- **Goal:** The end toward which effort is directed: the terminal point in a race. These are always specified in time and magnitude so they are easy to measure. Goals have key ingredients. First, they specifically state the target for the future state and second, they give the time interval in which the future state will be accomplished. These are key inputs to every strategic plan.
- **Goal-based questions** pose the end goal without specifying the means or locking you into particular attributes.
- **Go-to-Market Investment:** This is the cost of slotting fees for distribution, trade spending, advertising dollars (creative development, media spend), promotional programs and digital, social media.
- **Governance** determines who has power, who makes decisions, how other players make their voice heard, and who is accountable. The corporate governance framework consists of (1) explicit and implicit contracts between the company and the stakeholders for distribution of responsibilities, rights, and rewards, (2) procedures for reconciling the sometimes conflicting interests of stakeholders in accordance with their duties, privileges, and roles, and (3) procedures for proper supervision, control, and information-flows to serve as a system of checks-and-balances (Wilfong and Ito, 2020).
- **HU Diagrams** are effective way of providing a visual picture of the interface between harmful and useful characteristics of a system or process.
- **Hitchhiking:** When a breakthrough occurs, it is a fertile area for innovators. They should hitch-hike on the breakthrough to create new applications and improvements that can be inventions.
- **I-TRIZ** is an abbreviation for Ideation TRIZ which is a restructuring and enhancement of classical TRIZ methodology based upon the modern research and practices. It is a guided set of step-by-step questions and instructions that aid teams in approaching, thinking, and dealing with systems targeted for innovation.
- **Ideal Final Result (IFR)** states that in order to improve a system or process, the output of that system must improve (i.e., volume,

quantity, quality, etc.), the cost of the system must be reduced, or both. It is an implementation-free description of the situation after the problem has been solved.

- **Idea Priority Index** prioritizes ideas based on the potential cost–benefit analysis, associated risks, and likely time to commercialize the idea.
- **Idea Selection by Grouping or Tiers:** Groups can be helpful in evaluation of tiers like top ideas, or worst ideas. Both grouping and tiers are only useful in a batch evaluation process, not a continuous process.
- **Idea Selection by Checklist or Threshold:** An individual idea's list of attributes must match the preset checklist or threshold in order to pass (e.g., be implemented in six months, profit at least $500,000, and require no more than two employees).
- **Idea Selection by Personal Preference:** A manager, director, line-employee, or even expert is used to screen an idea based on his or her own preferences.
- **Idea Selection by Point Scoring:** Uses a scoring sheet to rate a particular idea on its attributes (e.g., an idea that can be implemented in six months gets +5 points, and one that can make more than × dollars gets +10 points). The points are then added together and the top ideas are ranked by highest total point scores.
- **Idea Selection by Priority Index (IPI):** The IPI prioritizes ideas based on the potential cost–benefit analysis, associated risks, and likely time to commercialize the idea, using the following relationship:

  1. Annualized potential impact of the idea = ($) × probability of acceptance
  2. IPI = Annualized cost of idea development ($) × time to commercialize (year)

- **Idea Selection by Voting:** Individual(s) can vote openly or in a closed ballot (i.e., blind or peer review). Voting can be weighted or an individual, such as expert, can give multiple votes to a given idea.
- **Image Board, Storyboarding, Role Playing:** These are collections of physical manifestations (image collages or product libraries) of the desirable (or undesirable if you are using that as a motivator) to help generate ideas, or to facilitate conversations with users about what they want.

- **Imaginary brainstorming** expands the brainstorming concept past the small group problem-solving tool to an electronic system that presents the problem/opportunity to anyone that is approved to participate in the electronic system. Creative ideas are collected and a smaller group is used to analyze and identify innovative, imaginative concepts.
- **Indexing:** Providing a tag for a fact, piece of information, or experience, so that you can retrieve it when you want it.
- **Influence Through Language and Ideas:** These people love expressing ideas for the enjoyment of storytelling, negotiating, or persuading. This can be in written or verbal form, or both.
- **Initiating Sponsor:** The individual or group with the power to initiate or to legitimize proposed project or program related to all of the affected people in the organization.
- **Innovation** is converting ideas into tangible products, services, or processes. The challenge that every organization faces is how to convert good ideas into profit. That's what the innovation process is all about.
- **Innovation:** (Preferred Definition) The process of translating an idea or invention into an intangible product, service, or process that creates value for which the consumer (the entity that uses the output from the idea) is willing to pay for it more than the cost to produce it.
- **Innovation:** In the latest version of ISO Standards 56000 innovation is defined as a "new or changed entity, realizing or redistributing value.

    Note 1 to entry: Novelty and value are related to, and determined by the perception of, the organization and relevant interested parties

    Note 2 to entry: An innovation can be a product, service, process, model, method etc.

    Note 3 to entry: Innovation is an outcome. The word "innovation" sometimes refers to activities or processes resulting in, or aiming for, innovation. When innovation is used in this sense, it should always be used with some form of qualifier, for example "innovation activities."

    Note 4 to entry: For the purpose of statistical measurement, refer to the *Oslo Manual 2018*, 4th edition, by OECD/Eurostat.*

- **Innovation Benchmarking:** Comparing one organization, process, or product, to another that is considered a standard.
- **Innovation Blueprint:** A visual map to the future that enables people within an enterprise or community to understand where they are headed and how they can build that future together. The blueprint is not a tool for individual innovators or teams to improve a specific product or service or to create new ones. Rather the Innovation Blueprint is a tool for designing an enterprise that innovates extremely effectively on an ongoing basis.
- **Innovation Culture:** A culture that requires continuous learning, practices and exceptions of risk and failure, holds individuals accountable for action and has aggressive timing.
- **Innovation management** is the collection of ideas for new or improved products and services and their development, implementation, and exploitation in the market.
- **Innovation management:** (Preferred Definition) ISO 56000 defines innovation management as management with regard to innovation.

  Note 1: Innovation management can include establishing an innovation vision, innovation strategy, innovation policy, and innovation objectives and organizational structures and innovation processes to achieve these objectives through planning, support, operations, performance evaluation and improvement.[*]

  Note 2: The authors prefer the definition of innovation management as the handling of all the activities needed to innovate, such as creating ideas, developing, prioritizing and implementing them, as well as putting them into practice.

- **Innovation Management System (IMS):** ISO 56000 defines IMS as a management system with regard to innovation.[*]
- **Innovation Master Plan Framework** consists of five major elements. They are strategy, portfolio, processes, culture, and infrastructure.
- **Innovation metrics** are measurements to validate that the organization innovate. They typically are:

1. Annual R&D budget as a percentage of annual sales
2. Number of patents filed in the past year

---

3. Total R&D headcount or budget as a percentage of sales
4. Number of active projects
5. Number of ideas submitted by employees
6. Percentage of sales from products introduced in the past × year(s)

- **Innovation Portfolios:** A portfolio is a centralized collection of independent projects or programs that are grouped together to facilitate their prioritization, effective management, and resource optimization in order to meet strategic organizational objectives.
- **Innovative Categories:** Most service innovations can be categorized into one of the following groups:

  1. Incremental or radical, based on the degree of new knowledge
  2. Continuous or discontinuous, depending on its degree of price performance improvements over existing technologies. Sometimes called evolutionary innovation.
  3. Sustaining or disruptive, relative to the performance of the existing products
  4. Exploitative or evolutionary, innovation in terms of pursuing new knowledge and developing new services for emerging markets

- **Innovative Problem Solving:** A subset of problem solving in that a solution must resolve a limitation in the system under analysis in order to be an innovative solution.
- **Innovator:** An innovator is an individual that creates a unique idea that is marketable and guides it through the innovative process so that is value to the customer is greater than the resources required to produce.
- **Insight:** A linking or connection between ideas and the mind. The connections matter more than the pieces.
- **Inspiration:** The word inspiration is from the Latin word *inspire*, meaning "to blow into."
- **Inspire Innovation Tools:** These are tools that stimulate the unique creative powers. Some of them are absence thinking, biomimicry, concept tree, creative thinking, ethnography, Harmful Useful (HU) diagrams, imaginary brainstorming, I-TRIZ, and storyboarding.
- **Integrated innovation systems** cover the full end-to-end innovation process, and ensures the practices and tools are aligned and flow easily from one to the other.

- **Intellectual Property Rights:** The expression "intellectual property rights" refers to a number of legal rights that serve to protect various products of the intellect (i.e., "innovations"). These rights, while different from one another, can and do sometimes offer overlapping legal protection.
- **Interclause of Different Sets of Knowledge:** Networking creates different relationships to be built across knowledge frontiers and opens up the participating organizations to new stimuli and experience.
- **Interested Party:** ISO 56000 defines interested party as a person or organization that can affect, be affected by, or perceive itself to be affected by a decision or activity.

  Note: This constitutes one of the common terms and core definitions of the high level structure for ISO management system standards.*
- **Intrapreneur:** An intrapreneur is an employee of a large corporation who is given freedom and financial support to create new products, services, systems, etc., and does not have to follow the corporation's usual routines or protocols.
- **Joint Risk Taking:** Since innovation is a highly risky activity, it is very difficult for a single firm to undertake it by itself and this impedes the development of new technologies. Joint collaboration minimizes the risk for each firm and encourages them to engage in new activities. This is the logic behind many precompetitive consortia collaborations for risky R&D.
- **Journey Map or Experience Evaluations:** It is a diagram that illustrates the steps your customer(s) go through in engaging with your company, whether it is a product, an online experience, a retail experience, a service, or any combination of these
- **Kano Analysis:** A pictorial way to look at customer levels of dissatisfaction and satisfaction to define how they relate to the different product characteristics. Kano method is based on the idea that features can be plotted using axes of fulfillment and delight. This defines areas of: must haves, more is better, and delighters. It

---

classifies customer preferences into five categories, Attractive, One-dimensional, Must-be, Indifferent, and Reverse

- **Kepner Trego:** This method is very useful for processes that were performing well and then developed a problem. It is a good step-by-step method that is based on finding the cause of the problem by asking what changed since the process was working fine.
- **Key Components of Successful Innovation:**

    1. Funding for innovation
    2. Trained and educated staff
    3. Collaborative environment
    4. Key individuals
    5. Corporate infrastructure

- **Knowledge Management (KM):** A strategy that turns an organization's intellectual assets, both recorded information and the talents of its members, into greater productivity, new value, and increased competitiveness. It's the leveraging of collective wisdom to increase responsiveness and innovation.
- **Leadership** is a process of social influence, which maximizes the efforts of others, toward the achievement of a goal.

    Note: Notice key elements of this definition. Leadership stems from social influence, not authority or power. Leadership requires others, and that implies they don't need to be "direct reports."
- **Leadership Metrics:** Leadership metrics address the behaviors that all managers and leaders must exhibit to support a culture of innovation.
- **Lemonade Principle** is based on the old adage that goes, "If life throws you lemons, make lemonade." In other words, make the best of the unexpected.
- **Link Between Climate and Organizational Innovation:** Nine areas need to be evaluated to determine this linkage. They are:

    1. Challenge, motivation
    2. Freedom
    3. Trust
    4. Idea time
    5. Play and humor
    6. Conflicts
    7. Idea support

8. Debates
9. Risk-taking

- **Live-ins, Shadowing, and Immersion Labs:** They are designed to resemble the retail or home environment and gather extensive information about product purchase or use. These labs are used to both test the known, launch new product, and to observe user behavior.
- **Lotus Blossom:** This technique is based on the use of analytical capacities and helps to generate a great number of ideas that will possibly provide the best solution to the problem to be addressed by the management group. It uses a six-step process.
- **Management Principle** is a comprehensive and fundamental rule. A management principal is a statement that every manager is committed to govern their interaction and behaviors. Principles are the conditions that the organization promises the stakeholders that these are the laws that the organization will live up to. Many organizations feel that principles are too strict requirements and instead have a set of beliefs or values.
- **Managing People and Relationships:** Unlike counseling and mentoring people, these people live to manage others on a day-to-day basis.
- **Marketing research** can be defined as the systematic and objective identification, collection, analysis dissemination and use of information that is undertaken to improve decision making related to products and services that are provided to external customers.
- **Market Research Tools:** The following are some typical marketing research tools:

1. Analysis of Customer Complaints
2. Contextual Inquiry
3. Empathic Design
4. Cross-Industry Innovation
5. Crowdsourcing
6. Lead User Technique
7. Netnography
8. Outcome-Driven Innovation
9. Sequence-Oriented Problem Identification
10. Sequential Incident Technique

11. Tracking, Panel
12. Analytic Hierarchy Process
13. Concept Test, Virtual Concept Test
14. Conjoint Analysis
15. Free Elicitation
16. Information Acceleration
17. Information Pump
18. Kelly Repertory Grid
19. Laddering
20. Perceptual Mapping
21. Product Test, Product Clinic
22. Virtual Stock Market, Securities Trading of Concepts

- **Matrix Diagram (Decision Matrix):** A systematic way of selecting from larger lists of alternatives. They can be used to select a problem from a list of potential problems, select primary root causes from a larger list or to select a solution from a list of alternatives.
- **Medici Effect:** The book by this name describes the interclause of significantly different ideas that can produce cross-pollination of fields and create more breakthroughs.
- **Mentor:** Coaches and guides innovation champions and teams.
- **Methodology Merger:** Each methodology brings with it certain strengths and weaknesses which serve to fulfill specific steps and activities represented on the problem-solving pathway. When combined together and properly utilized, these methodologies create a very effective and useful outcome.
- **Mind Mapping:** An innovation tool and method that starts with a main idea or goal in the middle, and then flows or diagrams ideas out from this one main subject. By using mind maps, you can quickly identify and understand the structure of a subject. You can see the way that pieces of information fit together in a format that your mind finds easy to recall and quick to review. They are also called Spider Diagrams.
- **Mini problem** is one that is solved without introducing new elements. We have to understand resources, since the emphasis is on solving the problem without introducing anything new to the system.
- **Moccasins/Walking in the Customer's Shoes:** Moccasins approach is more often called walking in the customer's shoes. This activity allows members of the organizations group to directly

participate in the process that the potential customer is subjected to by physically playing the role of the customer.

- **Myers-Briggs (MBTI):** This is a survey-style measurement instrument used in determining an individual's social style preference.
- **Network-centric approach** is taught in colleges and based on collaborative brainstorming. The concept is that more minds are better than one at a given time.
- **Networker:** Works across organizational boundaries to engage stakeholders, promotes connections across boundaries, and secures widespread support.
- **Nominal Group Technique:** A technique for prioritizing a list of problems, ideas, or issues that gives everyone in the group or team equal voice in the priority setting process.
- **Non-Algorithmic Interactions:** Actions with cognitive and physical materials of a project whose results you can't predict for certain, those results you don't know.
- **Nonprobability sampling techniques** use samples drawn according to specific and considered characteristics and are therefore based on the researcher's subjective judgment.
- **Nonprofit** is an organization specifically formed to provide a service or product on a not-for-profit basis as determined by applicable law.
- **Normative reference** in ISO parlance is equivalent to a referenced document. It is indispensable to the application of the standard.
- **Objective:** ISO 56000 defines objective as: result to be achieved.
  - **Note 1 to entry:** An objective can be strategic, tactical, or operational.
  - **Note 2 to entry:** Objectives can relate to different disciplines (such as financial, health and safety, and environmental goals) and can apply at different levels (such as strategic, organization-wide, project, product, initiative and process).
  - **Note 3 to entry:** An objective can be expressed in other ways, e.g., as an intended outcome, a purpose, an operational criterion, as an innovation objective), or by the use of other words with similar meaning (e.g., aim, goal, or target).
  - **Note 4 to entry:** In the context of innovation management systems, innovation objectives are set by the organization

consistent with the innovation strategy and the innovation policy, to achieve specific results.

- **Note 5 to entry:** This constitutes one of the common terms and core definitions of the high level structure for ISO management system standards. The original definition has been modified by adding "initiative" to Note 2 to entry and "innovation strategy" to Note 4 to entry.*

  Note: It is important to understand that ISO 56000 uses objectives rather than goals. This requires a greater depth of specific in defining future performance for the IMS.

- **Observation** in this context means the recording of behavioral patterns of people, objects, and events in order to obtain information.
- **Online Collaboration:** Convening an online brainstorming or idea generation session so members can participate remotely, instead of organizing a group in a room together,
- **Online Management Platforms:** These are used to foster innovation enable large groups of people to innovate together — across geographies and time zones. Users can post ideas and value propositions online and can collaborate with others to make these stronger. The community can rate and rank ideas or value propositions, post comments and recommendations, link to resources, build on each other's ideas, and support each other to improve each other's innovations.
- **Open Innovation:** The use and application of collective intelligence to produce a creative solution to a challenging problem, as well as to organize large amounts of data and information. The term refers to the use of both inflows and outflows of knowledge to improve internal innovation and expand the markets for external exploitation of innovation. The central idea behind open innovation is that, in a world of widely distributed knowledge, companies cannot afford to rely entirely on their own research, but should instead buy or license processes or inventions (i.e., patents) from other companies.
- **Opportunity-driven model** is more representative of street-smart individuals who take an idea at the right time and the right place,

---

devise a solution, know how to market it, and capitalize on their breakthrough. They also appear to be lucky,

- **Organizational capability metrics** focus on the infrastructure and process of innovation. Capability measures provide focus for initiatives geared toward building repeatable and sustainable approaches to invention and reinvention.
- **Organizational Change Management (OCM)** is a comprehensive set of structured procedures for the decision making, planning, executing and evaluation activities. It is designed to minimize the resistance and cycle time to implementing a change.
- **Organizational Effectiveness Measurements:** The following is a typical way of measuring the organizations innovation effectiveness. Typically it is measured in key areas of management, processes, product, sales, internal services, and sales and marketing. Each area is typically evaluated in a combination of the following:

  1. Committed leadership
  2. Clear strategy
  3. Market insights
  4. Creative people
  5. Innovative culture
  6. Competitive technologies
  7. Effective processes
  8. Supportive infrastructure
  9. Managed projects

- **Organizational Master Plan (OMP):** The organizational master plan is the combination of the business plan, strategic business plan, the strategic improvement plan, and the annual operating plan.
- **Organization Internal Boundaries:** Employee silos often isolate chains of command and communication, which can impede the progress of a valuable idea through product development
- **Osborn Method:** Original brainstorming method developed by Alex F. Osborn by primarily requiring solicitation of unevaluated ideas (divergent thinking), followed by convergent organization and evaluation
- **Outcome-Driven Innovation (ODI)** is built around the theory that people buy products and services to complete tasks or jobs they value. As people complete these jobs, they have certain measurable outcomes that they are attempting to achieve. It links a company's

value creation activities to customer-defined metrics. Included in this method is the opportunity algorithm which helps designers determine the needs that satisfied customers has. This help determine which features are most important to work on. Most important is this intention of trying to find unmet needs which may lead to new and innovative products/services.

- **Personality** is defined as an individual or group's impact on other individuals or groups.
- **PESTEL Frameworks** focus on the macroeconomic factors that influence a business. These factors are: 1. Political 2. Economic 3. Social 4. Technological 5. Environmental.
- **Patents:** A government-granted right that literally and strictly permits the patent owner to prevent others from practicing the claimed invention.
- **Performance Engine Project:** A project that seeks, to improve a current level of performance and not to create a new value proposition.
- **Permeability to Innovation Idea Sources:** Information and idea seeking differs greatly among companies.
- **Physical contradictions** are situations where one requirement has contradictory, opposite values to another.
- **Pilot in the Plane Principle** is based on the concept of *control*, using effectual logic and is referred to as *non-predictive control.* Expert entrepreneurs believe they can determine their individual futures best by applying effectual logic to the resources they currently control.
- **Pipeline model,** as driven by chance or innate genius, is a somewhat common perception of the innovation process. Inventors who work in research drive the pipeline model and development environment on a specific topic, explore new ideas, and develop new products and services.
- **Plan-Do-Check-Act (PDCA):** A structured approach for the improvement of services, products, and/or processes. It is also sometimes referred to as plan-do-check-adjust. Another version of this PDCA cycle is OPDCA. The added "O" stands for observation or as some versions say "Grasp the current condition." The Plan-Do-Check-Act (PDCA) cycle is a very simple approach to project management that can be used effectively on non-complex programs and for implementing corrective action.

   Note: Often it is incorrectly called "The Deming Cycle."

- **Planning:** As a result, the one that we will use is the following: Planning is thinking about the activities required to achieve a desired goal. Planning combines forecasting with preparation of scenarios and how to react to them. It involves the creation and maintenance of a plan.
- **Platform:** A consumer need-based opportunity that inspires multiple innovation ideas with a sustainable competitive advantage to drive growth.
- **Portfolio Management:** The ongoing management of innovation to ensure delivery against stated goals and innovation strategy.
- **Post-Fordist:** Companies after the Henry Ford efficient production era where managers wielded inordinate responsibility for profit and loss and the new postmodern leaders of the global economy, who are responsible for developing talented teams.
- **Potential investor presentation** is a short PowerPoint presentation designed to convince an individual or group to invest their money in an organization and/or a potential project. It can be a presentation to an individual or group not part of the organization or the management of the organization that the presenter is presently employed by.
- **Practices:** To look at all the inputs that we have available for selection and all the available operations or routines that we can perform on those inputs, then to select those inputs and operations that will give us our desired results.
- **Primary data** is data collected from the field or expected customer.
- **Primary sources** are gathered directly from the source; for instance, if new customer opinions were required to justify a new product, then customer interviews, focus groups, or surveys would suffice.
- **Principles of Invention:** A set of 40 principles from a variety of fields such as software, healthcare, electronics, mechanics, ergonomics, finance, marketing, etc., used to solve problems.
- **Proactive Personal Creativity:** Proactive strategies to be especially effective in increasing the originality and effectiveness of personal creativity:

  1. Self-trust
  2. Open up
  3. Clean and organize
  4. Make mistakes

5. Get angry
6. Get enthusiastic
7. Listen to hunches
8. Subtract instead of adding
9. Physical motion
10. Question the questions
11. Pump up the volume
12. Read, read, read

- **Probability sampling techniques** use samples randomly drawn from the whole population.
- **Probe-and-Learn Strategy:** Where non-working prototypes are developed in rapid succession, tested with potential customers, and feedback is sought on each prototype.
- **Problem Detection and Affinity Diagrams:** Focus groups, mall intercepts, mail, and phone surveys that ask customers what problems they have. They are all forms of problem detection. The responses are grouped according to commonality (affinity diagrams) to strengthen the validity of the response. Developing the correct queries and interpreting the responses are critical to the usefulness of the method
- **Problem Solving:** Generating a workable solution.
- **Process:** A series of interrelated activities or tasks that take an input, add value to it, and produces an output.
- **Process innovation** is the innovation of internal processes. New or improved delivery methods may occur in all aspects of the supply chain in an organization.
- **Process Redesign:** A methodology used to streamline a current process with the objective of reducing cost and cycle time by 30% to 60% while improving output quality from 20% to 200%.
- **Process Re-Engineering:** A methodology used to radically change the way a process is designed by developing an aggressive vision of how it should perform and using a group of enablers to prepare a new process design that is not hampered by the present processes paradigms. Use when a 60% to 80% reduction in cost or cycle time is required. Process reengineering is sometimes referred to as New Process Design and/or Process Innovation.

- **Product innovation** is a multidisciplinary process usually involving many different functions within an organization and, in large organizations, often in coordination across continents.
- **Project Management:** The application of knowledge, skills, tools, and techniques to project activities in order to meet or exceed stakeholders' needs and expectations from a project (Source: PMBOK Guide).
- **Proof of Concept (POC):** A demonstration, the purpose of which is to verify that certain concepts or theories have the potential for real-world application. A Proof of Concept is a test of an idea made by building a prototype of the application. It is an innovative, scaled-down version of the system you intend to develop. The Proof of Concept provides evidence that demonstrates that a business model, product, service, system, or idea is feasible and will function as intended.
- **Pyramiding:** A search technique in which the searcher simply asks an individual (the starting point) to identify one or more others who he or she thinks has higher levels of expertise
- **Qualitative research (survey)** represents an unstructured, exploratory research methodology that makes use of psychological methods and relies on small samples, which are mostly not representative.
- **Qualitative Research:** Gathered data is transcribed, and single cases are analyzed and compared in order to find similarities and differences to gain deeper insights into the subject of interest. In *quantitative research*, the data preparation step contains the editing, coding, and transcribing of collected data.
- **Quality Function Deployment (QFD),** *aka* **the House of Quality:** This creates a matrix that looks like a house that can mediate the specifications of a product or process. There are subsequent derivative houses that further mediate downstream implementation issues.
- **Quantitative Analysis:** These people love to use data and numbers to figure out business solutions. They may be in classic quantitative data jobs, but may also like building computer models to solve other types of business problems. These people can fall into two camps: 1. descriptive and, 2. prescriptive.
- **Quantitative research (survey)** can be seen as a structured research methodology based on large samples. The main objective in quantitative research is to quantify the data and generalize the results from the sample, using statistical analysis methods.

- **Quickscore Creativity Test:** A 3-minute test that helps assess and develop business creativity skills.
- **ROI metrics:** ROI metrics address two measures: resource investments and financial returns. ROI metrics give innovation management fiscal discipline and help justify and recognize the value of strategic initiatives, programs, and the overall investment in innovation.
- **Radical Innovation:** A high level of activity in all four dimensions, while incremental innovations (low degree of novelty), are only weakly to moderately developed in the four dimensions.
- **Ranking or Forced Ranking:** Ideas are ranked (1, 2, 3, etc.) – this makes the group consider minor differences in ideas and their characteristics. For forced ranking, there can only be a single #1 idea, a single #2 idea, and so on.
- **Rating Scales:** An idea is rated on a number of preset scales (e.g., an idea can be rated on a 1 to 10 on implementation time, any idea that reaches a 9 or 10 is automatically accepted).
- **Reverse Engineering:** This is a process where organizations buy competitive products to better understand how the competitor is packaging, delivering, and selling their product. Once the product is delivered, it is tested, disassembled and analyzed to determine its performance, how it is assembled, and to estimate its reliability. It is also used to provide the organization with information about the suppliers that the competitors are using.
- **Risk analysis** is the process of analyzing, determining, and defining the risk of danger to government agencies, not-for-profit organizations, for-profit organizations both product and service-type organization.
- **Robust design** is more than a tool; it is a complete methodology that can be used in the design of systems (products or processes) to ensure that they perform consistently in the hands of the customer. It comprises a process and tool kit that allows the designer to assess the impact of variation that the system is likely to experience in use and, if necessary, redesign the system if it is found to be sensitive.
- **Role Model:** Provides a living example of innovation through attention and language, as well as through personal choices and actions. Key stakeholders often test the leader's words, to see if these are real. For innovation to move forward, the leader must pass these inevitable tests – to show that, yes, he or she is absolutely committed to innovation as essential to success.

- **Root Cause Analysis (RCA):** A graphical and textual technique used to understand complex systems and the dependent and independent fundamental contributors, or root causes, of the issue or problem under analysis. This is a technical process in that it provides specific direction as to how to execute the method.
- **Rote Practice:** Those activities where it looks like people are engaged in finding the right routines and inputs to obtain the desired result, but are just going through the motions.
- **S-curve** is a mathematical model also known as the logistic curve, which describes the growth of one variable in terms of another variable over time. S-curves are found in many fields of innovation, from biology and physics to business and technology.
- **SCAMPER:** SCAMPER is a mnemonic that stands for -Substitute -Combine -Adapt - Modify -Put to another use - Eliminate. It is a tool that helps people to generate ideas for new products and services by encouraging them to think about how you could improve existing ones by using by using each of the six words that SCAMPER stands for and applying it to the new product or service in order to generate additional new ideas.
- **Scarcity of Innovation Opportunities:** Markets have matured into commoditized exchanges.
- **Scenario analysis** is a process of analyzing possible future events by considering alternative possible outcomes (sometimes called "alternative worlds"). Thus, the scenario analysis, which is a main method of projections, does not try to show one exact picture of the future. Instead, scenario analysis is used as a decision making tool in the strategic planning process in order to provide flexibility for long term outcomes.
- **Scientific method** is a classical method that uses a hypothesis based on initial observations and validation through testing and revision if needed.
- **Secondary data** is data collected through in-house (desk research).
- **Secondary data sources** involve evidence gathered from someone other than the primary source of the information. Most media outlets, magazines, books, articles, trade journals, market research reports, or publisher-based information are considered secondary sources of evidence.

- **Scope** is defined as all the work that needs to be done in order to achieve the entity objectives. In other words, scope involves the process of identifying and documenting specific goals, outcomes, milestones, tasks, costs, and timeline dates specific to the entity objectives. Scope provides guidance for the establishment, implementation, maintenance, and continuous improvement of an Innovative Management System for use in all establish organization.
- **Service innovation** is not substantially different than product innovation in that the goal is to satisfy customers' jobs-to-be-done, wow and retain customers, and ultimately optimize profit.
- **Seven Key Barriers to Personal Creativity:**

  1. Perceived definitions of creativity
  2. Presumed uses for creativity
  3. Overdependence on knowledge
  4. Experiences and expertise
  5. Habits
  6. Personal and professional relationship networks
  7. Fear of failure

- **Simulation** as used in innovation is the representation of the behavior or characteristics of one system through the use of another system, especially a computer program designed for the purpose. As such, it is both a strategy and a category of tools – and is often coupled with CAI (computer-aided innovation), which is an emerging simulation domain in the array of computer-aided technologies. CAI has been growing as a response to greater industry innovation demands for more reliability in new products.
- **Six Sigma:** A method designed for the reduction of variation in processes. The general steps used within the DMAIC (define, measure, analyze, improve, and control) and DMADV (define, measure, analyze, develop, and verify) methodologies are mostly administrative in nature. Combining Six Sigma with other tool sets pushes the process strongly toward the technical end of the scale.
- **Six Thinking Hats:** It is used to look at decisions from a number of important perspectives. This forces you to move outside your habitual thinking style, and helps you to get a more rounded view of a situation. The thinking is that if you look at a problem with the "Six

Thinking Hats" technique, then you will solve it using any and all approaches. Your decisions and plans will mix ambition, skill in execution, public sensitivity, creativity, and good contingency planning.

- **Social business** is the practice of using social technologies to transform business.
- **Social innovation** relates to creative ideas designed to address societal challenges – cultural, economic, and environmental issues – that are no longer simply a local or national problem but affect the well-being of the planet's inhabitants and ultimately, corporate profits and sustainability.
- **Social media** refers to using social technologies as media in order to influence large audiences.
- **Social Networks:** Networks of friends, colleagues, and other personal contacts; strong social networks can encourage healthy behaviors. They are often an online community of people with a common interests who use a website or other technology to communicate with each other and share information, resources, etc. A business-oriented social network is a website or online service that facilitates this communication.
- **Sponsor:** The individual or group with the power to sanction or legitimize projects.
- **Spontaneous order** is a term that Hayek uses to describe what he calls the Open Society. It is created by unleashing human creativity generally in a way not planned by anyone, and, importantly, could not have been.
- **Stakeholder:** A "Stakeholder" of an organization or enterprise is someone who potentially or really impacts on that organization, and who is likely to be impacted by that organization's activities and processes. Or, even more significantly, perceives that they will be impacted (usually negatively).
- **Statistical Analysis:** A collection, examination, summarization, manipulation, and interpretation of quantitative data to discover its underlying causes, patterns, relationships, and trends.
- **Storyboarding** physically structures the output into a logical arrangement. The ideas, observations or solutions may be grouped visually according to shared characteristics, dependencies upon one another, or similar means. These groupings show relationships between ideas and provide a starting point for action plans and implementation sequences.

- **Substantial Platform, Transformational, Adjacencies Innovation:** Innovations that deliver a unique or new benefit or usage occasion, within an existing or adjacent category.
- **Sustaining Sponsor:** The individual or group that can use their logistics, their economic and/or political proximity to the individuals affected by the change to convince them that they should support, help implement, and comply with the project/program.
- **Synectics:** It combines a structured approach to creativity with the freewheeling problem-solving approach used in techniques like brainstorming. It's a useful technique when simpler creativity techniques like SCAMPER, brainstorming, and random input have failed to generate useful ideas. It uses many different triggers and stimuli to jolt people out of established mind-sets and into more creative ways of thinking.
- **System:** ISO 56000 defines a system as a set of interrelated or interacting elements.[*]
- **Systematic Innovation** can be viewed as occurring in stages
  - Concept stage
  - Feasibility stage
  - Development stage
  - Execution stage, preparation for production
  - Production stage
  - Sustainability stage
- **Systematic Innovation Tools:** The following is a small sample of systematic innovation tools.
  1. Theory of inventive problem solving (TRIZ)
  2. Scientific method
  3. Analogical thinking and mental simulations
  4. Edison method
  5. Osborn method
  6. Six Hats
  7. Problem detection and affinity diagrams
  8. Ethnography

[*]©ISO. This material is excerpted from ISO 56000:2020, with permission of the American National Standards Institute (ANSI) on behalf of the International Organization for Standardization. All rights reserved.

9. Function analysis and fast diagrams
10. Abundance and redundancy
11. Hitch-hiking
12. Kepner Trego
13. Design of experiments
14. Failure mode effects analysis
15. Five whys
16. Medici effect
17. Technology mapping and recombination

- **System Operator** (also called *9 windows* or *multiscreen* method) is a visual technique that is used frequently in the initial stages of TRIZ as part of problem definition.
- **System Operator:** The construction of a 3 × 3 matrix, with the rows labeled as the system, subsystem, super system; and the columns labeled past, present, and future.
- **Systems Engineering:** These methods are more technical than administrative processes, as they are fairly specific as to how to create and utilize the various systems engineering models. However, these methods guide the problem solver to understanding that full system analysis is necessary in creating truly effective solutions. Therefore, these methods may be more administrative in nature than technical.
- **Systems Engineering, System Analysis:** A technique to ensure that full system effects, impacts, benefits, and responses are understood when looking at changes or problems within a system.
- **Systems thinking** is an approach to problem solving, by viewing "problems" as parts of an overall system, rather than reacting to specific part, outcomes or events and potentially contributing to further development of unintended consequences.
- **Team charter** is a management-written commitment or contract stating the purpose and objectives of an assignment. It stipulates resources, performance targets, participants, and review authorities.
- **Team objectives** are closely aligned with the charter, the objectives specifying a team's direction over a period of time.
- **Team project plan** is a document formally approved by management used to guide the project execution and control.

- **TEDOC Methodology:** TEDOC stands for target, explore, develop, optimize, and commercialize data to solve problems creatively. As such, TEDOC brings repeatability, predictability, and reliability to the problem solving process with its structured and algorithmic approach.
- **TRIZ** (pronounced "treesz") is a Russian acronym for "Teoriya Resheniya Izobretatelskikh Zadatch," the Theory Of Inventive Problem Solving; originated by Genrich Altshuller in 1946. It is a broad title representing methodologies, toolsets, knowledge bases, and model-based technologies for generating innovative ideas and solutions. It aims to create an algorithmic to the innovation of new systems and the refinement of existing systems and is based on the study of patents of technological evolution of systems, scientific theory, organizations, and work of arts.
- **Technical contradictions** are the classical engineering and management trade-offs. The desired state can't be reached because something else in the system prevents it. The TRIZ patent research classified 39 features for technical contradictions.
- **Technical process** specifies not only what needs to be done, and in what order, but also provides specific details of *how* to execute the various tasks.
- **Technically Focused Brainstorming:** This methodology guides the generation of solution concepts by ensuring that those solution concepts support the resolution of contradictory requirements of the system under analysis and renders that system to be of higher value than it was before the solution was applied.
- **Technology Mapping and Recombination:** A matrix-based method that lists the various technologies that can perform a function and then examines combinations that have not been tried to see if there is enhanced performance or features.
- **Theory Development and Conceptual Thinking:** These people love thinking and talking about abstract ideas. They love the *why* of strategy more than the *how*. They may enjoy business models that explain the reasons behind the competitive position of a business
- **Things that are Not Innovation:** The following maintenance or change management activities are *not* types of innovation:
  - Cost savings
  - Ingredient or product changes

- Regulatory change
- Label change

- **Thinking innovatively:** Thinking innovatively is soliciting ideas from everyone – it is a challenge. There is a need for training people in asking questions, thinking of ideas, and articulating their ideas in words or graphics.
- **Thrashing:** A term used to describe ineffective human workgroup activity, effort lost in unproductive work.
- **Time of Day Map:** This tool focuses the participants not on a task or an experience, but rather what happens or doesn't in 2- to 4-hour chunks in a person's day and what opportunities may appear.
- **Top-Down Planning for Innovation:** Generally a revenue goal-driven process that is usually set from the top by the senior leadership team. It is usually a dollar revenue goal or a percentage of revenue target from innovation.
- **Trademarks:** Words or logos that are used by someone to identify their products or services and distinguish them from the words or logos of others.
- **Trade Secrets:** Essentially refers to the legal protection often granted to confidential information having at least potential competitive value.
- **Tree Diagram Breakdown (Drilldown):** A technique for breaking complex opportunities and problems down into progressively smaller parts. Start by writing the opportunity statement or problem under investigation down on the left-hand side of a large sheet of paper. Next, write down the points that make up the next level of detail a little to the right of this. These may be factors contributing to the issue or opportunity, information relating to it, or questions raised by it. For each of these points, repeat the process. This process of breaking the issue under investigation into its component part is called drilling down.
- **Trends:** Those dimensions on which lead users are far ahead of the mass market.
- **Trial and Error:** Attempts at successful solutions to a problem with little benefit from failed attempts.
- **Values:** Values are things that an organization believes are sacred – things that should never be sacrificed.

- **Value Analysis:** The analysis of a system, process, or activity to determine which parts of it are classified as Real-Value-Added (RVA), Business-Value-Added (BVA), or No-Value-Added (NVA).
- **Value proposition** is a document that defines the benefits that will result from the implementation of a change or the use of an output as viewed by one or more of the organization's stakeholders. A value proposition can apply to an entire organization, parts thereof, or customers, or products, or services, or internal processes.
- **Venture Capitalist:** Secures funding for innovation, evaluates and selects projects to receive resources, and guides implementation.
- **Vision:** A documented or mental description or picture of a desired future state of an organization, product, process, team, a key business driver, activity, or individual.
- **Vision Statements:** A group of words that paints a clear picture of the desired business environment at a specific time in the future. Short-term vision statements usually are between 3 and 5 years. Long-term vision statements usually are between 10 and 25 years. A visions statement should not exceed four sentences.
- **Work Breakdown Structure (WBS):** A work breakdown structure is a hierarchical decomposition of the total scope of work to be carried out by the project team to accomplish the project objectives and create the required deliverables.
- **Zones of conflict** refers to the temporal zone and the operating zone of the problem—loosely the time and space in which the problem occurs.

Appendix B

Most Used Tools

LIST OF THE MOST USED AND/OR MOST EFFECTIVE

Innovative Tools and Methodologies in Alphabetical Order

Book I – Organizational and/or Operational IT&M

Book II – Evolutionary and/or Improvement IT&M

Book III – Creative IT&M

Note: IT&M = Innovative Tools and/or Methodologies

P = Primary Usage   S = Secondary Usage   Blank = Not used or little used

	IT&M	Book Ill	Book II	Book I
1.	5 Why questions	S	P	S
2.	76 standard solutions	P	S	
3.	Absence thinking	P		
4.	Affinity diagram	S	P	S
5.	Agile Innovation	S		P
6.	Attribute listing	S	P	
7.	Benchmarking		S	P
8.	Biomimicry	P	S	
9.	Brain-writing 6-3-5	S	P	S
10.	Business case development		S	P
11.	Business Plan	S	S	P
12.	Cause and Effect Diagrams		P	S
13.	Combination methods	P	S	
14.	Comparative analysis	S	S	P
15.	Competitive analysis	S	S	P
16.	Competitive shopping		S	P
17.	Concept tree (concept map)	P	S	
18.	Consumer co-creation	P		
19.	Contingency planning		S	P
20.	Co-Star	S	S	P
21.	Costs analysis	S	S	P
22.	Creative problem solving model	S	P	
23.	Creative thinking	P	S	
24.	Design for Tools		P	
	Subtotal number of points	7	7	10

(*Continued*)

IT&M	Book III	Book II	Book I
25. Directed/Focused/Structure Innovation	P	S	
26. Elevator Speech	P	S	S
27. Ethnography	P		
28. Financial reporting	S	S	P
29. Flowcharting		P	S
30. Focus groups	S	S	P
31. Force field analysis	S	P	
32. Generic creativity tools	P	S	
33. HU Diagrams	P		
34. I-TRIZ	P		
35. Identifying and Engaging Stakeholders	S	S	P
36. Imaginary brainstorming	P	S	S
37. Innovation Blueprint	P		S
38. Innovation Master Plan	S	S	P
39. Kano analysis	S	P	S
40. Knowledge management systems	S	S	P
41. Lead user analysis	P	S	
42. Lotus Blossom	P	S	
43. Market research and surveys	S		P
44. Matrix diagram	P	S	
45. Mind mapping	P	S	S
46. Nominal group technique	S	P	
47. Online innovation platforms	P	S	S
48. Open innovation	P	S	S
49. Organizational change mgt	S	S	P
50. Outcome driven innovation	P		
Subtotal number of points	15	4	7

(*Continued*)

IT&M	Book III	Book II	Book I
51. Plan-Do-Check-Act	S	P	
52. Potential investor present	S		P
53. Pro-active Creativity	P	S	S
54. Project Management	S	S	P
55. Proof of concepts	P	S	
56. Quickscore creativity test	P		
57. Reengineering/Redesign		P	
58. Reverse Engineering	S	P	
59. Robust design	S	P	
60. S-Curve Model		S	P
61. Safeguarding Intellectual Properties			P
62. SCAMPER	S	P	
63. Scenario Analysis	P	S	
64. Simulations	S	P	S
65. Six Thinking Hats	S	P	S
66. Social Networks	S	P	
67. Solution Analysis Diagrams	S	P	
68. Statistical Analysis	S	P	S
69. Storyboarding	P	S	
70. Systems thinking	S	S	P
71. Synetics	P		
72. Tree diagram	S	P	S
73. TRIZ	P	S	
74. Value analysis	S	P	S
75. Value propositions	S		P
76. Visioning	S	S	P
Subtotal number of points	7	12	7
(P) priority rating	CREATIVE	EVOLUTIO-NARY	ORGANIZA-TIONAL
TOTAL	29	23	24

IT&M in Creativity Book 29
IT&M in Evolutionary Book 23
IT&M in Organizational Book 24

Appendix C

H. J. Harrington's Value Statements

THE MAN I WANT TO BE!

A man who would be concerned with how he could help me instead of himself, who would give me loyalty instead of demanding of me, who would think of himself as my assistant, instead of my boss, who would think it was his job to help me do my job better.

A man whose pride was peculiar because his pride was in his people. A man who could walk around the organization and say, "Yes, it was well done but not by me. I just happen to be lucky enough to have the best team in the whole organization." That is where his pride lies. Anything worthwhile that comes out of the department, his team did. If something goes wrong, he feels that maybe he was not on the ball. Maybe he had not directed or guided or taught or led his team properly. He will take the blame for anything that goes wrong.

A man who never made a promise he didn't intend to keep, merely to slough me off. I would pick a man who might say, "Gee, I'm so busy, Jim, I just don't know if I'll ever get done. But let's not wait until tomorrow when it is more convenient for me. Let's sit down right now and go at it. Now is the time."

A man who knew that I was not a genius. If I come to him with an idea, I don't want him to give me that objective stuff. I don't want him to say, "You have a suggestion. Here is the form. Fill it out. Stick it in the box and three months later if it is any good we will give you an award for it."

I want him to get excited about my brain child. I want him to treat my brain child carefully, because it is the most wonderful idea in the world at the moment. I gave birth to this child of mine. I want him to treat it tenderly. Especially tenderly if it is a feeble-minded brain child. The man who is going to get an award doesn't have to worry. It is I. If I don't get one, I will feel low. I want my boss to pick me up and encourage me.

A man who would handle every grievance right now, not like the fellow who has a 40-room mansion, but no garbage pails, and who says, "We just kick it around until it gets lost."

A man who in many ways reminded me of my father whom I loved dearly. But who had the knack if I stepped out of line, of lowering the boom so fast I didn't know what struck me until too late. But who, if he thought I had been pushed around, would fight for me every step of the way up the line even to the president of the company and the chairman of the board if necessary to see that I got a fair shake and a square break.

By: Dr. J. L. Rosenstein

Modified by: Dr. H. James Harrington, CEO,
Harrington Management Systems

Appendix D

ISO 56000:2020 Standards

ISO 56000:2020 STANDARDS

ISO 56000:2020	Innovation Management — Fundamentals and vocabulary
ISO 56002:2019	Innovation Management — Innovation Management System — Guidance
ISO 56003:2019	Innovation Management — Tools and methods for innovation partnership — Guidance
ISO/TR 56004:2019	Innovation Management Assessment — Guidance
ISO 56005:2020	Innovation Management — Tools and methods for intellectual property management — Guidance
ISO ISO/DIS 56006	Innovation Management — Tools and methods for strategic intelligence management — Guidance
I ISO/AWI 56007	Innovation Management — Tools and methods for idea management — Guidance
ISO/AWI 56008	Innovation Management — Tools and methods for innovation operation measurements — Guidance

Note:
Aligns with existing standards:

- ISO 9001 on Quality
- ISO 7001 on Information Security
- ISO 4001 on Environment

Innovation Management Principles:

1. Realization of value
2. Future-focused leaders
3. Strategic direction
4. Culture
5. Exploiting insights

6. Managing uncertainty
7. Adaptability
8. Systems approach

Index